FAST AND FURIOUS

Ian Botham celebrates breaking the world record for the most number of wickets

FAST AND FURIOUS

A celebration of Cricket's pace bowlers

by Grantlee Kieza

With
COLIN COWDREY, GREG CHAPPELL, BARRY RICHARDS, NEIL HARVEY
and TONY GREIG

WARD LOCK

First published in Great Britain in 1990 by Ward Lock
Villiers House, 41/47 Strand,
London WC2N 5JE, England

A Cassell imprint

© Grantlee Kieza 1990

ISBN 0 7063 6988 2

Printed by Tien Wah Press in Singapore

Contents

Tales of Terror From Colin Cowdrey

Colin Cowdrey, one of Test cricket's greatest batsmen, had his arm broken by Wes Hall and at an advanced age was called on to help fight the fire of Lillee and Thomson who were rampaging against England.

Cowdrey played against some of the fastest men ever and his lengthy career included bouts against the champions of two eras — Lindwall and Lillee. He recalls his last Australian summer.

'In December 1974, my long career was winding down. So imagine how I felt when I received a phone call from Mike Denness in Australia where his team was being blitzed by Lillee and Thomson. He asked me to join him. Dennis Amiss and John Edrich had bones broken and the side was down on batsmen. I said "Yes, of course. I'll come out to lend a hand" but it was a bit annoying because our season had ended and I wasn't as fit as I would have liked to have been. Within 24 hours I was on a plane to Perth.

The Test was due to start in four days and I didn't really think they'd call on me to bat so soon. But anyway I took the time to practise with old friends Graham McKenzie and Tony Lock and schoolboys came to the ground to bowl at me so I'd be ready to bat a little later in the tour.

The night before the Test, Mike Denness dropped a bombshell on me. "You're in the team, mate. And you're batting at No. 3."

Lillee and Thomson were extra fast on a quick wicket. They were a handful. Ray Lindwall was the best bowler I ever faced but I'm sure Lillee was every bit as good as his career went on. I think he peaked near the end of the '70s. Dennis had similar speed to Ray, a lovely build, fine run-up, everything perfect. He swung the ball — and was a very hostile character.

Thommo was different. He was very strong. He was rather like Charlie Griffith. He had a wonderful physique and learned as he went along.

Lillee and Thomson formed a terrifying combination just as Hall and Griffith had done and before them Lindwall and Miller. But part of the great joy and excitement of cricket for a batsman is the duel against the fast men. There's nothing like it.'

Jeff Thomson, frighteningly fast at his peak.

INTRODUCTION

The Men Who Put Dynamite Into Cricket

Harold Larwood used to say fast bowlers put the dynamite into cricket, and from the days of the legendary Brown of Brighton and Alfred Mynn through to Charles Kortright, Larwood, Frank Tyson, Jeff Thomson and more recently Michael Holding and Imran Khan, the fast men have been cricketers who could make the game explosive.

The fast bowler is the man who initiates the action and sets the challenge. The great ones can tear through a batting lineup, and, in the words of John Snow, watch it bleed. Pace bowlers are the first men on display as they try to dictate the course of a game in the opening overs.

Some of the pacemen in this book were not express speed but, like Richard Hadlee, Ian Botham and Maurice Tate, they mastered the quick man's gifts of swing and cut so well that they were often more lethal than their faster contemporaries.

This book is about the great fast and fast-medium bowlers from around the world who have been thrilling fans ever since a short ball from Happy Jack Ulyett made Charlie Bannerman retire hurt in the very first Test match.

Since then, fast bowlers have been centre stage in some of the most heroic moments in the game such as when Rick McCosker came out to bat in the Centenary Test with his jaw wired or when Stan McCabe smashed away against Larwood, George Gunn danced down to the bouncers of Learie Constantine, Colin Cowdrey came out to face Wes Hall with a broken arm, and Slasher Mackay took Hall's best shots on the body rather than give a chance.

All of these and many more mentioned in this book were special moments in cricket brought about by the duel between brave batsman and fiery fast bowler.

Grantlee Kieza

The Art Of Fast Bowling Is Born

George Brown, of Brighton, was a fast underarm bowler who is said to have been so quick that longstops felt safe only with a sack of straw tied to their chests. According to the stories of beleaguered batsmen, he once bowled a ball that beat the bat, wicketkeeper, long stop, tore through a man's coat on the boundary and killed a dog on the other side.

Nearly as fantastic were the feats of Alfred Mynn, the Lion of Kent. The round armer's best success came when he fired them down from around the wicket, making the ball hum.

It was said that Mynn the Merciless was so fast and so powerful that when he bowled, the earth trembled.

But it was not just England who had all the fast men before the Test era began. In Australia, there was the bearded Tom Wills, who played for Kent, MCC and Cambridge and invented Australian rules football to keep cricketers fit in winter. He also coached Victorian and Aboriginal teams. He was decidedly quick when he wanted to be but he had a suspect action.

One of the Aborigines to rise to prominence in the Wills era was Johnny Mullagh, the best-performing member of the 1868 Aboriginal team to visit England. A fast-medium bowler and free-hitting batsman, he suffered from racism all his life, throwing his wicket away in his only match for Victoria when the opposition captain called him "nigger".

By the time Alfred Shaw, a round-arm medium-pacer, sent down Test cricket's first delivery, Mullagh was living alone back in a bush shack away from the white man's game.

England and Australia were both at less than full strength for that first Test, on the sparse Melbourne Cricket Ground wicket in 1877.

The English keeper, Edward Pooley, was in jail after a brawl in New Zealand, and the home team was without its two best quick bowlers, Frank Allan and The Demon, Spofforth.

Allan, a left-armer described by at least one contemporary report as "the bowler of the century", skipped the match because he wanted to see some old friends at an agricultural show, prompting the *Melbourne Argus* to write: "Great as is Allan's value on the field, his capriciousness is still greater; and we trust that for the future he will studiously be left in that retirement which he professes to be so loath to leave."

But he was not. He took 4-80 in the Test of 1878-9, it being said he developed his amazing swing, a veritable boomerang ball, from throwing an Aboriginal waddy at possums.

The Australian pace attack for the very first Test match was led by two fast-medium bowlers John Hodges and Tom Garrett and the medium-paced round-arm spinner, Billy Midwinter. Left-armer Hodges, a bootmaker from the Richmond club, had never even played for Victoria and was very much in the shadow of Frank Allan, but he took 3-34 in the match. He is more famous for quitting as umpire in the fifth Test of the 1884-5 series because of complaints from the English players.

Alfred Shaw, a shrewd paceman who opened England's attack in 1878

tour of England was "kidnapped" by W.G. Grace to play for his native Gloucestershire, prompting a wild carriage chase through the streets of London.

He was dynamic in the first Test, taking 5-78 and 1-23, though the English-born Victorian slow-bowler Tom Kendall bowled Australia to its historic 45-run victory.

England's attack was led by the shrewd Alfred Shaw and the Yorkshire paceman George "Happy Jack" Ulyett and Allen Hill, who was tall, had a model action from a short-run up and was one of the best seamers of his day, usually bringing the ball back from outside off-stump. Three years earlier, he had taken a hat-trick for the Players against the Gentleman at Lords.

Ulyett played for Yorkshire for 20 years and played in 23 Tests for England as a superb all-rounder. He toured Australia five times, and against NSW in 1879 took four wickets in four balls.

He was a zestful man who used to say Yorkshire chose him for whistling and good behaviour, and England so that he could go in first with W.G. Grace and give the doctor confidence.

Hill took Test cricket's first wicket bowling Nat Thompson, and at the end of the first day Australia was 6-166 with Bannerman undefeated on 126 before a crowd of 3000.

The following day when he was on 165, a short, fast one from Ulyett split Bannerman's finger and, though he had not given a chance in five hours at the crease, he retired hurt.

In the second innings Bannerman batted with a bandaged hand and was clean-bowled by one of Happy Jack's extra-quick deliveries.

Ulyett's two half-centuries in the second Test won the match for England, even though Spofforth and Blackham were finally chosen.

The development of the English fast bowlers came despite the mastery of W.G. Grace, who forced many counties to open with slow bowlers. Most quicks operated on dubious pitches. There

Tom Garrett, a top sprinter from Wollongong, NSW, was only 18, but he could swing the ball both ways from his high action. He finished with match figures of 2-31 in the first of his 19 Tests for Australia.

Midwinter, who grew up on the Victorian gold fields and was known as the Bendigo Giant, stood 187 centimetres and weighed 89 kilograms. He played for and against Australia, and on the 1878

were no groundsmen at Lords, for instance, until 1864, when Sussex refused to play there because of the dangerous conditions of the pitch.

In 1868 at Lords, W.G. was cheered wildly after blocking the first four balls, all shooters along the ground, and two years later there, George Sumners, the young Nottinghamshire batsman, was hit in the head by the first ball he received and died three days later.

At Lords in 1878 and again in 1882, Harry Boyle proved the perfect foil for Fred Spofforth, remarking that if Spofforth was a demon, then he was the "very devil himself".

Boyle was a medium-pacer of unwavering line and length who invented the dangerous silly mid-on position to snare balls popped up off Spofforth's off-cutters. He made the position his own, despite warnings from W.G., who predicted a painful and early death from such damn foolishness.

Brian Crowley once wrote that while Spofforth dug a grave for the English batsmen, Harry Boyle kept the coffin lid firmly shut with his unerring length and deceptive flight.

Born in Sydney, Boyle grew up on the Bendigo gold fields with Billy Midwinter and played all his cricket in Victoria, riding for hours on horseback from Bendigo to play with the East Melbourne club. While playing for a Victorian XVIII, Boyle was the first Australian to bowl Grace.

Spofforth and Boyle routed the MCC for 33 and 19 in 1878, Boyle taking 6-3 in the second innings, five of them bowled. Spofforth's match figures were 10-20, Boyle's 9-17. On the Test-less tour, Boyle took seven wickets with his last eight balls, against the 18 of Elland.

On the 1880 tour of England, Victoria's fast-medium George Alexander stood in for Spofforth at The Oval, where three brothers Grace all played for England. The Nottinghamshire fast bowler Fred Morley took 5-56 in Australia's first innings.

He rose to prominence after the retirement from Notts of the left-arm speedster, James "Jemmy" Shaw, a 173 centimetre, 67 kilogram round-armer whose duels with W.G. are part of cricket legend and who in partnership with Alfred Shaw was devastating for Notts and England.

In 1882-3, Morley was a member of Ivo Bligh's touring team, but he suffered a broken rib in a ship collision at Colombo on the way to Australia and died 18 months later of "lung congestion and dropsy". Australia lost the Oval Test of 1880 but emerged with some great results from the tour, George "Joey" Palmer taking 266 wickets supporting The Demon.

The 1881-2 series was dominated by quick bowlers, Ulyett averaging 55 with the bat and Tom Garrett and Joey Palmer taking 42 wickets between them, Palmer with 7-68 in the second

Test at Sydney and Garrett with 6-78 there in the third.

Garrett took 5-80, Midwinter 4-81, in the fourth Test, at Melbourne, which ended in a draw after four days because the Englishmen had to catch a boat home. It was the last drawn Test in Australia until 1946-7.

Palmer bowled off-breaks at fast-medium and in later years developed the leg-cutter so that it became his stock delivery. Though his legend has not survived as well as The Demon's, many Englishmen rated him a better bowler than Spofforth. He almost bowled W.G. with the first ball he sent down to him, a yorker that went under the bat and clipped the stumps without dislodging the bails. A knee injury caused his premature retirement at 27, and he died at 50 from pneumonia.

In the first Test of Australia's 1884 tour, at Manchester, Lord Harris withdrew from the team because of the selection of Lancashire's Jack Crossland, who many said was a chucker. Monkey Hornby took over as England captain, but Crossland never got to play a Test, being replaced by Reg Barlow.

Stanley Christopherson, of Kent, one of the best quicks of his day, played his sole Test at The Oval during that tour, later becoming president of the MCC.

In the 1884-5 series England won 3-2, the medium-pacer Billy Barnes of Nottinghamshire topping both batting and bowling averages.

As George Lohmann, Charlie Turner and Jack Ferris emerged in the following years, Sammy Woods was also progressing.

He backed Ferris and Turner in England in 1888, though it was not one of his more memorable summers.

A strapping, genuinely fast bowler from Glenfield near Sydney, Woods stood 182 centimetres and weighed 86 kilograms and once took seven wickets in seven balls in a Sydney match.

He has one of the most distinguished records of any sportsman, leading Somerset and The Gentlemen at cricket, playing three Tests each for Australia and England, leading Cambridge at rugby union and later playing for England as an innovator in back-row play.

Sir Pelham (Plum) Warner, the English captain and later manager of the Bodyline team, wrote that Woods was the most subtle and artistic fast bowler he ever saw.

George Lohmann
(1865-1901)

The Good Die Young

Fair-haired, blue-eyed and handsome, George Lohmann posted the finest Test average of any long-standing bowler, taking 112 Test wickets at 10.75 each in 18 appearances for England.

He was one of the great Surrey trio of quick bowlers, with Bill Lockwood and Honest Tom Richardson. Essentially a medium-pacer with a surprise fast ball, he picked up wickets through deception more than speed.

Lohmann made three tours of Australia between 1886 and 1892 and toured South Africa in 1895-6, taking 35 wickets in three matches on the matting. Partnering Sammy Woods, Lohmann took a haul in South Africa that included 7-38 and 8-7 at Port Eliza-beth and 9-28 at Johannesburg. This was the best Test bowling until Jim Laker took all 10 in an innings at Old Trafford in 1956.

He made his Test debut against the touring Australians in 1886 in a series England won 3-0 as Spofforth, Palmer and Garrett neared the end of their careers.

In the third Test, at The Oval, he took 12 wickets (7-36 and 5-68), and England won by an innings.

In 1886-7, he took a record 8-35 to help England to a 71-run victory in the second Test, at Sydney, having helped it win the first with a top score of 17 in a first-innings total of 45.

He was an accomplished batsman in first-class cricket, with three centuries, and as a slip fieldsman he drew gasps from crowds with his reflexes.

Startling bowling performances seemed to occur every time Lohmann played.

At Sydney, in the only Test of 1887-8, he put up match figures of 9-52, and Bobby Peel 10-58, to rout Australia even though Charlie Turner's 12 wickets kept the game alive.

Lohmann's 62 runs in the second Test of the 1888 series, at The Oval, came as England made 317, the only decent score of the series, and he was again a hero – with 11 wickets at 13 runs each.

His career was one of triumph topping triumph. He took eight or more first-class wickets in an innings 20 times (four of them in Tests) and took 13 or more wickets in a match 14 times.

After his all-conquering feats in South Africa, Lohmann decided to stay there, hoping the climate would help his breathing problems. He managed the South African tourists to England in 1901 but was then, at the age of 36, dying of tuberculosis.

Charlie Turner
(1862-1944) and
Jack Ferris
(1867-1900)

The Terror And The Fiend

Charlie Turner, "The Terror", and Jack Ferris, "The Fiend", were the most successful pace-bowling partnership Test cricket has seen.

In only eight matches together, they shared a phenomenal 104 wickets. All the other Australian bowlers put together managed 21. No bowling partnership has so dominated a Test attack.

Such was the immediate rapport these two small medium-pacers had that on their debut Spofforth was put out to pasture.

Turner was born on November 16, 1862, at Bathurst and, although he did not make the First XI at Bathurst Grammar, he was possessed of strength and stamina.

He had strong legs and huge hands that could make

The prodigiously talented George Lohmann

Charlie Turner, small but dangerous.

the ball do wonders. Turner started out as a stable boy for the stagecoach company Cobb and Co. At 16, he played for Bathurst against Lord Harris's Englishmen and at the age of 19 was chosen for Twenty-Two of Bathurst to take on Alfred Shaw's touring Englishmen in 1881-82.

He amazed spectators and the Englishmen with 17 wickets in the match, 7-33 followed by 10-36. But, even with a growing reputation, he had to wait until the following year for NSW selectors to deem him worthy of a place in their team.

Turner stood 170 centimetres, weighed about 76 kilograms and bowled with a chest-on action. Tests during the 1888 tour of England at Woolwich Arsenal, using equipment to measure the speed of artillery shells, clocked his bowling at 88km/h, fairly tame compared with that of such bowlers as Larwood or Thomson.

But he was a terror because, as one contemporary report said, the Englishmen who faced him often did so in a state of panic.

His stock ball was a quick off-break, but he combined this with clever changes in pace, a well-disguised slower ball, a fast round-arm delivery and a deadly yorker.

Like Maurice Tate, he had the knack of making the ball seem to gather pace once it had pitched, and Sir Stanley Jackson rated him the best medium-pacer he played against.

Such was Turner's accuracy that Jack Blackham was able to take six Test stumpings off his bowling. Turner played 17 Tests before being dumped by the Australian selectors, and in that time he took 101 wickets at 16.53 each, an average that has never been bettered by any leading Australian bowler. He took five wickets in a Test innings 11 times.

He made his Australian debut at 24 after taking 13 for 54 for NSW against Arthur Shrewsbury's English tourists in 1886-7.

In the first Test, in January, 1887, he opened the bowling with another debutant, Ferris, the left-hander.

Ferris was born in Sydney on May 21, 1867, attended St Aloysius College and was known as "The Tricky" while playing for the Belvedere club at the start of the 1886-7 season when he was 19.

He was a small, thin, sharp-faced teenager of 168 centimetres who, in his debut, bowled across the batsmen, angling the ball into the marks left by Turner's follow-through and slanting the ball away towards slips. Usually, he came around the wicket, bowling a medium-fast leg-break spun with his fingers. In their first match together, the pair bowled unchanged, dismissing England for 45, Turner taking 6-15 and Ferris 4-27.

Remarkably, England recovered to win both the first and second Tests and retain The Ashes through the marvellous contributions of Billy Barnes and George Lohmann.

This was largely the story of Turner and Ferris as a pace-bowling combination. Australia did not have the batting strength to support them, and they were star performers in losing teams, winning one Test from the eight they played together.

In their first two matches against England, Turner and Ferris shared 35 of the 40 wickets to fall.

George Giffen, the slow-bowling all-rounder, wrote that Turner "owed more to genius than skill", and certainly his genius was evident in 1887-8, when he became the only cricketer to take more than 100 wickets in an Australian first-class season, with 106 at 14 from 12 matches.

Even allowing for the fact that wickets in those days were not covered, it was another Turnerism in the record books.

Turner and Ferris bowled Australia to victory at Lords in 1888 only to see England win at The Oval and Old Trafford to keep The Ashes again.

At Lords, the two wrecked England for 53 and 62, and in the second innings were the only two Australian batsmen to reach double figures.

Though England batted in only four innings in the three Tests, Turner took 21 wickets at 12 runs each. Ferris 11 at 15. Turner not only hit 103 against Surrey at The Oval but, more importantly, took 314 wickets at 11. Ferris, barely 21, took 220 at 14. Their total wickets were more than four times that of all the other Australians combined.

At Old Trafford against Lancashire, Ferris took 8-41. At Stoke against an English XI, Turner took 9-15.

Against another English XI, at Hastings, The Terror finished with match figures of 17-50, 14 of his victims clean-bowled.

Jack Ferris was a star in losing Australian teams.

After the 1890 Ashes tour had finished with Ferris taking nine wickets at The Oval in another losing Test and another losing series, W.G. Grace arranged for The Fiend to join him at Gloucestershire.

Ferris was only 23, but he decided to give up Test cricket and chance his fortune in England.

In eight Tests for Australia he had taken 48 wickets at 14.25. Strangely, his bowling form deserted him (perhaps in the absence of The Terror at the other end) but he performed well with the bat, putting together some big partnerships with Grace, and in 1893 he topped 1000 runs in an English first-class season.

In 1891-2, he and the former Australian skipper Billy Murdoch turned out for England against South Africa at Cape Town, with Ferris taking 13 wickets in the match for 91 runs, including 7-37 in the second innings. This time his batsmen did not let him down.

The Fiend returned to Australia late in 1895, but at 28 could no longer find the line that had made him such a feared cricketer.

He played once for South Australia in 1895-6 and twice for NSW in 1897-8.

He joined the Imperial Light Horse at the outbreak of the Boer War and returned to South Africa for another sort of tour, dying of enteric fever at Durban in November, 1900, at just 33.

Even without Ferris, Turner performed well in the next few years, opening with the likes of Bob McLeod, Harry Trott, Arthur Coningham and Ernie Jones.

In the 1891-2 series, he took 16 wickets at 21, and Australia won the Ashes 2-1. On the losing 1893 tour, he took 11 at 29.

When the Englishmen next came to Australia under Stoddart, he was having a good season in a series dominated by the wholehearted efforts of Honest Tom Richardson.

After four Tests, Australia had fought back from 2-0 down to be 2-2. But, despite 18 wickets for the series at 19 each, Turner was left out of the fifth and deciding Test to make way for another Bathurst bowler, the medium-paced off-spinner Tom McKibben, an alleged chucker. England won the fifth Test and the series.

Turner was furious about the lack of support selectors had shown him, after years without support from his batsmen. When he was asked to tour England with Harry Trott's side that winter he declined, saying he was too busy.

Turner kept playing for NSW on occasions until 1910. In 1908, he took 9-22 in a match between the Ramblers and the Union Bank at Sydney Showground.

He never forgot his long lamented partner. During the Bodyline series, when Harold Larwood was sending them down faster than Turner could have done with a hurricane behind him, the old man would sometimes be seen drinking alone under a plaque commemorating Jack Ferris.

Writing in 1920, the NSW batsman Frank Iredale called Turner the greatest bowler Australia had produced and perhaps the unluckiest. He could not recall a match in which fewer than three catches were dropped off The Terror's bowling.

Turner died at Manly, Sydney, in 1944 at 81.

Fred Spofforth
(1853-1926)

The Demon

The son of a Yorkshire bank manager, Fred Spofforth had the same sharp features as Dennis Lillee. He was 188 centimetres tall, lean and strong, with a long, thin face, a hawkish nose, a bristling moustache and eyes that could scorch the heart of any batsman.

He killed England at The Oval in 1882, and Australia and the Old Country have been playing for the remains ever since, The Ashes.

In the 1880s Spofforth was to bowling what W.G. Grace was to batting. He was the most famous cricketer in Australia and a fast bowler to be feared, if not always for his pace, which could be sharp, then for his intelligence, variety and cunning. He said bowling was just as artistic "as many of the so called higher arts".

On the 1882 tour of England Joey Palmer, something of a rival of Spofforth, was out of action for The Oval Test, the only one of the tour, and Spofforth had to share the bowling with Tom Garrett and his old faithful partner, Harry Boyle.

Spofforth had taken 7-46 in England's first innings,

only to see Australia bundled out cheaply twice. England went out to bat in the final innings of the match needing just 85 runs to win with the strongest batting line-up it had ever fielded. But, snarling to team mates, "This thing can be done", The Demon was not about to let the Englishmen win easily.

Questions had been raised by some of the Australians about Spofforth's work rate on the tour, and there were whispers that he was not trying as hard as he might have in some of the county games.

But on the afternoon of August 29, 1882, when the chips were down, he bowled as only he could.

After a sleepless night, Spofforth started from the Gasworks end and bounced the ball straight at W.G. Grace with the fieldsmen close in.

The Demon had been enraged when W.G. ran out Sammy Jones as he left his crease to pat down a bump on the pitch, and he let all the Englishmen taste his fury.

With just 15 runs on the board, Spofforth had removed Dick Barlow and Monkey Hornby. But then Grace and Happy Jack Ulyett dug in their heels and took the score to 51, just 34 short of victory.

Spofforth switched to the Pavilion end, and Ulyett, playing for The Demon's fast off-break, failed to read a fast, straight one and hit an edge to Blackham. Two runs later, W.G. miscued a drive off Boyle, and Bannerman caught him at mid-off, 4-53.

After 12 straight maidens, Bannerman deliberately misfielded to give Lyttelton a single and bring him down to face Spofforth. Four more maidens, and The Demon sent down the break back to shatter Lyttelton's stumps, 5-66, 19 still needed.

Lucas hit Boyle for four, but in one over The Demon dismissed Steel and Read. The score was then 7-70. England still needed 15 runs and, at 75, Lucas played on to Spofforth, 8-75. Boyle took the last two wickets, and Australia won by seven runs.

After the match, Grace lamented that he left six men to get 30 runs and they could not get them.

Spofforth finished with 7-44 and match figures of 14-90, the best by an Australian in England until Bob Massie's performance nine decades later.

The *Sporting Times* published the famous obituary for English cricket, and The Ashes have been the prize in England-Australia contests since.

Spofforth, born in the Sydney suburb of Balmain on September 9, 1853, spent much of his childhood in Hokianga, near Auckland, New Zealand.

At 10, he saw the first English team to visit Australia play NSW and watched the fast English round-arm bowler, George "Tear 'Em" Tarrant, frighten the local batsman to such an extent that the youngster decided he would like to be a fast man too.

His approach was 16 paces and he accelerated in a crouch, which he said prevented back strain. William Cooper, a contemporary legbreak bowler, said Spofforth could be as fast as Larwood. But The Demon, a bank manager who knew the value of preserving assets, varied his pace according to the opposition and the pitches on which he bowled. Most of his deliveries were fast-medium, sometimes with a slower ball tossed in and sometimes with a fast yorker.

Spofforth bowled fast off-breaks and leg-breaks mainly and even sought the guidance of a university professor on the physics and aerodynamics of pace bowling. He learned to vary his pace by altering the amount of ball in his grip and devised signals to let Jack Blackham know what to expect behind the stumps.

Spofforth's relationship with Australia's first keeper was anything but cordial to begin with. He declined to play in the very first Test in Melbourne in 1877 because Blackham had been preferred to Spofforth's regular keeper, Billy Murdoch. But, realising the Australian team could still perform without him, he made up for lost time, playing in the second 1877 Test, in which the stumping of Alfred Shaw gave Spofforth his first Test wicket.

As with Lillee, Spofforth's presence was enough to scare runs out of batsmen, and in the next decade he played 18 Tests and took 94 wickets at 18.41.

In 1878, he took 764 wickets in Australia, America and England at 6.08, and at Lords against the MCC took 10 for 20 in a match that lasted just over five hours.

At the finish Spofforth was still seething at a remark from an MCC member that the Australians were not black like the last lot – the Aboriginal team that had toured England a decade earlier. With Harry Boyle at the other end, England was dismissed for 33 and 19.

In the sole Test of 1878-9, at Melbourne against "the Gentlemen of England with Ulyett and Emmett", the two best professional cricketers of the day, Spofforth took 13-110, including the first hat-trick in Tests.

An injured finger kept Spofforth from the only Test in England in 1880 and he barely featured in the 1881-2 series, though he bowled out all 20 of his opponents in a Victorian country game after riding almost 640 kilometres on horseback from Sydney.

He took 11 wickets against England at Sydney in 1882-3, including a haul of 7-44, even though England reclaimed the Ashes Spofforth had created. In England the following season, he took more than 200 wickets, including 7-3 in a total of 26 against an English XI at Birmingham, finishing the match with 14-37.

Two years later, after his 14 wickets had failed to stop a 3-0 sweep by England, The Demon married a Derbyshire girl, brought her to Australia and played his final Test at Sydney in the long shadows created by the little medium-pacers, Turner and Ferris. The Demon had to wait until the second innings to get a bowl, and after 12 overs he had just one wicket.

He was left out of the second Test, perhaps because England had lost its big gun, Billy Barnes, a plucky all-rounder who broke his hand on a wall when trying to punch the Australian captain, Percy McDonnell.

The Demon moved to England and played twice for Derbyshire against Yorkshire in 1889, taking 15 wickets in one match. In 1891, he joined the Hampstead side in London, taking at least 50 wickets a season until his 50th birthday.

In later years, Spofforth settled into a mansion at Long Ditton, Surrey, showing off his garden and becoming chairman of a tea company. He left an estate worth 164,000 pounds, which would have made him the equivalent of a multi millionaire today.

The Demon Spofforth and (INSET) the "very Devil himself" Harry Boyle.

Ernie Jones, first of the truly fast Australian bowlers

The Days Of The Demons

Arthur Mold was a bowler of such pace that Wilfred Rhodes, at 90, still winced when recalling him. Born in Northamptonshire but a star for Lancashire, Mold developed his great pace from a run-up of just four strides. In 1890, he demolished the Australian batting with 9-43 for the Lyric Club, and between 1889 and 1900 he took eight or nine wickets in an innings 17 times and 13 or more wickets in a match 14 times. Against Nottinghamshire in 1895, he took four wickets in four balls and the following year he sent one of George Lohmann's bails about 60 metres.

But he found enemies with his pace and action. At Trent Bridge in 1900, the South Australian umpire Dimboola Jim Phillips called him for throwing and he sent down just one over. A year later in the Lancashire-Somerset match at Old Trafford, Phillips called him 16 times in 10 overs, writing a finish to his career. Mold later lamented that he wished he had been called years earlier, because the controversy spoiled the great performances of his life.

Overs were increased from four balls to five when the Australian team managed by Harry Boyle arrived in England in 1890.

With it was the gangling, big-nosed, big-eared, kind-hearted and scholarly Hugh Trumble – "that great camel", as Plum Warner called him – one of the game's finest medium-pacers. Exploiting his 190 centimetres to their ultimate effect, Huge Hughie was the master of the quick off-break and could swing the ball when it was new.

He was a mainstay of Australian bowling for 12 years and at Melbourne against England he took two Test hat-tricks – in 1901-2 and 1903-4 – the second in his final Test, in which he took 7-28 to give Australia victory.

In The Oval Test of 1890, Frederick "Nutty" Martin, the Kent left-arm medium-pacer, took 12-102 in the match during a halcyon year when he took 190 wickets. But he never played against Australia again.

When the Englishmen arrived for the 1891-2 tour, they pinned much of their bowling hopes on John "One-eyed" Sharpe, another Surrey speedster.

The loss of an eye in his youth seemed to be no handicap, and he was famous for his off-cutter and extra-fast yorker. He took more than 100 wickets in 1890 and 1891.

Sharpe took 6-84 with his fast-medium pace in the first Test, at Melbourne, but he tried to make his slight frame work too hard and, instead of bowling faster, he burned himself out.

Charlie Turner took 16 wickets in the series, and three years later he bowled the last great innings of his career with 5-32 at Melbourne, opening with the dapper debutant, Arthur Coningham, who took 2-76 in his only Test, snaring Archie MacLaren with the first ball of the match.

Bill Howell, from bee farm to Test arena

Coningham was a left-arm, fast-medium all-rounder who had been a controversial selection on the previous tour of England in 1893.

He was the first man to score a first-class century for Queensland and would have had a longer international career except for his eccentric behaviour.

He won a bravery medal on the 1893 tour for saving a boy from drowning in the Thames, and he was a champion runner, shooter, billiards player and rugby hero whom women found irresistible.

But on tour he often disappeared without notice and once, in a cold match, he built a fire in the outfield.

After his cricket career ended, he became a bookmaker, failed in a tobacco business, and won money at billiards and shooting birds.

In 1899 he sued his wife for divorce, naming a priest as his wife's lover and claiming he could not have fathered his wife's child because of a knock he had taken playing cricket.

In two sensational trials, Coningham was once relieved of a loaded revolver in court and after the case against the priest was dismissed, he broke court furniture in attacking him.

Conspiracy on both sides was established.

Coningham was jailed for six months in New Zealand for fraud and was divorced in 1912 on the ground of his own adultery. He also admitted he had pointed a revolver at his wife.

He died in an asylum.

Despite Coningham's marvellous start to his Test career, England took a 2-0 lead in that 1894-5 series. Australia recovered to win the next two matches, thanks largely to the big-hitting quick bowler, Albert Trott, of Victoria.

"Alberto" scored 110 runs in the two unbeaten innings of the third Test at Adelaide (38 and 72) and picked up 8-43 in the second innings.

The match also marked the debut of another quick-bowling all-rounder, Syd Callaway, who took 5-37 in England's first innings.

Callaway twice took 15 wickets in a first-class match, and, after twice touring New Zealand with NSW teams, settled there and became an important figure in the early days of Kiwi cricket.

Trott was one of Australia's best players that summer but, even though his brother Harry was captain of the 1896 tourists to England, Alberto was left out of the team because the selectors had chosen their side before his heroic performances.

One of those chosen for the tour was Charles John Eady, of Tasmania, like Alberto a quick bowler and savage hitter, whose greatest feat came in 1902, when he hammered 566 out of 908 for Break O'Day against Wellington.

Alberto packed his bags, joined Middlesex, and became the most successful all-rounder in county cricket at the turn of the century. He bowled with a similar action to Spofforth's; but, though he had the pace, he lacked The Demon's cunning.

He played twice for England against South Africa and he gained a reputation for huge hits, blasting Poor Fred Tate to the top of the Lords pavilion and slamming the medium-paced Australian, Monty Noble, over the pavilion in 1899.

His career at times floundered because he tried to live up to the big-hitting reputation no matter what the circumstances.

Alberto took 100 wickets in a season seven times and made eight centuries, took 10-42 for Middlesex against Somerset in 1900, and in a benefit match at Lords in 1907 he ruined what could have been a big payday for himself by taking four wickets in four balls and then a hat-trick.

He became an umpire after retiring, but hard

drinking ruined his health and his marriage. At his London boarding house at Willesden Green on the day before World War I began, he shot himself, leaving his wardrobe and a few pounds to his landlady.

Monty Noble, the victim of Alberto's biggest hit, was one of Australia's finest all-rounders, bowling medium-pace off-breaks using a grip he later discovered was the same used by American baseball pitchers – the ball squeezed between thumb and forefinger to produce great swing.

In the 1897-8 summer against England, Noble and Trumble both took 19 wickets behind Ernie Jones's 22 to help Australia to a 4-1 series victory, even though Honest Tom Richardson and Old Jack Hearne took 42 wickets between them.

That series also saw the debut of Farmer Bill Howell, who had not played first-class cricket until he left his bee farm at Penrith, near Sydney at 25.

Farmer Bill had potential as a big-hitting batsman, but he made his name as a fast-medium bowler in 18 Tests.

He made his debut at Adelaide and on the 1899 tour of England took 10-28 in the first innings against Surrey off 23.2 overs and then chipped in with 5-29 in the second.

The 1899 series previewed the Golden Age Of Cricket with some astonishing performances.

In the third Test, in which Headingley was first used as a Test ground, the tragic spinner Johnny Briggs had a fit and was rushed to Cheadle Asylum where he died three years later.

The bowling duties for the match fell to the Essex express, Harding Isaac "Sailor" Young, a left-armer.

In the fourth Test, at Old Trafford, he was partnered by another debutant, the Kent amateur Bill Bradley, who had taken hat-tricks that season against Essex and Yorkshire and who once took six wickets in six balls for Lloyd's Register against the Mitcham club.

Both were made to do an enormous amount of hard work in the Tests and were never the same again.

While England and Australia had been engaging in a decade of Ashes conflict that saw both teams building up for war in the new century, England had also been sending teams to South Africa and the West Indies to encourage the development of the game.

In Barbados in 1895, England had encountered the powerful Clifford Goodman, forerunner of generations of Barbadian demons. In South Africa, it had nurtured its own quick men.

The delicate George Lohmann was the hero of the 1895-6 campaign and he was backed on the tour by Hugh Bromley-Davenport a fast, left-arm bowler and Cambridge blue who played for Cheshire, Middlesex and The Gentlemen.

Hampshire's Christopher Heseltine was also a right-arm fast bowler on the tour. Unlike Bromley-Davenport, he did not win a blue at Cambridge. Nor did he even make the Eton First XI. But by the age of 27 he had developed his pace and skill enough to make tours to India, The West Indies and South Africa, where he played two Tests.

Three years later, the South Africans led England on the first innings in their two Tests but lost both, largely because of Albert Trott, who took 17 wickets in two matches.

At Cape Town, he and Schofield Haigh, with 6-11, dismissed the locals for 35.

Haigh, known as the Sunshine of the Yorkshire XI, formed a sticky partnership with George Hirst. After inspecting a pitch he considered helpful, he came up with one of cricket's best lines: "Methinks they'll deviate somewhat".

They often did, no matter what the condition of the pitch, and he took 100 wickets or more in a season 11 times, collecting five hat-tricks along the way.

Arthur Mold, a terrifying bowler with just a four-stride run-up.

Ernie Jones
(1869-1943)
The Mighty Jonah

In a match between the touring Australians and Yorkshire in 1896, Ernie Jones, the South Australian miner turned fast bowler, came within a whisker of badly hurting the head of an opening batsman called Johnny Brown.

The distraught Yorkshireman took off for a single and then refused to turn for what would have been a comfortable second run.

As the angry crowd yelled at the Australian captain, Harry Trott, "Take him off, Trott, he'll kill someone", Johnny Brown looked up the pitch at his opening partner and said: "I've got a wife and family. No more of that stuff for me."

Such was the effect of the Mighty Jonah, the first of Australia's true express fast bowlers and a man who cared little about the reputations of others.

Whether he was sending a short ball whizzing through the beard of the imperious W.G. Grace, cracking the ribs of the eminent Stanley Jackson, or crushing the hand of the future King of England with a bone-jarring shake, Jones was always the same belligerent speedster.

As a young man he was fond of wrestling his team mates naked in the dressing room to prove his strength and toughness, and he was something of a champion at this peculiar challenge until thrown by the pugnacious captain, Joe Darling.

Jones, introduced to Test cricket as Australia's answer to Tom Richardson, had plenty of bluster.

Thirty years after he retired from big cricket, Jones would row out from Fremantle in Western Australia to meet the ocean liners bringing over the latest English Test teams to confront the Australians.

Megaphone cupped to his mouth, he would shout out to startled visitors: "Hundred to one England for the Tests!" or "You haven't got a chance!"

Ernie Jones was born at Auburn, near the South Australian capital, Adelaide. He sometimes worked as a stevedore but it was at Broken Hill, where he went to work as a miner, that his fast bowling began to make men quiver, earning him the nickname of the Broken Hill Catapult.

The mines gave Jones a big chest and powerful shoulders, which helped his cricket no end and, when he returned to Adelaide to further his cricket career, he became a sensation, taking five NSW wickets in South Australia's first Sheffield Shield match in December, 1892.

Affie Jarvis, his wicket-keeper in the South Australian side, who once took a stumping off him, found out the hard way that he had to stand back a long way from the stumps or get hurt.

In one Adelaide Club match, Jonah's keeper let through 48 byes off Jonah's bowling, and sometimes two long stops were used to save giveaway runs. There are reports of Jonah knocking over one of the long stops who failed to handle a really quick one.

Jonah was coached heavily, and he developed from a raw speedster good for only a few overs at a time into a quick bowler who could bowl long spells and deliver the knockout ball off a fairly short run.

In England in 1896, he was overshadowed by the guile of Hugh Trumble. But in the first match of the tour against Lord Sheffield's XI at Sheffield Park, Sussex, he took 7-84 with the wickets of six of the all-time best – Grace, Jackson, Arthur Shrewsbury, William Gunn, Ranji, C.B. Fry – and a lesser light, George Davidson.

He subjected the Englishmen to an ordeal they had seldom suffered from an Australian bowler. Against W.G. Grace, he sent down a bouncer that knocked the regal figure back on his heels.

Grace remonstrated: "What do you think you're at, Jonah?" The big fast man replied: "Sorry, Doctor. She slipped".

The real recipient of pain and suffering in that match was Jackson. He made 95 not out but suffered a cracked rib. He remembered gingerly how he and the good doctor had been made to "dance about a bit" when Jones let go with "short and bumpy" stuff on a dry wicket. Jackson's cracked rib kept him out of cricket for three weeks.

When he next met Jones, the big Australian apologised profusely, pumping the Yorkshireman's hand. Jacker was not quite sure which hurt the most, the cracked rib or Jonah's grip.

Jones was the spearhead of Australia's bowling attack from 1894 to 1902, playing 19 Tests and taking 64 wickets at 29.01 each. He toured England three times – in 1896, 1899 and 1902, taking 121, 135 and 71 wickets, respectively.

C.B. Fry, a master batsman, world long-jump champion, soccer hero and occasionally a fast bowler with a suspect action, rated Jones the fastest bowler he faced over a prolonged period. But he reckoned Kortright could bowl the fastest ball.

Stanley Jackson called Jonah the best fast bowler of his time. Jones was also a magnificent fielder, especially at mid-off.

Jonah was called for throwing by the umpire, Dimboola Jim Phillips, in the match between South Australia and Stoddart's XI at Adelaide in the 1897-8 series and again in the second Test, at Melbourne.

But this was put down to overzealousness. In fact, that season was a magnificent triumph for the speedster. He took 22 Test wickets at 25 each and for South Australia against Stoddart's men had match figures of 14-237.

At Lords, where Australia won by 10 wickets in 1899, Jonah took his best Test figures, 7-88, and in the series took almost twice the wickets of anyone else from either side, 26 at 25.

Against New Jersey, in America, he took 8-6, and at the age of 54 he took 8-38 and hit 116 out of 123 in 35 minutes (11 sixes and 11 fours) for Queenstown Church of Christ.

The Mighty Jonah as seen by a contemporary artist.

As Dr Grace lay dying in 1915 he was aggrieved by the German zeppelin airships hovering over England, cursing them until friends and family became concerned at the effect his vexation was having on his deteriorating health.

Someone said he should not be afraid, since he had once been brave enough to stand up to the deadly bombs of Jonah Jones.

"Yes," growled the indignant doctor. "But I could see him."

Kortright's pace and accuracy took a swag of wickets.

Charles Kortright (1871-1952)

The Bail Breaker

In the *Book Of Cricket*, Plum Warner estimated the speed of Charles Kortright's bowling to be about 2000 feet a second, about 50 feet a second quicker than that of the other champion fast bowlers of the early 20th century, Tibby Cotter and Kodgee Kotze.

This works out at about 2160 kilometres an hour, or nearly 14 times faster than Jeff Thomson.

It is not known whether Plum Warner had just been hit in the head by Korty when he made his calculation, but perhaps his estimation was merely a way of emphasising that Kortright bowled a cricket ball as fast as humanly possible.

Indeed, those who faced the powerfully-built, tall Essex speedster at his peak believed no man could ever bowl as fast.

He never thought much about swing or cut; he was so fast, he did not have to. He believed in bowling as quickly as possible at the stumps and not wasting opportunities by pitching short. In his later years, he often advised another Essex express, Ken Farnes, always to keep the ball up.

Kortright took a run-up of 13 metres – a long run for the times - and wicket-keepers defied the convention of the day by standing well back to him.

He revelled in bowling to Surrey, perhaps because it contained Lohmann, Lockwood and Richardson, who, together with his injuries, prevented Korty from playing Test cricket.

Against Surrey at Leyton in 1893, he took 8-29 and 5-35, bowling unchanged through both innings with Walter Mead. Two seasons later on the same ground, he took 6-4.

In 1900, he was still quick enough to shock Yorkshire with 8-57.

Kortright achieved his almost mythical speed with a ball larger than the one used by modern fast bowlers, with smaller stumps to aim at and with a narrower crease that reduced the angle of his delivery.

He began his career as a high-scoring batsman, hitting 158 in an hour and three-quarters at Southampton in 1891, and in 1900 his eye was still good enough for him to hammer 131 out of 166 against Middlesex at Leyton.

Kortright used the yorker better than most fast bowlers. His first victim in county cricket, Billy Brockwell, was yorked, and in later years Kortright claimed the impact of ball on the stumps caused the bails to fly forward, one of them breaking above his own head.

Kortright was an amateur in every sense. He claimed proudly never to have done a day's work in his life. In fact, he was a dedicated cricketer from his days at Brentwood School when he would creep out through his bedroom window at 4am and practise bowling against the chapel wall until dawn.

When he did not have a cricket ball, he would practise his action using stones aimed at trees and posts, and in an article in Wisden in 1948 he said all his life he had wanted to project things further and faster than anyone else.

For several years, Kortright's opening partner at Essex was the strongly-built Harry Pickett, who played for the county from 1880 to 1897 and who in 1895 at Leyton took 10-32 in the first innings against Leicestershire on the spring bank holiday.

Kortright took 8-63 in the second innings and Arthur Woodcock took 12-115 for Leicester.

Pickett is believed to have committed suicide. His body was washed up at Aberavon, Wales, several weeks after it was reported missing; and Arthur Woodcock, once rated second only to Kortright in England for sheer pace, poisoned himself. Woodcock had once opened with Honest Tom Richardson for the Mitcham Club and later coached at the Haverford College in America, coming back to England to play for Leicestershire.

Once, in a minor match for the MCC against Lewes Priory at the Dripping Pan Ground in 1908, when Woodcock was 42, he bowled a batsman and sent a bail about 48 metres.

Unlike his two peers, Kortright lived to a ripe old age — 81. His life was one of wealth, prosperity and a spot of sport when he felt like it.

Bill Lockwood
(1868-1932)

The Moody Artist

Bill Lockwood had more than his share of tragedy and upheaval in his illustrious career.

He was a moody and temperamental paceman who with Tom Richardson formed for Surrey and England the first true fast-bowling combination.

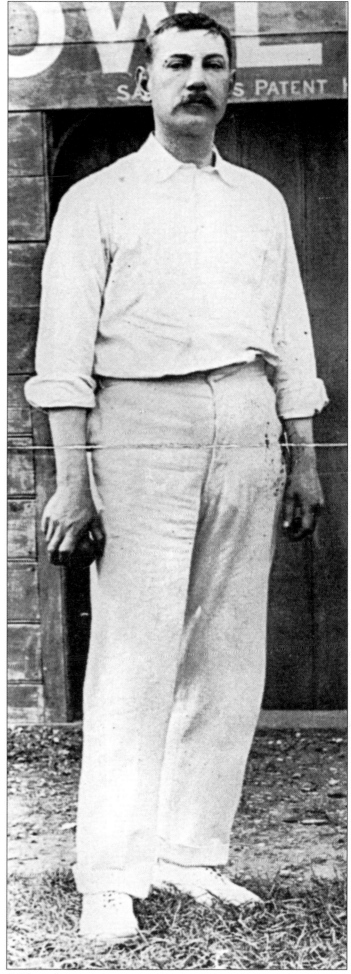

Bill Lockwood, a victim of his temperament

Neville Cardus wrote: "Lockwood had nicer technical shades than Richardson. But Lockwood had not a great spirit. He was a bowler at the mercy of a mood, an artist with an artist's capriciousness."

Lockwood also seemed to be injury-prone, suffering more than his share of strains and pains.

He took to heavy drinking after the death of his wife and child and lost his place in the Surrey team because of it.

But he was a rare talent and had enough heart to fight his way back to the top of English cricket after Richardson had burned himself out on the 1897-8 Australian tour.

For five years from 1898, Lockwood was the best bowler in England, though he had passed 30 and was constantly plagued by a thigh injury.

Born on March 25, 1868, he was noted for his high action and a powerful body swing that generated pace and cut.

Like that of Richardson and so many bowling champions of the day, his stock ball was the off-cutter, which he bowled to such effect that it would land outside off-stump and the keeper would have to dive down the leg-side to collect it.

He could bowl the slower ball better than any paceman of his era, sending it down with no change in action, and he was the master at using the width of the crease to vary the angle.

Lockwood was born in Nottingham but, after a handful of matches for his native county, he moved to Surrey at the age of 19. In the next 12 years, Surrey was county champion nine times, thanks to his efforts and those of Lohmann and Richardson.

"Lightning" Lockwood studied Lohmann's methods diligently and developed his pace so much that by the age of 24 he took 114 wickets in 16 county matches to emerge as England's most successful bowler.

Ranji, Billy Murdoch and C.B. Fry all thought Lockwood was a more dangerous bowler than Richardson.

Lockwood made his Test debut in the drawn match at Lords against the 1893 Australians, taking 6-101. He finished the series with 14 wickets at 15 each and, with Johnny Briggs, he won the series for England, taking eight wickets at The Oval where England won by an innings.

Lockwood had mixed fortunes and deep depressions over the next few years, but in 1898 he fought his way back into the Surrey team, for which he took 134 wickets and scored nearly 1000 runs.

Only the great workload of Lockwood's bowling prevented his batting from developing fully, but he twice did the double of 1000 runs and 100 wickets and he scored 15 first-class centuries.

Recalled to the England side in 1899, he took 7-71 against Australia at The Oval and was set to level a losing series against Joe Darling's tourists. But he had to leave the field during the second innings because of his thigh injury, and Australia managed to survive for a draw.

Lockwood's injury created doubts about his ability to cope with a long tour of Australia in 1901-2, so he

stayed home. But in 1902, when Darling's men returned to England for one of the finest series, Lockwood was again recalled at the age of 34.

He made a half-century but did not get a bowl as Rhodes and Hirst wrecked Australia for 36 in the rained-out match at Edgbaston. He did not get a bowl because of the rain at Lords either, and missed the match at Sheffield when Sydney Barnes returned for one Test.

But in the last two matches Lockwood finished his Test career by playing two of the greatest matches in cricket history. He topped five wickets three times in an innings, finishing the series with 17 at 12 runs each.

When Australia sneaked home by three runs in Poor Fred Tate's match at Old Trafford, Lockwood took 6-48 after being unable to bowl on the slippery turf before lunch, and then 5-28 in the second innings.

At The Oval, where Gilbert Jessop hammered his 75-minute century, Lockwood took 1-85 and 5-45 in England's one-wicket victory. His career lasted 12 Tests, in which he took 43 wickets at 20.55.

He retired from county cricket in 1904, ending an erratic but marvellously successful combination with Richardson.

In later years, Lockwood moved back to Radford, Nottinghamshire and was crippled by arthritis.

Tom Richardson (1870-1912)

Honest Tom

Tom Richardson was the first of England's truly fast Test bowlers. He was a man immortalised by the prose of Neville Cardus and by the honest labours of his big heart, which carried him through two tours of Australia and 14 Test matches before finally giving out at the age of 41.

In the words of David Frith, "Honest Tom" was born for bowling. His team mate, C.B. Fry, the master batsman, called him "a cheerful, brown-faced, Italian-looking brigand with an ivory smile".

He had rare stamina and his pace would not drop no matter how much work he had to do under the blazing Australian sun or on the merciless Oval wicket.

Honest Tom, who played his first full season for Surrey in 1893, built up his pace off a fairly long run, culminating in a high leap that made Cardus catch his breath and reach for a pen.

Richardson's accuracy was a byword, and he bowled a fuller length than most fast bowlers, swinging the ball into the batsman.

His greatest weapon was the off-cutter. Every few

Tom Richardson, a toiler in all conditions

deliveries, he would tear his fingers across the seam and make the ball cut back — sometimes, as much as 30 centimetres from outside off-stump, even on the tamest wickets.

With half his matches played on the heartless Oval wicket and with only one ball available through an innings, he took 290 wickets in 1895, still easily the highest tally for a fast bowler in a season. Some of his critics expected him to be drained that year, after a strenuous tour of Australia.

In 1896, he took 246 wickets; in 1897, 273.

Richardson was often abused by Australian crowds because of his dangerous pace and a suspicion that he was trying to maim the local batsmen.

Bowling to the little Victorian, Harry Graham, Richardson had the Test dasher continually dodging the short-pitched ball by falling to his knees.

Once, at Bramall Lane, Sheffield, Richardson pounded the Yorkshire batsmen to cries from the crowd of "Take him off!" and "Fetch the ambulance!"

He finished with 9-47 in the first innings, and, when he batted in the customary No.10 position, the crowd called for another cheerful fast man, George Hirst, to give him a taste of his own medicine.

Hirst's third ball hit Richardson on the thigh, to a great roar of approval from the crowd.

But there was not a malicious bone in the Surrey man.

Herbert Strudwick, the Surrey keeper, often spoke of Richardson's reluctance to bowl at his fastest after he had injured a batsman.

Dick Lilley who stood up to the stumps when he first kept wicket to Richardson in the Tests noted Honest Tom's pace dropped markedly after a ball had struck the keeper in the chest.

W.G. Grace soon intervened, saying: "You stand back, Dick, or he won't bowl full out."

Honest Tom made his Test debut in the drawn third Test of the 1893 Australian tour, at Old Trafford, taking 10 for 156.

In Australia in 1894-5, he took 32 wickets at 26 runs each, and his 6-104 in the final Test helped England win The Ashes.

By 1897-8 he was overweight, tired and needing additional financial encouragement to make another tour to Australia. But he plodded on in searing heat to take 22 wickets at 35 each in a losing series.

During Richardson's career, the Surrey side were county champion four times. Asked once whether he approved of plans to increase overs from five balls to six, he replied heartily: "Give me 10."

He ended his Test career as he had begun it with 10 wickets against Australia - this time at Sydney, where he collected 8-94 in the final match of the 1897-8 series.

He played 14 consecutive Tests for England and took 88 Australian wickets at 25.22 against the likes of Clem Hill, Syd Gregory, Joe Darling, George Giffen and Monty Noble, his last series being endured through painful rheumatism, increasing weight and stifling heat.

Honest Tom played out his career with Somerset and in retirement became a publican. There has always been some speculation that his sudden death was suicide. In any case the Gentleman v Players match of 1912 was suspended on the afternoon of his funeral.

Sadly, the finest achievement of this big-hearted fast bowler ended in futility in the 1896 series against Australia, in which he took 24 wickets at 18.

It came at Old Trafford and, even though Honest Tom played nine more years of first-class cricket, it was generally believed he was no longer quite the same bowler.

Australia needed a mere 125 to win, despite a seven-wicket haul off 68 overs by Honest Tom in its first innings. Richardson bowled and bowled and bowled, never slackening his pace, though, as Cardus wrote, each hour seemed an eternity.

At 7-100, it seemed the Gypsy king could do it and, as the other English bowlers began to falter, Richardson kept roaring in with what Cardus described as an action "like a great wave of the sea about to break".

With nine runs left, James Kelly gave a chance to his rival wicket-keeper, Lilley, who jarred his elbow and dropped the catch.

"The heart of Richardson might have burst at this," wrote Cardus. "But it did not. To the end he strove and suffered. Australia won by three wickets, and the players ran from the field - all of them save Richardson."

Honest Tom had taken 13 of the 17 Australian wickets in the match for 244 runs off 544 balls. All had been in vain.

He was dazed, wrote Cardus: "His body still shook from the violent motion. He stood there like some fine animal baffled at the uselessness of great strength and effort in this world ...

"A companion led him to the pavilion, and there he fell wearily to a seat."

Another version of the story is less romantic.

It says the beloved and thirsty Tom was first into the pavilion and had sunk two pints of beer before any of his team mates had time to take off their boots.

Tom Richardson was born in a gypsy caravan and born for fast bowling.

Hugh Trumble, a superb medium-pacer who captained Australia, and little Sid Gregory.

THE 1900s

The Golden Age

Neville Cardus once wrote of Walter Brearley gazing out from the Long Room at Lords and passing judgment on another generation of fast bowlers. "He could seldom bear to look for long," Cardus wrote. "His eyes popped almost out of his head; the explosive red of his face heightened. 'Ah could throw my hat down the pitch quicker!' he would say."

Maybe he could have. In his days, Walter Brearley was the fastest bowler in England, a 95 kilogram strongman who derived his speed from sheer strength and the fact he loved the challenge – wallowing in work, as Cardus put it.

He made his Test debut at Old Trafford against Joe Darling's Australian team in 1905, and took four wickets in each innings. He began his medium-length run with a step to the left rather like Richard Hadlee's in his early days. He had a powerful thrust of his body at the point of delivery and a total disdain for batsmen, labelling them all "a bunch of ruddy teetotallers".

Against the 1905 tourists, he dismissed Victor Trumper five times, and in the same season took 9-47 and 8-90 against Somerset at Old Trafford, bowling the last two batsmen in the first innings and taking the first two wickets in the second with four consecutive deliveries.

Brearley came into the England team after Arnold Warren's six-wicket haul at Headingley.

Warren was the first Derbyshire player to take 100 wickets in a season and, although he played for the county for 23 years, he played only one Test, twice taking the wicket of Trumper and picking up Monty Noble, Warwick Armstrong, Joe Darling and Frank Laver, a medium-pacer who at the the age of 36 took 7-64 at Trent Bridge and four years later as player-manager on the 1909 tour managed 8-31 at Old Trafford.

This fabulous century had begun with a pair of Trinidadian fast bowlers, Woods and Cumberbatch, touring England in 1900. Plum Warner wrote that they were often quite unplayable: "(Woods) bowls very fast with a rather low and slinging delivery, while Cumberbatch, who is perhaps the better of the two, bowls medium-pace right hand with a little work both ways."

Woods was the bowling success on the first West Indian tour of England, and his exuberance summed up a golden era when quick men would bowl a full length, enticing the batsman to hit, giving rise to the glorious action photographs of Trumper, Ranji and C.B.Fry.

One bowler who may have been even quicker than Walter Brearley was a South African, Johannes Jacobus "Kodgee" Kotze, whom Plum Warner rated second only to Kortright for sheer pace in the history of cricket.

The burly Kotze took a long, pounding run and had an awesome catapult in his final leap.

He gripped the ball between thumb and forefinger and seemed to hold it just a little longer before release than most bowlers, and many felt this gave the ball greater thrust.

His body swing helped move the ball through the air, and he was assisted by the brilliance of his wicket-keeper, Barberton Halliwell, who used raw steak inside his keeping gloves and could stand up at the wicket to Kotze, even taking stumpings down the leg side.

Kotze could bowl fast all day, but he was often discouraged by dropped catches and big hitting. He was instrumental in having turf wickets introduced to South Africa and was groundsman at the Newlands Stadium in Cape Town for many years, until his death in 1931.

Like Kotze, the Kent speedster, Arthur Fielder could bowl marathon spells of sheer pace. He made his debut at Melbourne in the 1903-4, series but the wicket was such a "sticky dog" that he did not get to bowl. The English pace bowling was handled mainly by George Hirst and Worcestershire's champion all-rounder Ted Arnold, who took 18 wickets with sharp medium pace that summer and in four consecutive seasons for his county achieved the double of 100 wickets and 1000 runs.

The series was something of a disappointment for Fielder, but four years later he had much better results.

Fielder played six Tests for England, all of them in Australia. He was the master of the off-cutter and away-swinger and played for Kent when it had fine slips men to snap up the edges.

Until World War One he led the Kent attack, and his 158 wickets in 1906 helped the county win its first championship. In the same season he set a record with 10-90 for the Players against the Gentlemen. In 1907-08 he took 25 wickets at 25 in his second Ashes series, bowling with Sydney Barnes.

Tibby Cotter took 14 wickets in the first two

John Barton "Bart" King, an American who could match the best

Tests of that series, but he was ruled out with a muscle strain and the NSW-born Adelaide fast-medium bowler, John O'Connor, took his place, bagging eight wickets on the Adelaide Oval. O'Connor bowled with a jerky action and, unlike most quick bowlers of the time, tended to concentrate on bowling outswingers rather than off-cutters.

Australia won the series 4-1, England's one-wicket victory at Melbourne almost ending in a tie as Gerry Hazlitt, then a frail 19-year-old, tried for a run-out. But his throw was wild.

Hazlitt was a fine medium-pacer who took 23 wickets in nine Tests. But he always had a weak heart, and he died at 27, four months after Victor Trumper.

The best of the English bowlers in 1907-8 was the bespectacled Jack Crawford, the Surrey all-rounder who played for South Australia for 10 years. He took 30 Australian wickets at 25 with lively medium pace.

He had been a hit on the 1905-6 tour of South Africa, partnering Schofield Haigh and his pacy Surrey pal, Walter Lees, who in his only Test series took 26 cheap wickets in five matches.

South Africa had a champion fast-medium bowler for that series in S.J. "Tip" Snooke, who took 24 wickets at 15, including 12 in the Third Test. Sixteen years later, he opened both batting and bowling for his country against England at the age of 41.

The South Africans also boasted the 190 centimetre Jimmy Sinclair, who first played against England as a 15-year-old in 1892. He scored South Africa's first half-century and century in 1899. It is said he once hit Wilfred Rhodes so hard that the ball went out of the Harrogate ground and knocked over a cabbie.

In 1901, Sinclair, who also played rugby for South Africa, escaped from a Boer prisoner of war camp and made it back to the British lines just in time for the cricket tour of England.

Partnering Snooke in 1905-6, he took 21 wickets.

When the South Africans toured England in their first official Test series in that country in 1907, Neville Knox, Walter Lees's senior opening partner at the county, played the only two Tests of an injury-marred career. He was as quick as anyone in the world, and in 1934 Jack Hobbs called him the best fast bowler he had seen.

Knox took a long run that started near deep mid-off, and often he played when not fit. From the age of 25 he was troubled by shin soreness from thundering down the Oval wicket, but he played first-class cricket until his mid-30s.

One of Knox's rivals for pace in the early 1900s was Worcestershire's William Beaumont Burns, who once scored a hat-trick and a century against Gloucestershire.

He was exceptionally quick and until World War One he partnered Dick Burrows, who was fast and strong and played 20 seasons for his county without a Test cap because he was often erratic.

But there was no doubting his speed. He once sent a bail a record 61.5 metres at Old Trafford in 1911 when he bowled Lancashire's Bill Huddleston and 10 years earlier he bowled Archie MacLaren and sent a bail 58.8 metres.

Another of the masterful quick bowlers at the time was an American, John Barton King, who never played Test cricket but knocked over the stumps of many who did.

King was the finest cricketer produced in America at a time when the game was popular there. The tall, balding bowler had great strength in his wrist and fingers, could bowl fast and, because of his early baseball training, swing the ball both ways.

He toured England three times, and on his first visit in 1897 bowled Ranji first ball in a tally of 7-13 for the Philadelphians against Sussex.

He once wrote that the secret of fast bowling was complete relaxation.

In 1909, he bowled all 11 of the Irish Gentleman in one innings. One was a no-ball.

That same year, left-armer, Bill Whitty, Sydney-born but Adelaide-based, took 77 wickets on tour with the Australians in England. But he failed to take a wicket in his one Test.

In partnership with the faster and more dangerous Cotter, he was, however, a great success against the first South Africans to tour Australia, in 1910-11.

He stood 182 centimetres and possessed a fluent action and sharp tongue, rebuking umpires who failed to agree with his opinions.

Once after being refused an appeal for a caught behind, he bowled a widish ball well clear of the batsman and appealed again.

The umpire berated him, and Whitty snapped back: "Just thought you might make two mistakes in one day."

In the second Test of that series, Whitty took 6-17 as he and Cotter wrecked South Africa for 80 after the tourists had made 506 in their first innings. Australia won the series 4-1, and the South Australian batsman, Arthur Richardson, called Whitty "the loveliest-actioned bowler" he had seen.

A year earlier in South Africa, England had used two talented fast men. The burly all-rounder George Thompson, known as The Northampton Nugget, was a hit with both bat and ball on tour, and Claude Buckenham, a tall, slim paceman, took nearly 1000 wickets for Essex between 1899 and 1914.

After England and Australia had both beaten South Africa, Plum Warner brought his Englishmen to Australia in 1911-2. But, after making 151 against South Australia, he became ill and was replaced by Johnny Douglas, a soccer international, pace-bowling all-rounder and conqueror of Australia's Snowy Baker for the 1908 Olympic boxing gold medal.

Douglas, who drowned at sea while trying to rescue his father during a business trip in 1930, was rated by Hobbs as the best new-ball bowler he faced. Cotter and Whitty may have bullied the South Africans, but this English team was even stronger than the last, that of 1907-8.

Sydney Barnes was backed by the left-armer Frank Foster, Douglas, and Surrey's Bill Hitch, a big-hitting, courageous fieldsman and fast bowler with a stuttering approach.

Foster and Douglas opened the bowling in the first Test but, miffed, Barnes was said to have given below his best and Douglas, deciding not to punch his head in, allowed Barnes the new ball.

From then, England romped away with the series, Barnes and Foster sharing 66 wickets and England winning the last four Tests convincingly.

Foster bowled around the wicket with a short run and easy action. He pioneered leg-theory bowling, spearing the ball into the batsman and trying to make him turn it to a ring of fieldsmen on the leg side.

Twenty years later, Bill Voce bowled much like Foster, with more venom, and Foster publicly condemned the Englishmen for the unsporting way they used his ideas.

Foster was one of cricket's best all-rounders in the Golden Age, hitting 305 not out against Worcestershire in 1914 and leading Warwickshire to its first championship in 1911.

He claimed his fast bowling team mate, Frank Field, was the best pace bowler in England from 1908 until World War One.

Herbert Strudwick, the English wicket-keeper, always thought Foster had it in for him in Australia because he wanted his county man, Tiger Smith, behind the stumps.

Strudwick claimed Foster would often signal him to expect a leg-side stumping and then send the ball whizzing down the off-side to be taken by Frank Woolley at first slip. No matter what his tactics, Foster and Barnes formed one of England's most successful opening attacks.

Australia's fast men that summer — Cotter, Whitty, and the medium-pacers, Charlie Kelleway and Roy Minett — were rendered ineffective against the batting strength of Hobbs, Rhodes and Woolley.

Such was the dominance of the Englishmen that Whitty lost his place after the second Test and Tibby Cotter was replaced by John "Ginger"

McLaren, who became the first Queensland-born Test player. McLaren missed the fourth Test after threats of industrial action because he had been used as a special constable in a police strike.

But he played in the fifth Test, plagued by dropped catches. The last thing Australian cricket needed after the hammering from Barnes and Foster was to lose its six best players.

But, in a row over the management for the 1912 Triangular Tournament, Cotter, Trumper, Armstrong, Clem Hill, Vernon Ransford and Hanson Carter all stayed home and the Australians again were no match for England, though they beat South Africa twice.

Hazlitt's 7-25 against England at The Oval could not compensate for poor batting.

When England went to South Africa the following season with the killer Barnes, Jimmy Blackenberg was the best of the local bowlers with his medium-pacers, and in support was Joe Cox, a good fast medium bowler who three years earlier had taken 8-20 (seven bowled) against Transvaal, helping Natal win its first Currie Cup.

At Port Elizabeth, Eric "Bill" Lundie bowled 46 overs into the wind. Like his quick-bowling team mate, Claude Newberry, he died during World War One.

That war also took Percy Jeeves, the paceman from Warwickshire, and Major Booth, from Pudsey, Yorkshire, who in 1913 scored 1228 runs and took 181 wickets at 18.5, showing at the age of 27 that he had mastered the off-break, swing and changes in pace.

Jack Massie survived World War One, but he spent the rest of his life wondering what might have been, watching men of less ability playing for Australia.

Massie was the finest left-handed Australian bowler Johnny Moyes ever laid eyes on. One hundred and ninety centimetres, a champion athlete, oarsman, footballer and fast bowler, he took 99 wickets for NSW and showed signs of greatness.

He had a long-striding run and a fast dipping ball that was a menace to even the best batsman.

He was shot in the shoulder at Gallipoli and shot through the foot in France. He never played big cricket again.

Sydney Barnes
(1873-1967)

A Tough Old Crow

By his own admission, Sydney Barnes was an obstinate cuss.

He was an intense man who bowled mainly fast spinners, wearing the skin off his fingers in many games so that the ball became smeared with his own blood.

He was brooding and gaunt. He scowled his way through matches and raged at misfielding. But to such batsmen as Archie MacLaren, Plum Warner, Charlie Macartney, Frank Woolley and Jack Hobbs among so many others, he was the finest bowler they ever faced.

Barnes stood 185 centimetres and was wiry. He was king of spin, swing and cut, sometimes delivered at genuine pace but usually no faster than brisk medium off a bounding, high-stepping run of 13 strides and a high action that saw the right arm coming over so straight that it brushed his ear.

His most dangerous ball was delivered wide of the crease, swinging into the batsman and changing course after pitching, so that it clipped the off bail.

Barnes seemed almost always to be at loggerheads with officials and he missed at least five years during his peak (1902-7) because Test selectors found him so difficult to handle.

But when he was bowling for England and he had it in his mind to get wickets, he was almost unplayable. Indeed, many believe Barnes may have been the finest bowler of any era.

His first Test wicket was a caught-and-bowled off Victor Trumper, and Charlie Macartney recalled another Barnes riddle that confounded the maestro.

It was the kind of delivery you might see when drunk, he said: "The ball was fast on the leg-stump but just before it pitched it swung suddenly to the off. Then it pitched, broke back and took Victor's leg stump."

Barnes was a master at bowling to his field, encouraging the batsman to play shots. He could mesmerise batsmen, putting a fielder in position and then somehow making the batsmen hit the ball straight to the man.

Barnes was a professional cricketer for 45 years, and in all classes of cricket he took 6225 wickets at 8.31 each. It was not until he was 61 that he was first dropped from a team for lack of form, and even in that year he went to another club and bowled brilliantly for them.

Twelve times in his career, he took all 10 wickets in an innings. In a match for Porthill in 1906 against Leek Highfield, he batted through the innings to score 76 and then took 10-12 with the ball.

In 1907, he took 112 wickets at 3.91 each, again took all 10 wickets against Leek Highfield and did the hat-trick twice in one innings against the powerful batting line-up of Silverdale.

In 1909, Barnes opened the bowling to the Leek

Sydney Barnes, a lifetime at the top.

captain, Harry Ellerton. The first ball swung at him and he was lucky to edge it past leg stump for a single. Barnes then took the next nine wickets without a run being scored and, when the last man came in, he was dropped first ball and went on to make a last-wicket partnership of 30 before Barnes rattled the stumps. But for the dropped catch, Barnes would have had 10 wickets for one lucky single.

In 27 Tests for England he took an amazing 189 wickets — seven a Test — at 16.43, and in just seven Tests against South Africa he took 83 wickets. Shortly before his death at 94 in 1967, Barnes estimated, without a trace of modesty, that had he been playing in the modern era he could have taken 500 Test wickets.

He was born on April 19, 1873 at Smethwick, Staffordshire, one of five children and the only cricketer in the family. His first hero was Tom Richardson, but he learned the off-cutter from Billy Bird, of Warwickshire, who coached Smethwicks First XI.

In his first game for the Smethwick Firsts, Barnes did not get a bowl and was out first ball. On the way back to the pavilion he heard someone say, "You're no bloody good"; and for the rest of his life he played the game as though he was forever trying to prove otherwise.

He played five matches for Warwickshire between 1893 and 1896, then joined Rishton in the Lancashire League doubling as groundsman.

At 28, he was playing for the Lancashire League side, Burnley, and bowling to the English skipper, Archie MacLaren, in the Old Trafford nets.

He was so impressive that, despite his limited first-class background and a reputation for being headstrong, he was invited to tour Australia as Yorkshire would not release its stars George Hirst and Wilfred Rhodes and there were doubts over the fitness of Bill Lockwood.

Barnes was then a little-known professional who had never seen a Test match. He was such a prickly character that even his mentor, MacLaren, exclaimed during a rough passage on the voyage, "At least if we go down we'll take that bugger, Barnes, down with us".

In his first game for England, Barnes took five wickets against South Australia, followed by 12-99 against Victoria, 5-65 in the first innings of the first Test and 13-163 in the second.

Monty Noble taught him to bowl an outswinger that cut back at the batsman after pitching, and Barnes practised it for hours in the nets, swinging the ball past a pole half-way up the pitch and then making it cut back five metres from the batsman.

But he had little opportunity to use the delivery, breaking down with a knee injury after seven overs in the third Test when his new spikes gripped the ground so firmly that his knee gave out.

Barnes fell foul of the England selectors and, though he played two seasons with Lancashire, did not play Test cricket again for five years.

He was back in Australia for the 1907-8 tour, opening with Arthur Fielder. Both had marvellous tours in an otherwise disappointing series, Barnes taking 7-60 in the final match at Sydney.

Barnes would gain revenge four years later.

Opening with Frank Foster, he took 34 wickets at 23, and England won the series 4-1.

Barnes bowled below his best in the first Test because the skipper, Johnny Douglas, took the new ball instead, But in the next match, at Melbourne, with his

ego massaged, Barnes began with one of the finest spells in Test cricket, having fought the flu the previous night .

At one stage he had 5-6 — with the wickets of Warren Bardsley, Charlie Kelleway, Warwick Armstrong, Roy Minett and Clem Hill, who was clean-bowled by a ball that changed direction twice.

Against South Africa in the 1912 Triangular series, he took more than half the wickets for England, finishing with 34 from the three matches at 8.29 with a best of 8-29 at The Oval.

In four Tests in South Africa in the 1913-4 season, when Barnes was 40, he finished his career with 49 wickets at 10.93.

His 17 wickets at Johannesburg (8-56 and 9-103) set a world record until Jim Laker topped him in 1956.

Jack Hobbs remembered that on tour Barnes was "practically unplayable, making the ball turn so much that three or four times an over he would beat the bat and miss the stumps."

Barnes took his 49 wickets in the first four Tests of the series but missed the fifth, at Port Elizabeth, saying he withdrew because South African officials, bitter because his bowling was ruining gate receipts, refused to pass the hat around to meet expenses for his wife and son on tour.

The South Africans claimed that while Barnes had always liked a quid, the real reason he withdrew was that Herbie Taylor was frustrating him as no other batsman had ever done.

Taylor played Barnes by looking for the way Barnes's fingers would cut down the ball — either for the off-cutter, or the "Barnes ball", as Neville Cardus called the leg-cutter, the delivery that first swerved in and then fizzed and cut towards off stump and the slips.

Barnes was still a feared bowler in his 60s.

In 1920, at 47, he was asked to tour Australia. But the MCC would not pay for his wife and son to accompany him, so he stayed home. In 1924, at 51, he took 5-32 off 16 overs against South Africa, and four years later he twice played for Wales against the West Indies, taking 7-51 and 5-67.

At 55, he headed the English first-class averages, and at 56 he bowled unchanged for three hours and took 8-41 bowling for Minor Counties against South Africa.

At 67, he was still taking wickets as a club professional. At 80, he bowled an over of brisk pace and immaculate length in a benefit game featuring some of England's great names.

But sometimes his reputation counted for nought.

Playing for Rochdale against Walsden, the wooden-spoon team in the Central Lancashire League, Barnes was bowling brilliantly when in came a kid from the third grade making up the numbers.

He promptly hit four boundaries in succession.

"Well played, lad," said his captain after the innings, "Do you know who the bowler was?"

"Nay. Ah don't," the boy replied.

"Well it wor Sydney Barnes," the captain told him, waiting for the shock to hit.

"Well all Ah can say," the lad replied, "is that Ah wish he'd bin on at both ends."

Tibby Cotter, echoes of "Thommo"

Albert "Tibby" Cotter (1883-1917)

The Stump Snapper

Albert "Tibby" Cotter died with a machine-gun bullet through the head when the Australian Light Horse cavalry advanced on Beersheba in 1917.

A stretcher bearer, he was not supposed to be anywhere near the ancient desert city but, in the tradition of the Australian larrikin hero, he defied orders and rode with his mates to meet death or glory.

Cotter was once the fastest bowler in the world — a small, marvellously muscled man that the Sydney journalist J.C. Davis described as a model for the sculptor.

He toured England in 1905 and 1909, and the last record of tremendous fast bowling from this handsome hero was the 5-215 he took in a Services game at Gezireh, in Palestine in 1916.

The pitch was a little more barren than the English wickets on which he had created so much havoc.

He was one of the great drawcards of his day, and there are more than 20 different accounts of his breaking stumps or snapping bails as well as batsmen's knuckles with his lightning deliveries, propelled from a slinging action similar to that used by Jeff Thomson 70 years later.

Cotter, born to wealthy parents in Sydney on December 3, 1884, was nicknamed "Tibby" as a child because he was smaller than the other boys against whom he played cricket.

As a boy he played with two future Test men, Warren Bardsley and Charlie Kelleway, and in later years Bardsley remembered that even as a child Cotter was so quick he would knock the palings from the fence against which he bowled.

At Sydney Grammar, Tibby blossomed as an athlete, excelling as a sprinter, rugby player, a fast-bowler and a bright-eyed, big-hitting batsman.

At 18, while playing club cricket with Glebe, he made his first class debut against Victoria.

Like Frank "Typhoon" Tyson, Cotter began his career with an excessively long run and found that by cutting it down he became a more effective fast bowler. In Cotter's case, the ball began to cut back from outside off-stump more dramatically.

Cotter stood just 170 centimetres but was solid in the chest and shoulders. Like Thomson, he threw his bowling arm back toward mid-off as he began his delivery stride, presenting the batsman with a brief look at his profile before snapping his powerful torso toward the stumps and slinging the ball through as though it were a spear.

But Cotter tended to drop his shoulder more than Thomson, skidding the ball through toward the stumps and causing some writers of the day to regard him as a fast round-armer. Like Thomson, he could also be dangerously erratic, giving the batsman no clue as to where the next one might land and, like the latter-day hero, he also suffered a severe shoulder injury that caused him to bowl the ball back to the wicket-keeper rather than throw it.

Both men seemed indifferent about whether they smashed a stump or a batsman's nose, and both bowlers possessed a yorker that was freakishly quick, difficult to sight and usually impossible to defend against.

In fact, one of Cotter's stump-breaking exploits was performed with the yorker against no less a master than Victor Trumper.

Johnny Moyes in his book *Australian Bowlers* once gave a chilling account of just how quick Cotter could be. Against South Australia with the wind at his back, "The ball flew fast and high, too fast indeed for one batsman, who could only turn his back and take the full force of the ball, which burrowed into his flesh and left a hole into which the ball could have been placed some time later."

Moyes also remembered Cotter as a good sport, quite prepared to cheer a batsman for a fine shot and able to bowl for hour after hour.

With another small, strong man, John Scott, he formed a truly terrifying fast-bowling combination for NSW. Cotter and Scott, who was also a rugby league champion for Newtown and later a Test umpire, were outstanding together at the outbreak of World War One, but it was Cotter who kept his partner out of the Test team before the war and Gregory and McDonald who ruined Scott's aspirations after it.

Cotter earned his Test spot by taking eight wickets and scaring several other batsmen for NSW against Plum Warner's 1903-4 tourists.

In his second Test match — the last of the series at Melbourne — Cotter took 6-40 in the first innings as he and Monty Noble wrecked England for 61 and Hugh Trumble bowled Australia to victory in the second.

On tour with Joe Darling's men in 1905, Cotter had great personal success in a losing series in England, taking 124 wickets at under 20 each and emerging from the match at Worcester with 12-34.

In a series in which Stanley Jackson, C.B. Fry, Johnny Tyldesley and Archie MacLaren dominated with the bat, Cotter, usually partnered by the veteran Frank Laver, took 13 Test wickets at under 33 each.

In the last Test, at The Oval, Tibby took 7-148 in England's first innings of 430.

Back in England in 1909, Cotter was the best of Australia's bowlers, with 17 wickets at 21, taking 6-95, including the scalp of the debutant Frank Woolley at The Oval and 5-38 at Leeds.

Cotter never dominated touring teams the way some expected, breaking down against England in 1907-8 after taking 14 wickets; and even his 22 wickets against South Africa in 1910-11 were overshadowed by Bill Whitty's bowling and the batting of the touring all-rounder, Aubrey Faulkner.

By the 1911-12 series against England, Cotter could only watch in dismay as Barnes and Foster wrapped up The Ashes, Cotter's 12 wickets costing 46 runs each.

Cotter was only 27, but he never played Test cricket again, withdrawing from the 1912 Triangular series along with five other top Australians. He was two months short of his 33rd birthday when he died.

In 21 Tests, he took 89 wickets at 28.64. Before riding off to Beersheba, Cotter is said to have tossed a ball of mud and remarked to a comrade: "That's my last bowl, Blue. Something's going to happen."

George Hirst mixed skill with laughs.

George Hirst (1871-1954)

The Happy Warrior

Like Wilfred Rhodes, his slow-bowling partner from Yorkshire, George Hirst was born at Kirkheaton, bowled left-handed, batted right-handed and held a claim to being the world's best all-rounder.

Hirst could bowl with great pace, but he spent most of his time as a fast-medium left-armer.

As his nickname suggested, he was a tough competitor but a jolly fellow.

He possessed a brutal in-swinger and, though he often made his team mates laugh, he could make a batsmen cry with his speciality, the ball that shot in late and leaped at the groin.

He took more than 100 wickets in a season 15 times, and as a batsman he had a quick eye and nimble feet, once hitting 341 against Leicestershire.

The next year, 1906, he performed the "double double" (208 wickets and 2385 runs for Yorkshire) a feat that will never be repeated, especially since the reduction of the county championship in 1969.

That year against Somerset, he scored 111 and 117 not out and took 6-70 and 5-45, his second century coming in just 66 minutes.

Two years later, he and his opening partner, Schofield Haigh, with the slinging action and vicious yorker, knocked over Northamptonshire for 27 and 15, Hirst taking match figures of 12-19.

The Happy Warrior played for Yorkshire for 39 years from 1889, made 32,231 runs at 33.96 and took 2569 wickets at 17.86. He was a brilliant fieldsman at mid-off, taking 550 catches.

By comparison with his record for Yorkshire, Hirst's role in 24 Tests was less significant — 59 wickets at 30 and 790 runs at 22.57 — but he did play a hand in some of the most memorable matches of the Golden Era.

In 1902, he helped Wilfred Rhodes bamboozle Joe Darling's Australians at Edgbaston, where the visitors, rated as one of the finest teams to visit England, were all out for 36, Rhodes with 7-17 and the Happy Warrior with 3-15. Rain forced a draw.

Three days later, Hirst took 5-9 and Stanley Jackson 5-12 in dismissing Australia for 23 against Yorkshire.

At The Oval in the fifth Test of that remarkable series, Hirst took 5-77 in the first innings and, after Gilbert Jessop's whirlwind 100 in 75 minutes, he helped Rhodes make the last 15 runs for a one-wicket victory.

Hirst's contributions to the match, one of the most famous in Ashes history, were 5-77, 43, 1-7 and 58 not out.

Hirst toured Australia twice, making his debut in the 1897-8 series, scoring 62 but going wicketless at Sydney.

Six years later, he took 15 Australian wickets at 30. His best series was at home against South Africa in 1907, when he took 10 wickets at 18.50 in a low-scoring series that England won.

Hirst coached at Eton for 18 years and was still playing village cricket in 1941 at the age of 70. He was one of the professional cricketers the MCC honoured with life membership in 1949.

As coach of Yorkshire in 1935 he had some timely advice for a teenage batsman trying to make it with the county.

"Booger off," said George. "There's nowt we can teach thee."

The batsman was Len Hutton.

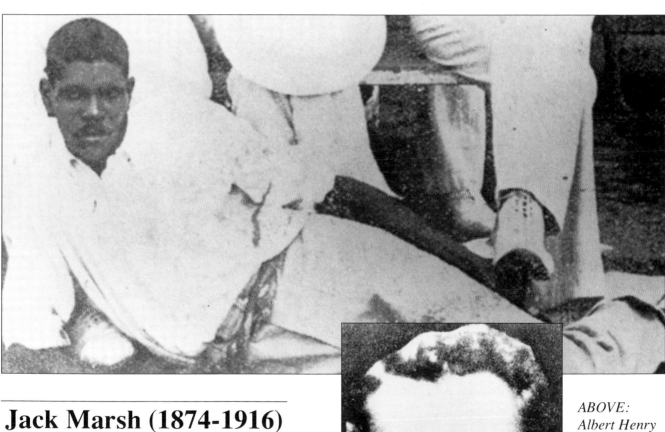

Jack Marsh (1874-1916) and Albert "Alec" Henry (1880-1909)

No Connections, Wrong Complexions

After being thrown out of big cricket because of a suspect action, Jack Marsh saw out his bowling days in a circus freak show until he was kicked to death

ABOVE: Albert Henry and LEFT: Jack Marsh. Both suffered racist taunts.

by two white men in a streetfight in the NSW country town of Orange.

His assailants were charged not with murder, but with manslaughter and, after the judge remarked that the once-fearsome fast bowler "might have deserved" the beating he took, they were acquitted without the jury retiring.

Like the American, Bart King, Marsh could occasionally make the ball wobble in the air, and *The Referee* newspaper said he was able to curve the ball significantly, had a peculiar dropping ball and possessed "phenomenal" break back even on perfect wickets, considering the pace at which he bowled.

He was a proud, dapper man, a full-blood Aborigine born at Yugilbar, in the Clarence River district in northern NSW, and, like his Queensland contemporary, Alec Henry, he had the misfortune of living in not only racist times but in an era when officials around the world were hounding chuckers from the game.

Marsh was discovered throwing a boomerang for tourists at La Perouse, Sydney, and at a NSW trial in November, 1900, he employed the whip of his sinewy arms and shoulders to uproot the stumps of Victor Trumper for one.

But the square-leg umpire, W. Curran, immediately labelled his deliveries illegal and said he would call Marsh for throwing if he played the next day.

According to the *Sydney Morning Herald*, Marsh felt so confident that his deliveries were fair, he offered to bowl in splints, forcing Curran to retire from the match.

That was only the start of the throwing allegations against Marsh that season.

Against Victoria in Melbourne, he was no-balled three times for throwing by an umpire, Bob Crockett, and lost his temper so much that after one delivery he took the return and then threw the ball at the batsman, Frank Laver.

In the return match in Sydney, Victoria brought Crockett as their own umpire for the occasion, and he no-balled Marsh 19 times, including three times in his first over to Warwick Armstrong.

The crowd booed Crockett every time he called Marsh, who had taken to bowling slower after his brush with Umpire Curran.

Although Monty Noble, a selector for NSW, said Marsh was a chucker and so erratic that he could not be relied upon, he took 58 wickets in grade cricket in 1902 at less than 10 runs apiece.

There were few complaints in Sydney about Marsh's action, and in 1903-4, when he took 5-55 for a Bathurst XV against Plum Warner's Englishmen, his action was passed as fair even though before the game Warner complained bitterly about having a dangerous fast bowler with a suspect action firing away at his men.

In 1905, there were suggestions that Marsh might tour with Joe Darling's team to England. But the Australian tennis hero and Lancashire all-rounder, Dr Leslie Poidevin, said such a thing was unlikely, given the country's "absurd white-Australia policy".

Warren Bardsley, the great left-handed opener, remarked many years later in his memoirs that the reason Marsh was kept out of big cricket was his colour.

Marsh was a popular figure wherever he played, often riding the Sydney trams with his blue NSW cap tucked under a straw hat. He was illiterate but was often seen reading a newspaper, even if it was occasionally upside down. He died from a fractured skull.

Marsh took 34 first-class wickets at 21.47.

In April, 1902, when NSW played Queensland at Brisbane, Marsh opened the bowling for the Blues and Alec Henry led the Queensland attack. It was the first time Aborigines had opposed each other in first-class cricket.

Henry took 2-63 and 1-38; Marsh 2-64, 3-67.

As with Jack Marsh, the Englishmen who faced Henry in 1903-4 rated him a great pace prospect, some calling him the fastest bowler they had ever seen but several agreeing that his action was not above suspicion.

Contemporary reports called Henry moody, fiery and unpredictable, and he bowled in bare feet for the South Brisbane Club. He played seven first-class games for Queensland, taking 21 wickets at 32.04, including 5-40 against NSW in 1902-03.

In a club match in 1904, the well-known umpire A.L. Crossart repeatedly no-balled Henry from square leg, sending the fast bowler into a rage.

Henry's reaction was reported to the Queensland Cricket Association this way: "Mr Henry, when the over was completed, deliberately went over to umpire Crossart and said words to this effect: 'You bastard! You no-ball my good balls, and the ones I did throw you never! You know nothing about cricket!' "

Alec Henry and Jack Marsh played their cricket at a time that was not good for Aborigines. Henry was once imprisoned at the Barambah (later Cherbourg) mission for a month for "loafing, malingering and defying authority", and from there he was made to live at the even more remote Yarrabah, where he died of tuberculosis at the age of 29.

In the words of the historian, Professor Colin Tatz, he died "defiant at the system, yet certain victim of it".

Sydney Barnes was really an old softie. Here he is on his 80th birthday with his grandchildren Penny and Peter.

George Francis specialised in quick balls straight at the stumps

THE 1920s

Tandem Terrors Of The Roaring Twenties

Fast men began hunting in packs in the 1920s. Australia had Gregory and McDonald, England uncovered Larwood and Voce, and the West Indies developed George John, George Francis, Herman Griffith and Learie Constantine. Early in the decade, the Englishmen were still recovering from World War One. When Johnny Douglas brought an understrength side to meet Warwick Armstrong's team in 1920-1, the Englishmen were relying on the Surrey veteran Bill Hitch again as well as Harry Howell, part of the Warwickshire attack that had included Frank Foster, Frank Field and Percy Jeeves before the war.

Howell's greatest moment came after the Australian tour when he took 10-51 against Yorkshire at Edgbaston in 1923. The year before, he and Freddie Calthorpe had dismissed Hampshire for 15, Howell taking 6-7 only to see Hampshire hit 521 in the follow-on and win the match.

Hitch and Howell were backed by Douglas and Abe Waddington, a support bowler to Emmott Robinson and George Macaulay at Yorkshire.

None of the English pacemen had much success, but at home to Australia the following season Jack Durston, the 192 centimetre Middlesex champion managed a five-wicket haul against the tourists at Lords in his only Test during a series dominated by Gregory and McDonald.

Two years later in South Africa, England won 2-1, thanks largely to the 31 wickets by Hampshire's fast-medium bowler, Alec Kennedy, and his inswing. For many years Kennedy and Jack Newman led the Hampshire attack, and Kennedy took 10-37 for the Players against the Gentlemen at The Oval in 1927. He had a long run, but it got results and he performed the double of 100 wickets and 1000 runs five times, 205 wickets and 1129 runs in 1922.

In that South African season, the left-arm, fast-medium bowler, Alf Hall, took 27 English wickets, including 7-63 at Cape Town. Born in Lancashire, he became a matting maestro for Transvaal and in the series against England was supported by another Transvaal fast-medium bowler, Doug Meintjes, who took six cheap wickets in two Tests.

The Cape Town Test also saw the debut of the medium-pace off-spinner, George Macauley, who not only took a wicket with his first ball in Test cricket but finished with 5-64 and hit the winning run in England's one-wicket victory.

In 1923, England had a bitter taste of the speed attacks that would haunt their pitches for decades to come.

Though Gregory and McDonald were the most feared fast bowlers in the world, the West Indies had a terrifying twosome of their own in George John and George Francis.

John was about 40 at the time, and only the West Indians saw him at his best a decade earlier.

The Trinidadian stood 175 centimetres tall and was powerfully built, bowling with a high arm and bringing the ball back from outside off stump.

C.L.R. James, the West Indian writer, recalled that many batsmen hit on the inside of the knee by his off-cutter collapsed like felled oxen.

John intimidated batsmen by his presence and had such a thrusting follow-through that he would collect the ball from the keeper only a metre or two from the batsman.

He would roll up his sleeves before every ball "like a man about to commit some long premeditated act of violence", and his 4-12 at Scarborough against Leveson-Gower's XI virtually assured the West Indies Test-match status for its next series in 1928.

On that first 1923 tour, though, John took 49 first-class wickets at 19.51, topping young Learie Constantine in the averages.

Leading the bowling was Francis — short, unemotional, undemonstrative and delivering very quick balls straight at the stumps as fast as he could.

He took 82 wickets on tour at 15.58, using his high leap at the crease, his outswinger, and his well-aimed yorker.

Against Surrey, he had match figures of 10-76. Against the MCC, he took 9-56 two years later as he and the cocky little Herman Griffith bowled Barbados to an innings win over Freddie Calthorpe's side during a series in which Walter Hammond became seriously ill.

Griffith might have toured England in 1923. He was certainly good enough, but he had a volatile nature — perhaps too volatile for a nation trying to emerge in the civilised world of cricket — and he had a bad habit of swearing at rival batsmen.

Five years later, he was on tour of England when George Francis bowled the first ball for the Windies in a Test at the age of 31.

Francis' first victim was Herbert Sutcliffe, and he also took 4-40 in the first innings of the Windies' first victory at Bourda, Georgetown, in February, 1930.

By 1924, when Herbie Taylor brought his South Africans to England for five Tests, the pocket-sized Sussex fast man, Arthur Gilligan, was the English skipper and he had high hopes for his 29-year-old friend, Maurice Tate, who was making his Test debut.

Together, the Brighton boys routed South Africa for 30 at Edgbaston and, even though the South Africans made 390 in the follow-on, England won by an innings, Gilligan taking 6-7 and 5-83.

Ted McDonald's decision to quit Test cricket meant that when Gilligan led England to

Herman Griffith was dogged by a volatile temper.

Australia in 1924-5, Charlie Kelleway was again Gregory's opening partner as eight ball overs were introduced to the Australian game.

Gilligan was always a fighter, making his maiden first-class century batting at No. 11, but in Australia his big heart was bruised.

In July, 1924, soon after his heroics against South Africa, Gilligan was knocked out by a blow over the heart from Worcestershire's strike bowler, Fred Pearson, in a Gentlemen v Players match at The Oval.

Though he scored 112 in the follow-on, he was never the same force, again. But he retained his good cheer and became a popular radio commentator in partnership with Victor Richardson and Alan McGilvray, giving rise to the catchphrase "What do you think, Arthur?"

In his old age, Gilligan became president of the MCC.

In England in 1926, Tate was supported by young Harold Larwood and Worcester's Fred Root, an exponent of Foster's leg theory, bowling inswingers at the toes of batsmen and enticing them to turn the ball into the leg-side field.

One of the few bowlers in the 20s to rival Larwood for pace was a South African, George

Bissett, who took 25 wickets in his four Tests against England in 1927-8, with a best of 7-29 in South Africa's win at Durban, forcing Bob Wyatt to retire hurt.

Wyatt could be a clever medium-pacer and, opening the bowling in an earlier Test at Durban, he took the wicket of Herbie Taylor for one run off his first 11 overs and was brought back into the attack after the eighth wicket had added 95, claiming the last two batsmen in his first over, thus finishing with 3-4 from 12 overs.

The year before, on an MCC tour, Wyatt scored a century and took a hat-trick against Ceylon. A few years later, the West Indians used him for target practice.

In the first Test on that South African tour, Leicestershire's George Geary took 12 wickets, including 7-70, before he threw his arm out and took no further part in the series.

Geary was a fast-medium bowler who played 14 times for England and would have played more but for injuries. He was struck by an aeroplane propeller during World War One, needed a plastic hip after 26 years of first-class bowling, suffered bruised hands taking slips catches for Larwood, and on the 1928-9 tour of Australia had his nose broken by a short ball from West Australian Ron Halcombe, who might have played Test cricket but for a suspect action.

Despite the mishaps, Geary was sharp enough to dismiss Don Bradman at Leicester with the same leg-cutter that impressed Alec Bedser. In 1929, he took 10-18 against Glamorgan, a world record for an innings until Hedley Verity's 10-10 three years later.

At Melbourne in the final Test of the 1928-9 series, he bowled one of the great marathon spells of all time, taking 5-105 off 81 overs, 36 of them maidens.

During the series, Jack Gregory broke down, Charlie Kelleway had food poisoning, and the Australians tried such new ball bowlers as Ted a'Beckett, Hunter "Stork" Hendry and Otto Nothling, who took Bradman's place in the Australian team but failed to take a wicket.

More successful were Ron Oxenham; Alan Fairfax; Percy Hornibrook, who could bowl pace or spin; and the rapid Tim Wall, who took eight wickets on debut in Australia's only win of the summer. The series was dominated by four centuries scored by Walter Hammond, who also took 83 wickets in 85 Tests with pace bowling.

England had prepared for the tour of Australia which unveiled Bradman by taking on the West Indies in its first official Test series, Douglas Jardine making his debut.

The promise of the 1923 West Indians was not realised, and England won all three Tests. Against what appeared a daunting fast attack — Learie Constantine, George Francis and Herman Griffith — Jack Hobbs still averaged more than 100 runs an innings.

Griffith, then 35, was the most successful of the West Indian bowlers with 11 wickets at 23, including 6-103 at The Oval.

Short, solid and cocky, he bowled a good outswinger at fast-medium pace. He and Francis were formidable against any side on the Empire pitch at Bank Hall in Barbados.

At Sydney on the first West Indian tour of Australia, Griffith was pushing 38; but his sound fitness held him in good stead and he made another niche in history, bowling Bradman for a duck, later calling Bradman his "bunny".

The England side was flushed with success after beating the West Indies and Australia when it took on South Africa in 1929, winning the Test series despite the all-round efforts of its chief rival, Denys Morkel, a fast-medium bowler who scored more runs and wickets than anyone else on tour.

Larwood bowled fast for England, but South Africa made some great progress, unleashing the left-armer, Neville Quinn, who took 6-92 at Headingley and would later be described by Bradman as second only to Maurice Tate as a medium-pacer.

Quinn died suddenly at the age of 26.

Arthur "Oosh" Ochse, a strong, stocky country boy, took 10 wickets on tour.

Pocket-sized paceman Arthur Gilligan.

At the end of 1929, England sent two teams abroad, one to the West Indies and one to New Zealand for the first Test tours there.

Freddie Calthorpe was a tall swing bowler with a curved run, and he had a young Nottinghamshire paceman, Bill Voce, with him for experience in the West Indies.

The locals had the same Constantine, Griffith and Francis attack they had in 1928, but this time they also had George Headley to score four centuries in four Tests.

At the same time as the West Indians were proving themselves, Harold Gilligan led another team of Englishmen to New Zealand for a four-Test series, included in their ranks the veteran Notts fast man, Fred Barratt, who had inspired the young Larwood.

New Zealand began their Test history badly on a fast Christchurch pitch.

At one stage the Kiwis were 7-21, but they limped to 112. The Essex speedster, Morris Nichols, who did the double eight times in his career, took the first three wickets, Duleepsinhji picking up two slip catches while the third went caught and bowled.

Then, Maurice Allom, a big amateur from Cambridge, bowled one of the most sensational overs in Test history.

The first ball hit Roger Blunt on the foot and was close to lbw. The second cut back to hit Stewie Dempster's off-stump. The third beat Tom Lowry. The fourth had him lbw. The fifth had Ken James caught behind off an inside edge. The sixth clean-bowled Fred Badcock. Four wickets in five balls, including the hat-trick.

Astonishingly, because of business commitments, Allom, later president of the MCC, played only four more times for England, three of those on the New Zealand tour, where the locals eventually began hitting the ball.

In the next Test, for instance, John Mills and Dempster posted an opening stand of 276 after two balls from Nichols flew over Dempster's head in the first over of the day.

Sir Learie Constantine embodied West Indies cricket

Sir Learie Constantine (1902-1971)

Old Electric Heels

From humble beginnings, Learie Constantine became a knight, Baron of Maraval and Nelson, Britain's first coloured life peer and High Commissioner for Trinidad and Tobago.

Everything he did seemed to be powered by a generator inside his short, stocky, long-armed body, and his flamboyance did much to put West Indies cricket on the map.

He embodied the vibrant spirit of the game, calypso style, playing all his life as he had done in his childhood, hitting the ball as hard and as far as possible and bowling as quickly as his muscular body could achieve.

Jack Hobbs said that for a few overs Connie bowled faster than anyone he faced, including Larwood, Jack Gregory and Ted McDonald.

"Electric Heels" was born on September 21, 1902, in Diego Martin and grew up in Maraval, a few kilometres from Port of Spain, Trinidad. The grandson of a slave, he was the son of Lebrun Constantine, an overseer on a cocoa estate and the first West Indian batsman to score a century at Lords.

In later years as a barrister and politician, knighted for his social work, he fondly recalled his childhood playing cricket on a pitch of rolled clay covered with matting which his family made for "Test matches" with neighbouring clans.

His mother kept wicket "almost as well as a Test keeper" and a sister showed as much aptitude for batting as the budding maestro himself. When not in such grand games the children practised with an orange or a lime for a cricket ball and a coconut branch for a bat.

In 1922, Constantine and his father both played for Trinidad against British Guiana (now Guyana) at Georgetown, in one of the few times a father and son appeared together in a first-class match.

On the West Indies tour of England the following year, he finished third in the bowling averages behind his fellow fast bowlers, George John and George Francis.

That tour also demonstrated to Connie that cricket could be his passport to a better life.

According to C.L.R. James, "He revolted against the revolting contrast between his first-class status as a cricketer and his third-class status as a man."

Sir Learie in 1970, one year before his death, with (from left): Gubby Allen, Keith Miller and Sir Len Hutton

On the West Indies 1928 tour of England — its first official Test series — his team lost all three Test matches but Connie was like a gymnast in the field and put together a remarkable tour double, hitting 1381 runs and taking 107 wickets as part of a powerful pace combination with Francis and Herman Griffith.

Against Northamptonshire, Constantine took 7-45, including a hat-trick, 6-67, and five sixes in a score of 107. Playing with a limp against Middlesex at Lords, he scored 86 out of 107 in less than an hour then took 7-57, including 6-11 in his second spell of 39 deliveries. He then scored 103 out of 133 in an hour, with two sixes, and 12 fours.

Bob Wyatt remembered going out to bat for Warwickshire against Connie, passing Bates, the preceding batsman, being carried from the field unconscious on a stretcher, and then having Constantine's first two deliveries glance off his head on the way to the boundary.

The next season, needing money to study law, Connie joined Nelson as the first coloured professional in the Lancashire League, the first in a long line of West Indian professionals there.

He was such an exciting performer that he was judged worthy of bigger contract offers than Bradman.

In his 10 seasons at Nelson the club won the league championship eight times and broke attendance figures wherever it played.

He provided an inspiration for other West Indians to try their luck in English league cricket, allowing poor, often uneducated youngsters from the Caribbean the opportunity of making good money and learning their craft in a tough arena.

In England's first Test tour of the Caribbean, Constantine was often restrained by team mates from bowling short to the touring skipper, Freddie Calthorpe, but in the first Test at Bridgetown he bowled a form of bodyline with only two men on the off-side.

George Gunn, then over 50, had his own method of playing Constantine's short bowling — advancing bravely down the wicket before the ball was bowled to offer a dead bat shoulder high as the ball leapt toward his face, then blowing Connie a raspberry and skipping back toward his crease. Eventually, Electric Heels hit the bullseye, slamming one into the veteran's armpit.

Opening with Francis, Connie took nine wickets, including 5-87 in the West Indies' first Test victory, on a lively pitch at Georgetown, and finished a drawn series with 18 wickets at 27.

His obligations to Nelson interfered with appearances for the West Indies in England in 1933, but he and Manny Martindale showed Douglas Jardine what bodyline felt like for a batsman at Old Trafford, even though Jardine's century was a testimony to his fighting qualities.

Constantine's 15 wickets at 13 each against England in 1934-35 helped the Windies to their first series win. At Port of Spain, Maurice Leyland was out to Connie with one ball remaining after the fast bowler had scored 90 and 31 and had been taken out of the attack after complaints for bowling too short.

He was, at 36, still sharp enough to take 11 wickets in the losing 1939 series in England, with 5-75 and 79 runs at The Oval.

In 18 Test matches, Constantine took 58 wickets at 30.10 and scored 635 runs at 19.24. They are modest figures, given his legendary status, but, as Gordon Ross, a chronicler of West Indian cricket, was to write many years after Connie's most magnificent deeds, it was not so much what he did on the field as how he did it.

"Anyone who saw him give his astonishing one man performance against Middlesex at Lords in 1928 will not think of him in terms of runs scored and wickets taken anymore than they count the number of crochets and quavers in a Beethoven symphony," he wrote.

"They remember the way he did it, that high voltage of energy that uprooted stumps and scored a century in an hour."

Jack Gregory
(1895-1973)

Big Jack

Jack Gregory was just another Australian soldier stuck in England at the end of World War One waiting for a ship home.

He had captained the exclusive Shore school XI in Sydney and played some lower-grade cricket before spending a year working on a cattle station.

But within a few months of being included in the AIF cricket team in England, Gregory had become the world's most celebrated all-rounder. A dashing bronzed digger who stood nearly 190 centimetres, he bowled right-arm fast off a run-up that resembled an elephant stampede, batted left-handed, scoring the fastest century in Test cricket, and, with either left or right hand, took magnificent slip catches.

Cyril Docker, who had been the key fast bowler for the AIF side, strained his back, and Gregory was seen as an ideal, if raw, replacement.

In the summer of 1919, he took 131 wickets and found himself fielding at slip after damaging a finger in a fall in the outfield.

Herbie Collins thought the slips were the best place for a man with a bad hand, and Gregory was to become one of the best catchers cricket has seen, taking 44 in 1919 alone.

Even though his cricket experience was limited, Wisden said he had a way of getting the ball to rise that reminded observers of Neville Knox in 1906.

Throughout his Test career Gregory was often criticised for bowling too short and dangerously.

Arthur Carr, who captained Larwood and Voce at Nottingham, said Gregory had a way of frightening batsmen more than most fast bowlers, remarking that it took "a lot of guts" to bat against Gregory, even though he was not quite as quick as little Tibby Cotter had been — a comparison supported by the Croucher, Gilbert Jessop, who had been pretty quick in his day as well.

Gregory, in fact, was a completely different proposition from the diminuitive Cotter. After a shuffling start, Gregory took 10 bounding strides to deliver the ball, and in his ninth stride he hopped like a giant kangaroo.

His delivery stride measured about 2.75 metres. Ray Robinson, the cricket writer, reasoned that, with his teeth bared and blue eyes bulging, Big Jack already had many batsmen beaten before he let the ball go.

He played 24 Tests, took 85 wickets at 31.15, an average that suffered in his later years, and averaged

LEFT: Big Jack Gregory could do it all

36.96 with the bat, blasting two centuries. His remarkable reflexes accounted for 37 catches.

Gregory's stock deliveries were the late outswinger or the ball that reared from just short of a length and, with him leading the way, the AIF team lost only four of its 28 first-class matches and beat a full-strength MCC at Lords.

In England, Gregory took six wickets in an innings six times. In South Africa on the way home, the AIF team played eight first-class matches; and at Durban against Natal Big Jack took 9-32 and ran out the other batsman. In Australia, he took 7-22 for the AIF against Victoria; and against NSW he scored centuries in both innings, took 8-130 in the match as well and held three catches in the slips.

Born at North Sydney on August 14, 1895, he was the son of Charles Smith Gregory, a NSW player in the 1870s, nephew of Dave Gregory, Australia's first Test captain and cousin of Syd, a veteran of 58 Tests.

After such a blazing start to his first-class career, he made his Test debut against Johnny Douglas's tourists in 1920-1, continuing his AIF form, averaging 74 with the bat, taking 23 wickets at 24 and latching on to 15 catches.

At Melbourne, he hit 100 and took 7-69 in England's first innings, and in the next Test at Adelaide was joined by Ted McDonald, forming a destructive combination.

He and Gregory swept through England in the first three Tests of the 1921 tour. Gregory finished with 19 Test wickets at 29 each, his 6-58 in the first innings of the series stamping Australian authority onto a team in the middle of eight losses against its oldest rival.

On the way home, Gregory kangaroo-hopped around South Africa at tremendous speed, taking 15 wickets in three Tests at 19 each. At Johannesburg, he did even better than that hitting a century in 70 minutes, still the fastest in Test cricket, although the South Africans still managed a draw.

By the time of the 1924-5 series against England, Gregory was on the wrong side of 29 and had not only begun to lose his own great pace but also the sharp speed of Ted McDonald to support him.

Eight-ball overs were introduced to the game, and Gregory told Arthur Gilligan, his English counterpart, that he bowled only six at top pace to preserve his waning stamina.

Gregory took 22 wickets at 37 each against Hobbs and Sutcliffe and, despite England figuring highly in both the batting and bowling for that series, Australia kept The Ashes with a 4-1 win.

In England in 1926, Hobbs and Sutcliffe gained their revenge, winning back The Ashes for the first time in 14 years. Gregory broke down with leg trouble and took only three wickets in the five Tests.

The end of Gregory's career came at the Brisbane Exhibition Ground in the first Test of 1928-9, in which Gregory bowled with his old fire, chipping the shoulder off Larwood's bat and taking three wickets in the first innings.

But he broke down with a knee injury trying to take a return catch after he had sent down 41 overs, and he was a dejected absentee for the rest of the game.

Don Bradman remembered the grim sight of the big fellow limping into the dressing room with his knee heavily bandaged and with tears in his eyes exclaiming: "Boys, I'm through, I've played my last game."

Gregory married a Miss Australia and lived out his days on the NSW south coast.

In the heady days between World War One and the Great Depression, Jack Gregory was Australian cricket's most celebrated hero.

Ted McDonald
(1892-1937)
The Satanic Bowler

Ted McDonald was a chainsmoking loner who attracted unsavoury friends and who, according to Don Bradman, had a beautiful, graceful action.

"Whence does McDonald draw his terrible strength and velocity?" asked Neville Cardus in a purple mood.

"His run to the wicket is so easy, so silent. He does not thunder over the earth like (Jack) Gregory — like a bull at a gate. No. He runs along a sinister curve, lithe as a panther, his whole body moving like visible, dangerous music. A more beautiful action than McDonald's was never seen on a cricket field, or a more inimical.

"The man's whole being tells of the sinister destructive forces of nature. He is a Satanic bowler."

Like Michael Holding half a century later, McDonald, slim and tall with the customary big shoulders for fast bowling, was so light on his feet that even

Ted McDonald, cricket's black sheep.

49

Ted McDonald's lethal grace.

after spells of 30 overs or more from his 18 metre, 15-pace run, he left no marks.

Though he did not try too hard against unskilled opponents, the sight of Hobbs, Sutcliffe or Hammond had a profound effect on increasing his pace and desire. He could bowl fast for long spells and could swing the ball either way.

"His greatest performances were when his side was in most urgent need," wrote Ian Peebles, the Scottish leg-spinner,

"This was typical of a curiously detached and somewhat taciturn nature. He had no interest in bowling out batsmen for the sake of compiling records. When catches went astray he was never heard to say an impatient word nor betray a flicker of expression."

McDonald followed in the footsteps of two other

Tasmanian quicks, Edward "Wack" Windsor and Ashley Facey, but unlike them, he was destined to bowl for his country.

Although he played only 11 Tests, McDonald is remembered as one of the great fast bowlers because he and Jack Gregory formed the first truly frightening Test combination and for the remarkable deeds he performed after his premature retirement to concentrate on county cricket.

With McDonald and Gregory opening the attack, Australia was never beaten. It had seven wins and four draws against England and South Africa.

McDonald was born in Tasmania, the son of a tinsmith, and as a bespectacled 17-year-old he went to work in an insurance company.

He first played for Tasmania in 1909-10 and moved to Victoria in 1911.

Despite some fine bowling after the outbreak of World War One, McDonald had to wait years for his big opportunity.

In 1919 he took 8-42 against NSW on a batsman's wicket at Sydney, and after other impressive results he was chosen to partner Jack Gregory against England at Adelaide in 1920-1.

Gregory bowled with the wind, was faster and could swing the new ball more, but McDonald had greater variation and was the master when the ball had lost its shine.

Plum Warner believed Gregory was quicker but McDonald the better bowler, particularly with the nasty off-cutter.

Although he took only six costly wickets (65 runs each) in his first Test series, McDonald had class.

Warwick Armstrong had beaten Johnny Douglas's inexperienced side in all five Tests in Australia and The Big Ship realised that Gregory and McDonald could create fear and victories in England.

McDonald took 27 wickets in the series at 24.74, and he and Gregory caused a tremendous run of bruises.

Australia won the first test by 10 wickets by the second evening, McDonald taking 5-32, his best Test figures, in the second innings.

In all matches on the English tour, Gregory and McDonald took 270 wickets between them at 16 each — McDonald's share was 150 — and in five Tests a desperate England used 30 players.

The Australian terror twins then rampaged against the South African batsman on the way home, though it was not until the third and last Test that they managed a win.

Early in the series, the South African opening batsman Jack "Billy" Zulch had asked Herbie Collins if McDonald was genuinely fast.

"Fairly quick," said Collins. "But he needs to warm up."

At Cape Town in the second Test, in which Jack Gregory scored his 70-minute century, McDonald had warmed up sufficiently behind the grandstand so that he was at top pace right from the start of South Africa's innings.

His second ball shattered Zulch's bat and sent a fragment of wood cannoning into the stumps, dismissing Zulch for a duck, hit wicket. Yet, overall, he was disappointing on that tour, his 10 wickets costing 37.10 with a best of 3-53.

After just a year as an international fast bowler, McDonald decided he had had enough, retiring from the Australian team with 43 wickets at 33.28 from his 11 Tests.

After taking 8-84 for Victoria against NSW in the summer of 1921-22, McDonald joined Nelson in the Lancashire League.

On June 21, 1922, Nelson played Church, who had engaged the crusty Sydney Barnes, then 49.

The duel between these two moody, intense pace bowlers, should have been filmed for posterity.

McDonald had helped establish Nelson as a cricketing power and, even though he did not bowl flat out, he managed 7-29 as Church collapsed all out for 59.

Barnes, not to be outdone by the Aussie upstart, took 6-19 as Nelson crashed, all out 44. Church then batted a second time and made only 38, McDonald bowling express and taking 5-7.

Maurice Tate's marvellous bowling action.

In 1924, McDonald joined the Lancashire county team as England's highest-paid cricketer on five hundred pounds a year and a guarantee of a benefit within five years.

Between 1924 and 1931, opening with Cecil Parkin and Richard Tyldesley, he took 1053 wickets for Lancashire. In 1925, he took 205 first-class wickets. Seven times he topped 100 wickets in a season, and he snared three hat-tricks, being a serious force in Lancashire's four championship titles between 1926 and 1930.

When Lancashire played the touring Australians in 1930, McDonald, then pushing 39, bowled Bradman for nine.

Early in the morning of July 22, 1937, McDonald was involved in a car accident near Bolton and, unhurt, he climbed from his vehicle.

He was trying to wave down traffic and help the other motorist when he was hit by another car and killed.

Few fast bowlers knew more about their craft than Ted McDonald.

Maurice Tate
(1895-1956)

His Father's Pride And Joy

Maurice Tate, with his big, wide smile and genial way, was 27 before he became a pace bowler and 29 before he represented England.

Despite this late start and the legacy of being Poor Fred Tate's son, he became one of the masters of Test cricket.

A big man with the face of a cherub and a hearty sense of humour, Tate was a born swing bowler. He had wide hips, big shoulders and immense hands and feet to cushion the force of pounding down outswinger after outswinger. Yet it was as a hard-hitting batsman and slow-medium off-break bowler like his father that Maurice first made a living out of cricket.

He was born at Brighton on May 30, 1895, into a cricketing family. His father Fred, yet to become "Poor Fred", was already into his ninth season for the county.

In 1902, when Maurice was seven, Poor Fred, a Sussex spinner, was brought into the English team for the fourth Test at Old Trafford.

Despite two decades of service for his county, Fred will be forever remembered for dropping a vital catch and losing his wicket, the last of the England innings, when his side needed only four runs to win.

With tears in his eyes, Poor Fred had announced in the dressing room that back home he had a little lad who would make up for his failures.

Maurice sensed how hurt his father was and in later years came to understand why he was never given encouragement to play the game.

Yet as a young cricketer Maurice played just like his father, and Sussex took him on in 1911 as an off-

Maurice Tate and his twin daughters.

spinner. He had only limited success and was fortunate that the county persisted with him after World War One. But at Eastbourne in 1922 when Sussex played Hampshire, Maurice became fed up with his inability to get through the defence of Phil Mead.

From his normal, six-metre off-spinner's approach, the big man trotted in and let the ball go as fast as he could. The ball pitched on Mead's off stump, cut back and knocked the leg stump clean out of the ground.

A star was born.

Arthur Gilligan, himself a lively pace bowler who had just taken over the captaincy of Sussex, encouraged Tate to perfect his new style of bowling, and in the next season Tate took 219 wickets, followed by 205 in 1924 and 228 in 1925. In each season he scored more than 1000 runs.

He made a Test debut which made Poor Fred and the rest of England cry with joy. Snaring the wicket of Fred Susskind with his first delivery for England, Tate finished his first Test innings with 4-12, helping Gilligan to rout South Africa for 30 in 75 balls after England had made 438 at Edgbaston. Eleven of the South African runs were extras.

Tate overtook Gilligan as England's premier strike bowler before long, and finished his first Test series with 27 wickets at 15.70, taking his best Test figures of 6-42 at Headingley. He never looked back.

Tate's action was all economy and strength. His short run of eight strides culminated in a classical wheeling action that propelled the ball at a lively pace. John Arlott once remarked that the ball seemed to fly off the pitch "as if by some mysterious acceleration".

Indeed, most batsmen who faced Tate believed the ball gained pace once it hit the wicket.

Wicket-keepers usually stood up to him because he was so accurate. Yet even they were sometimes startled by the sudden speed of the ball after it landed.

Without a hint of boastfulness, Tate remarked in his later years as a round red-faced Sussex publican that he had never bowled a no-ball and had sent down only one wide in his whole career, a slower ball caught by a sudden gust of wind.

Tate was quick to perfect his outswinger and leg-cutter and, although he took nearly 3000 first-class wickets in 25 years, he was often plagued by the sight of the ball just missing the outside edge of the bat. He was largely responsible for turning the wicket at Hove, previously a paradise for batsmen, into the stuff of cricketing horror stories, swinging the ball around everywhere but where the batsmen wanted it.

Ian Peebles called him the greatest seamer the game has known, and John Arlott wrote of the difficulty bewitched opponents had in playing him on heavy seaside mornings.

"The inswing and outswing were there as a matter of course but, as every man who batted against him will testify, the ball would sometimes seem to begin to swerve and then straighten again before it struck the ground," Arlott wrote. He could be very fast, too. In 1927, at Eastbourne again, he wrecked Lancashire with 6-28 on a batsman's wicket, making the ball jump at chests on what had seemed a tame pitch.

In the 1924-5 Ashes series in Australia, Tate bowled more overs than any two other English bowlers put together, all his bulk coming down on his left foot, particularly his big toe.

In the first Test at Sydney the toenail was pushed inwards and the toe turned septic, prompting doctors to consider amputation. But "Chub," as he and Poor Fred were both known, kept bowling. He took 11-228 in the match out of Australia's 902 runs. He kept bowling, finally tearing the toenail from the flesh at Adelaide two Tests later.

England lost the series 4-1, but Tate finished with 38 wickets from five matches at 23 runs each, as many wickets as the next three English bowlers combined.

Tate finished his first-class career in 1937 having taken 2783 wickets (18.16) and having hit 21,698 runs (25.02) For many years, he opened the bowling and batting for Sussex, hitting 23 first class hundreds and even going in first for England at one stage.

Against the mighty 1930 Australian team without Bradman at Hove, he had the visitors at 6-69, dismissing Bill Ponsford, Stan McCabe, Archie Jackson, Alan Fairfax, Victor Richardson and Ted a'Beckett while conceding just 18 runs.

Douglas Jardine could not find a place for Tate, then 37, in the Bodyline series, but Tate kept playing for England until 1935 and for Sussex until 1937.

In his prime, it was said Tate was the world's best bowler on a batsman's wicket. His career highlights included 9-71 for Sussex against Middlesex (five bowled, three lbw, one caught) in 1926; match figures of 14-58 for Sussex against Glamorgan at Hove in 1925; 100 not out for England against South Africa at Lords in 1929; and 203 for Sussex against Northamptonshire at Hove in 1921. Tate played 39 Tests for England and took 155 wickets at 26.13.

Sussex success . . . the famous English combination of Gilligan and Tate.

THE 1930s

Jardine And Bodyline

Before the England team left for Australia in 1932-3 Douglas Jardine, its haughty, intense, steel-willed captain, dined with Harold Larwood, his Nottinghamshire and England opening partner Big Bill Voce and their county skipper, Arthur Carr, at the Piccadilly Hotel, London.

They decided short-pitched bowling with a ring of leg-side fielders seemed the best way of curtailing Bradman's unprecedented scoring feats.

"Any scheme that would keep [Bradman] in check appealed to me," Larwood wrote later. "That's where [Bodyline] all started as far as I was concerned."

So a plot was hatched that created cricket's most controversial summer, the Englishmen using the Australian batsman as targets, relationships between the two countries becoming dangerously strained, and Jack Hobbs the great old English batsman, declaring someone would end up getting killed. Bill Woodfull, felled by Larwood, said only one team was playing cricket, and telegrams of protest echoed all the way back to London.

Bodyline was devised primarily because of Bradman's dominance in England in 1930. Alan Fairfax took 12 cheap wickets and averaged 55 with the bat; and Percy Hornibrook, who opened the Queensland attack with Alexander Hurwood, took 7-92 at The Oval with a mixture of pace and spin.

The rawness of Tim Wall, who had made a fine debut in the last Test of the previous Ashes series, was evident in England that year. The South Australian troubled England frequently with the sharp pace he derived from a kicking action and a long 27-pace approach. Although his accuracy was unquestioned in Australia, his line and length went astray in England.

Wall and Ernie McCormick, a lanky Victorian, were Australia's two best quick bowlers of the 1930s. Wall was the best of the Australian fast bowlers against South Africa in 1931-2, taking 5-14 in the first Test played at the Gabba ground, Brisbane.

The series also marked the test debuts of Queensland's Pud Thurlow and Tasmania's Laurie Nash. Thurlow did not take a wicket in his sole appearance for Australia, but he played 30 times for his State and was well known for his speed and his habit of kicking over the stumps accidentally because of his right-foot kick at the point of delivery.

Thurlow once put Bill Woodfull out for a season with a broken finger, and he flattened Alan Kippax with a bouncer.

Nash never played Sheffield Shield cricket, but he played 17 times for Tasmania and once for Victoria against the MCC. He was an instant success in Test matches. He could be exceptionally quick. In the last Test of the series against South Africa at Melbourne, where the flamboyant batsman Stan McCabe opened the bowling for Australia, Nash took 4-18 and 1-4 as he and Bert Ironmonger dismissed the tourists for 36 and 45.

Harold Larwood's skill and killer instinct were well used by Jardine.

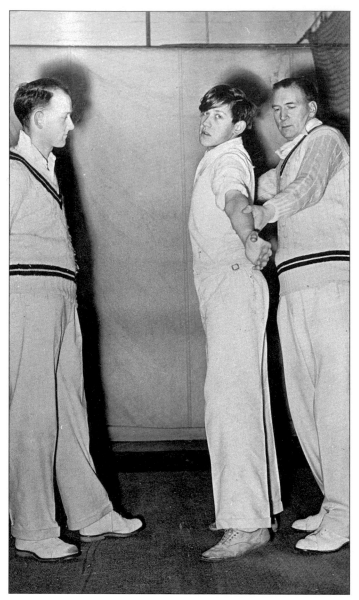

Alf Gover gives 15-year-old Nicholas Alwyn some tips while a young Frank Tyson watches with interest

Nash was also one of the finest Australian rules football players, and his regard for that game cut down his cricket appearances.

Tim Wall virtually carried the Australian bowling during Bodyline, but he could not match the fury of the visitors, partly because he lacked Larwood's speed and partly because Woodfull showed restraint in using the bouncer, not wishing to set a bad example for Australian children.

Another Victorian, Lisle Nagel, his elbow bandaged after it was struck by a flying crank handle, had taken 8-32 for a Combined Australian XI against MCC.

But the tall swing bowler from Bendigo made little impression in his sole Test.

Another Victorian, the short and powerful Harry "Bull" Alexander, hit Jardine three times in one over at Sydney and broke the bat of Bob Wyatt. But he took only one wicket in his only Test match.

Bradman called Wall the best fast bowler he faced when the ball was new, praising his stamina and late swing.

In a series England dominated, Wall still took 16 wickets at 25.56 each. That same season, he wrecked NSW with an innings haul of 10-36, taking Bradman for a duck and sending down a spell of 9-5 after lunch that included four wickets in one over.

It was 33 years before another fast man, Peter Allan, became the next Australian to take 10 wickets, with 10-61 at Melbourne.

When Australia visited England in 1934, Wall had as a support bowler a Victorian from the country town of Avoca, Hans Ebeling, who possessed a fine inswinger.

He took a wicket with his first ball in England but had to wait until the final Test at The Oval for his only Test appearance, taking the prized scalp of Walter Hammond and helping clinch the series with the wickets of Gubby Allen and Hedley Verity.

Ebeling's career was cut short by business commitments, but he stayed close to the game all his life and was the man behind the historic Centenary Test in 1977.

Under his aggressive captaincy, Victoria won the Sheffield Shield four times.

McCormick ran in even further than Tim Wall — 31 paces, his arms stiff as boards.

During his first match in England, in 1938 at Worcester, he was no-balled 35 times and joked that he would not get called again because the umpire was too hoarse.

McCormick was genuinely quick and brought the ball back into the batsman sharply, though he never could master the outswinger. That deficiency and constant lumbago prevented him from joining the truly great quick men of Australia.

McCormick began his Test career on the 1935-6 tour of South Africa, where at Johannesburg, the Springbok quick Eric Davies took 4-75, figures that would have been even more impressive had he not suffered a spate of dropped catches.

Against Gubby Allen's England tourists in 1936-7, McCormick removed Stan Worthington with the first ball of the first Test at Brisbane, and soon after he had Walter Hammond for a duck and Arthur Fagg for four. But, with 3-26 off eight overs, his back was so sore he had to retire.

McCormick's opening partner for the match was Morris Sievers, who took 5-21 in the third Test, his last appearance for Australia. A tall Victorian fast-medium bowler, he could extract great lift.

In England in 1938, McCormick showed fire at Lords, but he had to miss the final Test at The Oval when England made 7-903 and Hutton a record 364 with Australia's pace attack based on McCabe and Mervyn Waite.

Hutton's batting emphasised the omission from the touring party of the debonair Sydney speedster John Grantley "Ginty" Lush, who had topped the Australian first-class bowling averages in 1936-7 but had missed a place in the final Test after the selectors opted for Laurie Nash, who had not played a first-class match all summer.

In February, 1937, against Allen's Englishmen at the SCG, Lush had taken 6-43 and 7-72, with three wickets in four balls and had also top-scored with 49, after going into bat after Arthur Chipperfield had his jaw broken by Ken Farnes. His captain for the match was Alan McGilvray. Angered at missing a spot against the Englishmen that summer and then seeing Ted White touring England in his place in 1938, Lush joined Sir Julien Cahn's professionals and later became a widely-read Sydney journalist.

During the 1930s he opened for NSW with the left-arm quick, Bob (later Sir Lincoln) Hynes, who once dismissed Bradman for a duck.

At the time Victoria's Barry Scott was emerging as the fastest bowler in Australia and was being groomed to take Ernie McCormick's mantle when World War Two began.

After the Englishmen had lost The Ashes series to the 1930 tourists, they undertook a five-Test series in South Africa.

The best of the local bowlers was Buster Nupen, who took 21 wickets at fewer than 20 each in three matches on matting, though he was left out of the two Tests on turf. Far less successful were John Cochran and Bob Newson.

When the South Africans came to Australia in 1931-2, Sandy Bell and Neville Quinn led their attack, Bell taking five wickets in an innings in three consecutive matches, despite pain-killing injections for a foot injury at Adelaide.

By 1935, when the South Africans came to England, their attack was led by Bob Crisp and Chud Langton.

Not quite as fast as George Bisset in the 1920s, Crisp stood 186 centimetres and had pace and aggression. He twice took four wickets in four balls for Western Province in the Currie Cup.

Crisp was an all-round athlete who played nine Tests. After a season with Worcestershire in 1938 and a stint with Sir Julien Cahn's team, he became an adventurer who twice climbed Mount Kilimanjaro, in a fortnight, swam naked in Loch Lomond, Scotland, ran a duck farm, wrote for newspapers, won medals as a tank commander in the desert during World War Two, and eventually became a semi-recluse with boat and donkey on the Greek island of Corfu.

Chud Langton was also 186 centimetres and bowled fast-medium in the manner of Maurice Tate.

He had sporadic success in 15 Tests, but he took 6-89 and added 101 in two hours with Bruce Mitchell when South Africa scored its first Test win in England at Lords in that 1935 series.

In November, 1942, while a flight-lieutenant flying over Accra on the Gold Coast, he was shot down and killed.

Langton had also been involved in a record ninth-wicket partnership at The Oval, where England's Hopper Read took 6-200 in the match, his only Test on a batsman's wicket. Read had a long approach, and with Ken Farnes he formed a very quick attack for Essex.

Another of England's really fast bowlers of the time was Nobby Clark, from Northamptonshire, a fair-haired, highly-strung and often brilliant left-armer who could make the ball cut across the batsmen like a fast leg-break. He gave the 1934 Australians plenty of concern with tactics not all that far removed from the despised Bodyline.

Clark had made his debut against the South Africans in 1929, when he was something of a veteran at the age of 27. But he lost little pace as he grew old and even after the Second World War, when he was in his mid-40s he was still considered as fast as anyone in England for a few overs.

Clark often concentrated on the Lancashire League, where he could make more money than at Northants, and England selectors often did not consider him for Test sides.

When the Indians made their second tour to England in 1936, the Surrey fast man Alf Gover was called into the England side only to find that the slips in Test matches could be just as clumsy as those at Surrey.

Gover had a frantic approach to the wicket, but his action was sound and his pace often frightening .

In 1935, Gover took four wickets in four balls at Worcester, and in 1936 he dismissed 200 batsmen — the first time since Tom Richardson in 1898 a Surrey fast bowler had scored a double century.

Gover was one of cricket's most popular characters in the 1930s. Once, Patsy Hendren, the famous hooker, asked Gover not to bounce him because his old eyes were not what they used to be. Just as Hendren expected, Gover sent down a fusilade of short balls and Hendren, licking his old lips, hit him all over the ground.

In retirement, Gover opened a coaching school in London, where his star pupils included some of the finest Test fast bowlers in the history of the game, among them Frank Tyson and Andy Roberts.

One of Freddie Trueman's favourite anecdotes concerned Gover on tour of India with Lord Tennyson's side in 1937-8.

Gover began one match with his usual long run-up, but as he charged in to the crease, he just kept running, past the startled batsman, the dumbfounded wicket-keeper and the guffawing gully, straight back into the dressing room. It was something in the curry. Also on Tennyson's tour was Arthur Wellard of Somerset who took 100 wickets in a season eight times and had a fierce off-cutter but is probably best remembered for his massive hitting — 500 sixes all told.

After the 1936-7 Ashes series in Australia, England returned home for a series against New Zealand. At The Oval it chose Austin Matthews for his sole Test after his 14-132 on a batsman's wicket for Glamorgan against Sussex at Hastings.

Among the debutants for the Kiwis in that series were Walter Hadlee and a powerfully-built fast bowler from Auckland, Jack "The Bull" Cowie.

In the three Test matches, only the second at Old Trafford was decided, England winning by 130 despite 10 wickets to "The Bull".

Cowie took 19 wickets in the series at 20.78, with a best of 6-67, and against Ireland at Dublin that year took 6-3 with his huge outswinger and menacing off-cutter.

He was New Zealand's best bowler for close on 20 years but, because of the war and New Zealand's minor status in international cricket at the time, he played only nine Tests, taking 45 wickets at 21.53.

Cowie had started as a legspinner, but he found he could bowl fast.

His first Test wicket was Walter Hammond's. Wisden said that if Cowie had been Australian, he might have been considered a wonder of the age.

Tim Wall was one of Australia's finest pacemen in the '30s.

After World War Two he was still effective, even though much of his pace had gone and could still make the ball swing away late even when it was old.

He was 37 when he toured England with Walter Hadlee's 1949 team.

In the first Test between Australia and New Zealand, when Cowie was 35, he took a splendid 6-40. After England had lost to Australia in the 1946-7 series, the team went to Christchurch, New Zealand, for a single Test, in which Cowie took 6-83 and had England punch-drunk when the rain prevented his figures from improving.

England followed its home series against New Zealand in 1937 and Australia in 1938 with another tour of South Africa.

In the fourth Test, Chud Langton took 5-58, his best performance of the series, and in the fifth Test the Worcestershire fast-medium bowler, Reg Perks, took 5-100.

Perks had been coached by Jack Gregory when the Australians toured England in 1926 and he modelled his final leap on the great jump of the big Australian.

Norman Gordon took 20 expensive wickets in the five Tests and looked a good bet for the proposed 1940 tour of England, cancelled because of war.

The best of the English pacemen was Ken Farnes, who had been the spearhead when

England toured the West Indies in 1934-5, partnering the burly, 190 centimetre Middlesex quick, Jim Smith.

In six seasons for his county, Smith took 676 wickets and, like Wellard, loved a six, hammering a half-century against Gloucestershire in 11 minutes in 1938.

The Bridgetown pitch for the first Test of that tour was in such a sorry state after rain that both teams opened their batting with their bowlers, Smith taking 5-16 in the second innings of his Test debut.

Four years later, the West Indians in England played the last Test series before the war.

Bill Copson, a Derbyshire red-head who bowled with fire, made his Test debut at Lords.

A coalminer, he first played cricket at the age of 17 during the General Strike of 1926 and progressed through the ranks from a colliery team, once taking 10-5 in a Derbyshire League match.

His first delivery for the county put paid to the England batsman, Andy Sandham. In 1936, he took 160 wickets to help Derbyshire win the county championship, and the next year took two hat-tricks and had 8-11 against Warwickshire, including four wickets in four balls.

He had toured Australia in 1936-7, but he missed out on a Test, but against the West Indies he made up for lost time with nine wickets at Lords.

In that match the West Indians introduced into their attack the tall, left-arm fast bowler from Trinidad, Tyrell Fabian Johnson, who took a wicket with his first ball on the tour and the wicket of Walter Keeton with his first ball in Tests.

The series also saw off the fast men of the 1934-5 series — Constantine, Martindale and Leslie Hylton, who played with George Headley at the Lucas Cricket Club, Jamaica. Hylton died on the gallows in 1955, for shooting his wife.

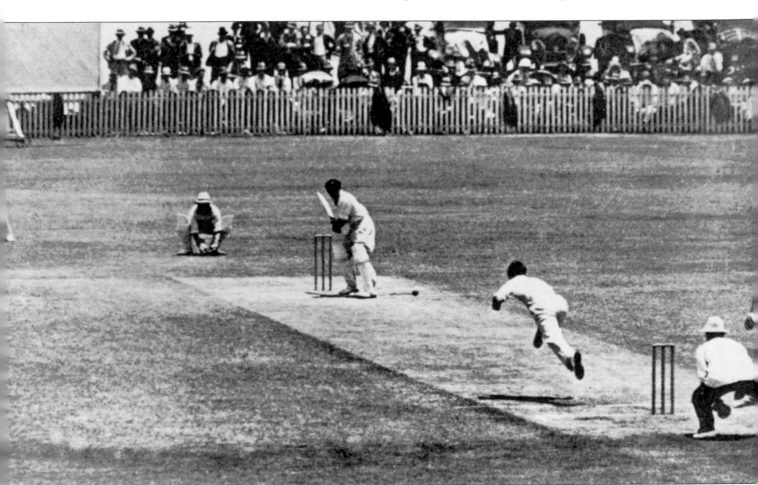

Gubby Allen defied the Bodyline edict.

Sir George (Gubby) Allen (1902-1989)

Honour And Glory

At the height of the furore over Bodyline, Douglas Jardine called a special meeting of his team to reassure himself of their support.

Sixteen of the 17 players in the English side raised their hands in a vote of confidence for Jardine's plan to bowl, short, fast and with a leg-side field against the Australians.

The only dissenting vote was that of Gubby Allen, an amateur, a Gentleman, educated at Eton and Cam-

Allen was a man of principle all his life.

In his old age, Allen, for many years one of the most powerful figures in English cricket, told the writer Philip Derriman Jardine had wanted him to bowl more bouncers and have a stronger leg-side field.

"I said, 'No, Douglas, I never bowl like that, and I don't think it's the way the game should be played'," Allen recalled.

Allen's strong principles and his belief that cricket should always be a manly game played by gentlemen were the basis of his platform as president and treasurer of the MCC, chairman of England's Test selectors and knight of the realm.

He often made controversial team choices based on ability rather than statistics, and he was often accused of meddling in cricket politics. But he was a great friend to the game all his life.

He was also a fine ambassador for cricket, chosen as England skipper to eradicate the sour taste of Jardine's unwelcome visit to Australia.

Gubby Allen was born in Sydney on July 31, 1902, the nephew of Reginald Charles Allen, who played for Australia against Shrewsbury's Englishmen in 1886-87.

As a fast bowler he had a powerful sprint to the stumps and a classical sideways action and dynamic follow-through that sometimes lifted his body well above the ground. He was a genuine all-rounder with a Test century to his credit, a Test batting average of 24, and remarkable reflexes close to the wicket.

He had varying successes for Eton, Cambridge and Middlesex, and made his Test debut in the 1930 series against Australia, in which he bowled faster than Larwood but, like the Northamptonshire speedster, he finished with few wickets for his effort. The year before, Allen had taken 10-40 at Lords against Lancashire.

In 1931, against the touring New Zealanders, he hit 122 at Lords, and at The Oval he took 5-14 in New Zealand's first-innings total of 193.

Although he refused to bowl Bodyline for Jardine there is no doubt that Allen benefited from the speed and hostility of Larwood and Voce, and only Larwood took more wickets than Allen, who finished with clean hands, clean conscience, and 21 scalps at 28 each.

He was made England's Test captain for the 1936 home series against India, taking 10 wickets at Lords in his first match as leader and then giving England the series with 7-80 at The Oval. Later, in Australia, he and Voce destroyed the home team in the first two Tests,

bridge and a man who championed the old-fashioned values of the game.

Patrick Murphy wrote about Jardine's meeting that Allen "symbolised the code of sportsmanship that had been drummed into generations of athletes at the English public schools and would have nothing to do with the tactic, to his eternal credit.

"Yet Allen was on safer ground than the rest of the team. He had influential friends at Lords and was unlikely to be blackballed out of the Test arena because of his genuine principles."

creating a belief that Don Bradman's first series as skipper was going to be a monumental disaster.

Australia was bundled out for 58 in the first Test after being 4-7 at one stage, Allen taking eight wickets in the match, including 5-36 in the second innings.

In the second Test, he took 3-19 in Australia's first-innings total of 80 and toiled away as Voce and Walter Hammond, who had already made a double century, made sure England did not have to bat twice to win.

But, after a crushing start to the series worthy of Jardine's approval, things went wrong for the Englishmen.

The third Test at Melbourne drew 350,534 people to the MCG, where, after the Australians had declared at 9-200, Allen kept England floundering on a wet wicket until reaching 9-76.

Then Australia went out to bat a second time, opening with the tailenders on a pitch that was drying out. Bradman made 270. Australia turned the corner and won The Ashes 3-2.

At 45, Allen was pulled out of retirement in 1947 to lead England to the West Indies. But, with the number of breakdowns his old body suffered, he might as well have saved himself the trouble.

Bradman falls to Bill Bowes' first ball.

Bill Bowes
(1908-1987)

One Great Delivery

Big Bill Bowes played in only one of the Bodyline Tests in Australia in 1932-33. Considering his potential and the high regard in which he was held, this was a personal disappointment. But Bowes, a tall, gangling, bespectacled, awkward-looking fellow who was often just as awkward to face, managed a couple of feats that startled every cricket fan.

He bowled Don Bradman first ball and made Jardine

dance with joy. England had won the first Test, at Sydney, by 10 wickets, thanks to some ferocious bowling from Larwood and centuries to Sutcliffe, Hammond and the Nawab of Pataudi.

In the second Test, Bradman was recalled to the team after being unfit for Sydney, and Australia was 2-67 at Melbourne when the Don made his way to the wicket.

He was the people's choice, the young bush boy who could turn back the tide of the England speedsters. Bowes was brought into the team at the expense of the slow bowler Hedley Verity, giving the Englishmen a five-pronged pace attack

The applause from the vast MCG crowd, a then world record of 63,993, was still echoing in the Englishmen's ears when Bowes ran to the wicket in his ungainly, shambling manner and then dropped in a fast one short outside the off-stump.

Bradman pounced, leaped into a pull shot, got a bottom edge and dragged the ball onto the stumps.

The huge crowd sat stunnned. But Bradman came back to hit an unbeaten century before running out of partners, and Bill O'Reilly spun Australia to its only win of the summer.

Bowes stood almost 190 centimetres and was a raw-boned fast-medium bowler able to swing the ball both ways from a high action.

A committed Yorkshireman, he played for his country from 1928 to 1947 and was a regular with the side from 1931, even though he was under contract to the MCC at Lords.

He was a clumsy-looking fielder, usually at mid-off, and he averaged a mere 4.6 runs with the bat in his 15 Test appearances for England against five countries. But what he lacked in grace, he made up for with commitment and deceptiveness, snaring 68 Test wickets at 22.33.

Big Bill made his debut against India in 1932 at Lords, where his 4-49 along with Jardine's bat allowed England to win its first Test against India.

In 1934, Bowes ploughed through an enormous amount of work in three Tests against the high-scoring Australians, finishing off the great start made by Ken Farnes. He finished the Test series with 19 wickets at an impressive 25.42, his best bowling 6-142 in the drawn fourth Test at Headingley, where Bradman made 304 and Ponsford 181.

Bowes also took 5-55 as part of a nine-wicket haul when Australia wrapped up the series 2-1 with its 562-run victory at The Oval, where Ponsford and Bradman both topped 200.

Four years later at The Oval, when Hutton hit 364, Bowes took 5-49 and 2-25 against the dispirited visitors, who sorely missed the injured Bradman and Fingleton.

Bowes and Morris Nichols bowled well against South Africa in 1935, and in the 1939 series against the West Indies, Big Bill snared his best Test figures of 6-33 in the rain-affected match at Old Trafford.

After the war he played one Test against India, and he spent two seasons as a medium-pace bowler for Yorkshire.

Ken Farnes
(1911-1941)

The Essex Express

Ken Farnes gave his heart and soul playing cricket for England and at 30 he gave his life fighting for her in World War Two.

Farnes was one of the most mourned cricketers to die during that war, because no-one represented the vitality and energy of fast bowling more than the strapping, 193 centimetre school-master from Worksop College.

Farnes took 60 wickets in 15 Test matches and was England's fast-bowling spearhead after Harold Larwood was bodylined out of the game.

Farnes took a run-up of 11 paces and achieved great bounce because of his height and the powerful flick of the wrist at the moment of delivery.

Playing in the Gentleman v Players match at Lords in 1936, he knocked the stumps out of the ground in dismissing Gimlett, Hammond, and Hardstaff; and in 1938 he generated one of the fastest overs seen at Lords.

The first delivery cannoned off a pitch the batsman thought harmless. The second roared off the glove of Bill Edrich and hit him in the head, leaving him dizzy

Ken Farnes' pace and bounce troubled Australia.

as the umpire gave him out caught. Price, the nightwatchman, managed to survive one more before touching another to a slips fielder, Wally Hammond, who had become a "Gentleman" to captain England.

Somehow, Eddie Paynter managed to last out Farnes's last two balls of the evening.

Farnes finished with 8-43. Hammond said it was the fastest bowling he had seen, and old-timers reckoned it was the fastest bowling they had seen at Lords since Charles Kortright was at his best.

Farnes spent three years opening the bowling for Cambridge University before joining Essex. In the University match of 1932 he was no-balled 21 times, but he was not troubled excessively by the problem throughout his career. The problem really existed for the batsmen who were constantly plagued by good-length deliveries leaping at their chests.

He took 10 wickets (5-102, 5-77) in his first Test against Australia at Trent Bridge in 1934, but Bill O'Reilly took 11 and bowled Australia to victory with 10 minutes left in the match.

On the rain-affected pitch at Bridgetown in 1935, Farnes had the Windies reeling at 5-31. England won by four wickets, even though the Windies were the only team to pass 100 runs for an innings.

Again in the 1936-7 series against Australia, Farnes bowled tremendously on a docile wicket to take 6-96 in the deciding fifth Test at Melbourne, in which most of his team mates needed treatment with ice packs in the intervals. But the English batsmen could not do justice to the efforts of the big fast bowler, and Australia won by an innings and 200.

At Lords against Australia in 1938, he narrowly missed a hat-trick, bowling O'Reilly, having Ernie McCormick caught by Charlie Barnett, then having Denis Compton drop Chuck Fleetwood-Smith in the slips.

Farnes would graciously write later that the miss might have saved England — the match was drawn — because Bill Brown, who carried his bat for 206, and Fleetwood-Smith batted for more than half an hour on a rain-affected pitch which could have been hazardous for the Englishmen had McCormick had the new ball.

Together with Bill Bowes, Farnes bowled England to victory over an Australian team without Bradman and Fingleton after Hutton had made his 364 to level the 1938 series at The Oval.

Farnes toured South Africa in 1938-9 and finished second in the bowling averages to the left-arm spinner Hedley Verity who, like Farnes would live only a few more years, dying in an Italian prisoner-of-war camp.

At the outbreak of war, Farnes joined the Royal Air Force, trained as a pilot officer in Canada and was killed when his plane crashed in Northamptonshire in October, 1941.

Eddie Gilbert — Bradman sang his praises.

Eddie Gilbert (1908-1978)

Fast Eddie

Just before Christmas, 1931, a little black man who lived in a tent in the backyard of a Queensland cricket official sent down five deliveries to Don Bradman which the champion batsmen recalled as the fastest bowling he faced.

"One delivery knocked the bat out of my hand,"

Bradman recalled, "and I unhestitatingly class this short burst faster than anything seen from Larwood or anyone else."

Eddie Gilbert shuffled only four quick steps before whizzing his arm over in such a blur that no-one could be certain whether he chucked.

Bradman was hit with the fourth ball of Gilbert's over, and caught behind off the fifth. He called his duck against such pace the luckiest duck he ever made.

In that Brisbane match, Gilbert finished with 4-74 off 21 overs, despite a rollicking 229 not out by the Test batsman Stan McCabe, who considered his performance against such ferocity the best innings of his career, even though he played three of the greatest innings in Test matches, including an unbeaten 187 against Larwood the next season.

After the match, the NSW manager accused Gilbert of throwing and said that four NSW players were sure Gilbert did not bowl with a fair action. Even Bradman was unsure, saying that, even if he did not actually throw the ball, Gilbert certainly jerked it.

Even slow-motion photographs could not determine whether Gilbert's action was fair; but they did show an unusually long bone formation where the wrist and forearm met, perhaps explaining the whip that Gilbert was able to generate.

Gilbert, a wiry man of 170 centimetres and about 57 kilograms, might have played for Australia had not controversy surrounded his style.

Gilbert's pace could be terrifying, even for a Bradman, but he did not have great stamina and was often moody on the field.

While he played for Queensland Gilbert lived in a tent in the Qeensland Cricket Association secretary's backyard. He came from the Barambah Aboriginal settlement, later renamed Cherbourg, and spent the last 29 years of his life in a Brisbane mental hospital, unable to speak.

Gilbert became a local terror at the Aboriginal mission, bowling fast on concrete pitches, and he made his Sheffield Shield debut for Queensland against South Australia in 1930-1.

That same season he had great success against the West Indies, taking 5-65 and 2-26 before injury slowed him.

Learie Constantine hit Gilbert for a huge six over square leg, and fast Eddie came down the pitch and shook the all-rounder's hand, saying it was the first time he had been hit for six. Later in the match, Gilbert hit Constantine for six over the fine-leg fence.

Gilbert was never free from controversy. In Melbourne in 1931, where he claimed the wicket of the Victorian batsman Jack Ryder, he was called 11 times in three overs by the umpire Andy Barlow and did not bowl again. But in his very next game, the Bodyline umpire George Hele passed his action in the match at Adelaide between Queensland and South Australia.

The next season as Australia cried out for a speedster to combat Larwood's team, Gilbert bowled with tremendous fury for Queensland against Jardine's Englishmen in Brisbane. Jardine was still gloating after the Englishmen had won the third Test at Adelaide. One of Gilbert's rockets tore into Jardine's hip and, although the stoic captain refused to show any sign of pain, he collapsed in his dressing room.

Cricket fans called for Gilbert's inclusion in the Australian side. The little man said he welcomed the opportunity to bowl leg theory at the tourists, but he was never given the opportunity.

Perhaps it was his colour that kept him out of the Australian team. More likely, it was his action.

That same Bodyline season, Gilbert developed shoulder trouble that curtailed his appearances for Queensland, but he was still quick enough in 1934-5 to take 6-64 and 3-114 against NSW and 5-77 in the match against Victoria.

Eddie Gilbert was erratic but had lightning pace.

ABOVE and RIGHT: Harold Larwood. Some say nobody has bowled faster than he did during the Bodyline series.

Harold Larwood (1904-)

Kill The Body And The Head Will Fall

Harold Larwood was just a little bit of a thing when he first turned up at Trent Bridge looking for a county trial.

At 18, he stood just 160 centimetres. He was frail, pale and untried, he was also very fast, and there are still some who saw him operating years later during the Bodyline series of 1932-3 who say no-one has bowled faster.

By the time he was fully grown, Larwood was anything but a giant. At his peak he stood 172 centimetres, but, from the English perspective at least, he was a superhero.

This sturdy little man from a mining village in the north of England became the most feared man in cricket.

Larwood was Douglas Jardine's supreme weapon in the war against Don Bradman. He was loyal, hard-working, deadly accurate and, above all, blindingly quick.

Like a well-drilled soldier, he did what he was told unflinchingly.

When Jardine told him the Australian batsmen were a cowardly lot — a pack of "yellow bastards" — Larwood roared into them with extra fury.

Even the old newsreel footage of him during Bodyline still quickens the pulse nearly 60 years later.

The controlled hostility of the run-up, gradually building the momentum in measured bounds like a cheetah chasing prey.

His action was as dynamic as it was classic. The final leap and sway back of the torso, both arms clutching at the sky, his left foot thumping down on to the wicket, then the powerful, violent thrust of the shoulders.

Larwood's pace came from a combination of supple strength, superb co-ordination, a natural fast-bowling rhythm and long arms.

When he arrived in Australia for the start of the Bodyline series, he wanted to settle some old scores with Bradman.

He had been disappointing against the Australians in England in 1930, but Jardine believed in Larwood.

At Trent Bridge against Kent in 1931, he had taken 9-41, and in the same season he scored 102 not out against Sussex in partnership with Bill Voce.

By taking 162 wickets at 12.86 and heading the England averages, he had done enough to convince Jardine he had the necessary pace and accuracy to execute Bodyline and perhaps kill the Bradman legend in the process.

Even though Bradman made a double century the last time he had faced Larwood at The Oval in 1930, the short stuff had clearly troubled the master batsman.

Larwood bowled a spate of bouncers at Bradman and the tragic youngster Archie Jackson. The spectators saw the Australians wince in pain, and it was said some in the crowd had tears in their eyes.

Larwood wrote that, although Jackson was "pinked" once or twice, he never flinched, "with Bradman it was different".

Larwood was 28 when Jardine decided to make him his No. 1 henchman. But he was fitter and stronger than ever before and, just in time for the greatest challenge of his life, he had found himself perhaps two metres quicker.

Although his best Test figures of 6-32 had come at Brisbane four years earlier, when Bradman made his debut, Larwood had only moderate success in that 1928-9 series with Percy Chapman's team.

Though quite sharp, he seemed to lose much of his effectiveness when the shine left the ball.

But by the time of Bodyline he was bowling on wickets of an uneven bounce, aiming at the batsman's body and with a string of close-in fieldsmen on the leg side.

Throughout the Bodyline series Larwood was jeered by fans.

He was mock-cheered after being dismissed for 98 in the final Test, and his name was at the centre of a rift that threatened to tear apart the sporting relationship between Australia and England.

Australians believed his sole purpose was to maim brave young batsmen, something he has always rejected, even though he never apologised for the Bodyline tactics.

In his autobiography, Larwood wrote that the short-pitched bowling put the dynamite into cricket, made it a manly game.

"I never bowled to injure a man in my life," he wrote. "Frighten them, intimidate them, yes. But I had a very unspectacular record of causing serious injuries to batsmen."

His serious injuries included hitting Bill Woodfull under the heart and fracturing Bert Oldfield's skull in Adelaide during Bodyline, hitting the South African batsman Jock Cameron on the head at Lords in 1929 and flattening Gloucestershire's Reg Sinfield in 1934.

In 1931, Patsy Hendren, a great hooker, mistimed a bouncer from "Lol" and was carried off the field with his legs twitching.

During Bodyline, Larwood kept pitching short, hitting the body and the stumps. He took Bradman's wicket four times out of seven and finished with 33 wickets from five Tests at 19.51. His best figures in the series of 5-28 came in the first Test at Sydney, in which he finished with match figures of 10-124.

Sixteen of his victims in Australia were clean-bowled, many of them positioned outside leg stump waiting for the ball aimed at the ribs. From such a position Larwood's blistering yorker was too fast to hit.

Certainly the short-pitched bowling worked against Bradman. He still managed to average more than 56 an innings, but that was only about half his normal rate and he did not bat with his customary gusto.

Though Bradman was hit by Larwood only once in the series — on the elbow in the last Test — he had to bat with uncharacteristic caution.

Often when Bradman would leap at least a metre outside leg stump in readiness to hit the ball to the off where fielders were scarce, Larwood would send the ball hurtling towards him rather than at the stumps.

The Larwood story had its origins in the Nottinghamshire mining village of Nuncargate, where he was born on November 14, 1904.

He left school at 13 and went to work as a pony boy in the coal pits. But at 17 he was awestruck by the sight of another miner, Fred Barratt, blasting out Jack Hobbs.

Barratt taught his young apprentice how to swing the ball, and Jim Iremonger taught him the importance of a balanced, rhythmic run-up and follow-through.

Larwood practised hard and did menial tasks for his seniors, cleaning bats and pads and once earning two bob for whitening the boots of Maurice Tate.

He made his debut for Notts in 1924 and in 1926 he played his first Test, taking three wickets in each innings at The Oval, where Sutcliffe and Hobbs made second innings centuries and England regained The Ashes after 14 years. George Geary took two sizzling catches off Larwood in the slips.

Stories of Larwood's speed have entered mythology. In a match against Tasmania in 1928-9 he is said to have sent a bail 60 metres.

In the days before sensitive timing equipment, his fastest deliveries were clocked at more than 150 km/h, but, according to the legends surrounding him, he may have bowled even faster than that.

Many stories are told of batsmen in England playing and missing but still walking off the field as though caught behind, relieved to have the opportunity to escape.

During Bodyline, Jardine always had a couple of team members working as Lol's chaperons, making sure he did not stay out too late or drink too much.

Bill Bowes, a regular minder, recalled that though Larwood did not drink a lot, "It didn't take much, two or three glasses, and he was quite prepared to sing".

He was quite prepared to bowl very fast, too.

In county cricket, it was always reckoned that the most dangerous time to face Larwood was after lunch, when he and Voce had sunk a few pints of ale and had their egos bruised by suggestions from their captain, Arthur Carr, that maybe the old speed was not there any more.

When the touring West Indians met Larwood in 1928, Lol reacted to suggestions that Constantine was quicker than him by hitting Frank Martin in the head and turning the cap of George Challenor back to front.

His lunch was always beer, because he said food prevented the stomach muscles from contracting quickly; and his only training for cricket was net practice and long walks.

The last Test of Bodyline was Larwood's last appearance for England. He fractured two small bones underneath his toes from the power of his delivery stride and, even though he could hardly walk, Jardine made him stay on the field as though his mere presence could unsettle Bradman.

When the Don was yorked on 71 by Hedley Verity, Jardine clapped his hands and said: "Right, Harold, you can go now."

Larwood limped off with Bradman, the two greatest figures in Bodyline leaving the controversial series together — Bradman to conquer new horizons, Larwood never again to play Test cricket.

Larwood condemned Australian spectators, officials and batsmen in the *Sunday Express* newspaper, refusing to apologise for his part in something the MCC now saw as an embarrassment.

He did not play Test cricket again, though part of the reason was his foot injury.

In 1933 he had an operation for a fractured sesamoid bone, and in 1934 he was bowling fast-medium off a short run and needing soft grounds. He topped the English bowling figures in 1936 but was unavailable to tour.

In 1950, Larwood emigrated with his wife and family to Australia, where he became a popular figure.

He was supported on his trip by the then Australian Prime Minister, Ben Chifley, and by one of the batsmen he had terrorised, Jack Fingleton.

He and Bert Oldfield, who suffered against the speedster, were to become great friends in their old age.

For many years, he had a great deal of bitterness toward the game and saw himself as a scapegoat. In 21 Tests he took 78 wickets at 28.41, and in eight county seasons topped 100 wickets, taking two first-class hat-tricks.

He always maintained that during Bodyline he did only what was necessary to win back The Ashes.

The menacing Manny Martindale.

Manny Martindale (1909-1972)

Black Bodyline

Bob Wyatt was fighting for his reputation as an English skipper when he went out to face Manny Martindale in the fourth and final Test of the 1934-5 series against England.

The crowd at Kingston, Jamaica, could taste Wyatt's blood. After all, the series was level at one Test apiece and now in this series decider England had to bat after George Headley had smacked 270.

Martindale was a powerful man of a mere 170

centimetres with big, strong legs, broad shoulders, a long run, a big inswinger, great pace and a vicious streak.

The Jamaican Prime Minister, Michael Manley said: "He imparted menace."

In his approach to the wicket everything seemed to focus on an axis, providing a straight track for the smooth, accelerating approach and the express-train speed.

In the second over of England's innings, Wyatt, a handy medium-pacer who occasionally opened England's attack, misjudged a fast ball outside his off-stump, ducked into it, and was struck in the face. He was taken to hospital unconscious with a fractured jaw.

David Townsend, George Paine, and Errol Holmes followed close behind on their way back to the pavilion and, with Wally Hammond out to Constantine, half the England team was missing with the score at 26. The West Indies won the match by an innings and 161 runs and had finally arrived as a power in cricket, taking their first series against England.

According to the West Indian journalist, Clayton Goodwin, Martindale relied on speed rather than guile and was consistently quick, unlike Constantine, who achieved even greater pace in short bursts.

Martindale, another Barbadian, was born on November 25, 1909. In the 10 Test matches he played he took 37 wickets at 21.72, and he had a number of successful seasons with Burnley in the Lancashire League.

Despite fracturing Bob Wyatt's jaw, he is probably better known for splitting the chin of Walter Hammond in 1933, when he and Constantine gave the Englishmen a tatse of the medicine they had been doling out to Don Bradman and his mates in Australia a few months before.

Martindale was savage with his speed in that Old Trafford match, in which he took 5-73 and made the Englishmen wish they had never heard of Douglas Jardine.

Indeed, the only batsman to defy them truly was Jardine, who stoically refused to give in or admit defeat. The man in the harlequin cap hit 127 to ensure a draw, even though he had almost as many bruises after Constantine caught him off Martindale's bowling.

A bloodied Hammond echoed the thoughts of everyone in Australia by saying that if this was what cricket had come to, he had had enough of it.

Martindale took 14 wickets at 17.92 on that tour, but the Englishmen won the series 2-0.

Two years later, in the Caribbean, Martindale took 3-39 and 5-22 at Bridgetown, where the first Test in the series was so affected by rain that both teams opened their second innings with the bowlers hoping the pitch would improve. Martindale finished the series with 19 wickets at 12.57.

Throughout an extraordinary series, Martindale's opening partner was the tigerish Jamaican, Leslie Hylton.

Both toured England in 1939, though neither could repeat their successes from their home series, and it was Constantine who took the bowling honours.

Martindale went off to play for Burnley and to coach in Barbados.

Mahomed Nissar (1910-1963) and Amar Singh (1910-1940)

India's First Speedsters

Mahomed Nissar earned his place in India's first Test team with a string of good performances in college cricket at Lahore.

He was a tall, strong, smiling man from the hills of the Punjab and, according to C.K. Nayudu, one of the few batsman to handle him well, he could bowl faster than Larwood on his day.

Nayudu played Nissar by marching down the wicket before the ball left the big man's hand, but at Lords in 1932, when India and England first met in a Test match, few of the batsmen were prepared to try such tactics against Nissar's pace.

At one stage the Englishmen were floundering at 3-19 in the first innings, but they managed to win the match by 158 runs, thanks to two lengthy innings by Douglas Jardine and support from Les Ames and Eddie Paynter. Nissar took 5-93 in his first innings of Test cricket.

For decades he was the best fast bowler produced by India. He had a bounding approach to the wicket and an easy action that generated surprising pace and swing and seam both ways.

During his first tour of England, Nissar took 71 wickets at 18.09. His opening partner was the powerfully built all-rounder, Amar Singh, who in that first Test took four wickets and top-scored with 51, batting at number 10. The pair was supported by the fast-medium bowling of Mohammed Jahangir Khan, who took 4-60 in England's second innings.

The three big Indians, all 22, formed an effective pace attack, even though they could not, in the infancy of their country's Test cricket, produce the much sought-after victory.

Jahangir remembers the Indian bowling in that match being better than the English led by Bill Bowes, even though the home side bundled out the inexperienced Indian batsmen.

In his old age, Jahangir, a four-time Cambridge blue, father of Majid Khan and uncle to Imran and Javed Burki, recalled that he was always confident he could trouble the left-handers Frank Woolley and Paynter and he dismissed both with the ball that moved away.

Despite his success in the first Test, Jahangir went wicketless in his next three appearances for India.

Nissar was the fastest of the three, but Amar Singh, who died of pneumonia at the age of 30, often gave batsmen the most trouble. Though he bowled mostly fast-medium, he could generate alarming speed.

Amar's run-up was only four paces, and at the end of it his left arm hardly moved, his right whizzing over in a blur.

The ball moved both ways and came off the pitch "like a crack of doom", to use the expression of Wally Hammond, who called the big Indian as dangerous an opening bowler as he had come across.

During that first tour to England, Amar took 111 wickets at 20.78. In India in the 1933-4 series, backed also by another fast-medium all-rounder, Nazir Ali, Amar took 7-86 against Jardine's Englishmen at Madras.

But England still won by 202, taking the series 2-0.

Nissar had taken 5-90 in England's nine-wicket victory at Bombay, and back in England two years later he managed 12 wickets from three Tests, including 5-120 in the third Test at The Oval, which England won by nine wickets.

Amar, then a professional in the Lancashire League, was almsot as impressive. He took 10 wickets in the Tests, including 6-35 at Lords.

Considering that Hammond averaged nearly 200 with the bat during those three matches, the bowling of the two Indians seemed pretty impressive.

Nissar took 25 English wickets in six Tests at 28.28, Amar Singh 28 from seven Tests at 30.64.

Bill Voce formed a damaging duo with Larwood.

Bill Voce
(1909-1984)

The Accomplice

In a preliminary match of the 1932-3 Bodyline tour between England and South Australia, Victor Richardson asked big Bill Voce what sort of team England had assembled.

"If we don't beat you, we'll knock your bloody heads off," Voce replied.

With Larwood, the tall, dark, and burly Voce formed one of cricket's most dangerous bowling combinations.

He was nowhere near as quick as his little Nottinghamshire opening partner, but Voce was a brisk left-armer who caused batsmen all sorts of problems bowling around the wicket, digging the ball in short and making it follow the body as if guided by radar.

Over the wicket he was always a threat, slanting the ball away from the right hander.

Voce was the one central character of the whole sordid Bodyline saga to survive the purge when the English team left Australia.

He toured down under again in 1936-7, but only after Gubby Allen threatened to quit as captain if he did not apologise in public for his role in the controversial series.

In 1946-7, when all the ales in the lunch intervals over two decades of cricket had caught up with him, Voce was still good enough to tour Australia with Hammond's team at 37.

Voce was born at Annesley Woodhouse, Nottinghamshire, on August 8, 1909, and died in Nottingham 75 years later.

The big speedster began his career as a teenage slow left-armer with Notts in 1927 but soon realised he could cause alarm with a menacing run to the wicket and powerful delivery stride.

In the 1929-30 series in the West Indies, he was a young speedster looking to make it big; and at Port of Spain he took 11 wickets, including his best Test figures of 7-70, in the second innings.

The next season, in South Africa, he took 23 wickets, more than anyone else, at 24.39; but his eight wickets in the first Test at Johannesburg could not prevent a South African victory in the only decided Test of the series.

In 1931, he hit 129 for Nottinghamshire against Glamorganshire at Trent Bridge, bringing up his century in just 45 minutes.

At the age of 23, five years Larwood's junior, he was an eager understudy on his first tour of Australia with Jardine's side.

Voce eventually toured Australia three times and played 11 Ashes Tests for England, all of them in Australia.

Although it was Larwood who caused most of the concern because of his remarkable pace and accuracy, Voce, known to players as "Tangy" was a difficult proposition at the best of times.

Bill Ponsford frequently turned his back on Voce's short bowling and let the ball strike his body rather than risk an edge.

At Adelaide, where Oldfield and Woodfull were struck by Larwood, Ponsford made a courageous 85, despite repeated bruising, before Voce bowled him behind his legs with a short ball that failed to rise.

Voce finished Bodyline with 15 wickets at 27 each, with a best of 4-110 in the first Test at Sydney.

Back in England, Voce, like Larwood, was unrepentant about his part in the controversial series; and in 1934 Arthur Carr, the former England captain and an important figure in the development of the Larwood-Voce combination, was sacked as the Notts skipper for supporting Voce in his wish to continue bowling Bodyline in county matches.

Often, even after the tactics had been condemned by the MCC and Larwood was no longer fit enough to produce the old fire, Voce would set his leg-trap field and jag the ball in towards the batsman's body, most notably in the 1934 match between Notts and the touring Australians, in which Big Bill took 8-66 at Trent Bridge and was "injured" with an alleged leg strain in the second innings after complaints from the tourists.

The Australians were heartily booed by the crowd when they took the field, and Voce was nowhere to be seen.

In 1936-7, Voce was presented with the opportunity of touring Australia again under Gubby Allen provided he expressed his regret over Bodyline in writing and the big man withdrew his earlier statement that he would play out his career with Notts.

Tangy gave the Australians plenty of spice in the first two Tests, taking 10 wickets for 57 runs in Brisbane and then 4-10 in the first innings at Sydney, where he had O'Brien, Bradman, and McCabe back in the pavilion in four balls with just one run on the board.

After such a dismaying start to the series, Australia managed to take The Ashes 3-2, but only after repeated back problems plagued England's spearhead.

Voce finished with 26 wickets at fewer than 22 each, and was the best bowler from either side.

He was still sharp enough in 1939 to take 8-30 for Notts against Somerset at Weston-Super-Mare, and after the war, when England was short of top-class bowlers, he played against India and toured Australia for a third time.

But by the age of 37 he was a lot fatter and slower than on his previous two tours, and in two Tests partnering Alec Bedser he conceded 161 runs without taking a wicket.

He finished his Test career after 27 matches and 98 wickets at 27.88.

He played his last game for Notts in 1952.

Harold Larwood (with cigarette) and Bill Voce watch Maurice Leyland playing darts. Spinner Tommy Mitchell (with glasses) is in the background

Ernie McCormick, his long run-up gave him plenty of pace.

Ray Lindwall, all silky-smooth rhythm, easy strength and accuracy.

The Post-War Warriors

Such was the strength of the Lindwall-Miller-Johnston pace-bowling combination for Australian cricket that many potential Test heroes hardly got a look-in in the late 1940s and early 1950s. Len Johnson, who carried Queensland bowling almost by himself between 1946 and 1953, had match figures of 6-74 against the '47-48 Indians at Melbourne, bowling them out with 3-8 in the second innings. But he never got another Test chance.

Two brilliant fast-medium bowlers who did not make the green and gold were the Sydney left-armer Alan Walker and the West Australian workhorse Charlie Puckett.

Walker was a rugby international who failed to get a Test place on the 1949-50 tour to South Africa and went off to play for Nottinghamshire, where he took four wickets in four balls against Leicestershire in 1955. Puckett might have been a Test regular at any other time — taking five wickets in an innings in Shield cricket 14 times — but he was in the right place at the wrong time.

Fred Freer, of Victoria, played against England in the Christmas Test of 1946 when Lindwall had chickenpox, and in 1948 he helped Rishton go from last to first in the Lancashire League. He, too, was denied opportunities.

The Adelaide swing bowler Geoff Noblet won three Test caps, one of them in the 1949-50 tour of South Africa, coming into the team for Lindwall, and another at Melbourne against the 1952-3 South Africans when Lindwall and Miller were left out of the Test side.

In 1956, the tall and gangly Pat Crawford, of NSW, played four Tests against England and India before injury got the better of him and he failed to live up to expectations as Lindwall's successor, his breakdown after just 29 balls in his Test debut at Lords inspiring a marathon spell from Keith Miller.

The Australian pace attack was virtually the same season in, season out, but England had Alec Bedser and a lot of guesswork to do.

Until Trevor Bailey arrived to partner the big man in 1949, Bedser's pace-bowling supports included Frank Smailes, who had taken 10-47 in an innings for Yorkshire against Derbyshire before the war; Dick Pollard, of Lancashire, who took 5-24 in 27 overs on debut against India in 1946; Alf Gover; Bill Edrich; Jack Martin, the Kent inswing bowler; Cliff Gladwin and George Pope, both of Derbyshire; Harold Butler, of Nottinghamshire; Alec Coxon, of Yorkshire; and Allan Watkins, the Glamorgan medium-pacer.

Not until the arrival in the early 1950s of Statham, Trueman and Tyson did England have a consistent pace attack. They were such a formidable trio that such a talented bowler as Peter Loader was limited to 13 Tests in a 12-year first-class career.

Loader and Alec Bedser were Surrey's magnificent opening combination in the county's championship run from 1952 to 1958. Loader had a long, high-stepping run to the crease, swung the ball when it was new and was a master at pace changes when the shine was gone.

He achieved high bounce on Australian wickets in 1958-9, and against the West Indies at Headingley in 1957 he took the first hat-trick in post-war cricket, getting Goddard, Ramhadin and Gilchrist and finishing with 6-36.

Loader had leapt to fame in 1953, taking 9-28 against Kent at Blackheath, and five years later he bagged 9-17 against Warwickshire at The Oval.

He left Surrey in 1964 and settled in Western Australia, becoming a cricket broadcaster. His 39 Test wickets cost 22.51 each.

Les Jackson did not even get to play a Test in the 1950s, making one England appearance in 1949 and another in 1961.

But in 1958 he and his Derbyshire partner, Harold "Dusty" Rhodes, combined to dismiss Hampshire for 23. He took 143 wickets at 10.99, the lowest county average since 1894, and against Worcester he did the hat-trick.

A miner, Jackson did not play first-class cricket until he was 27 in 1948, and he played his last test at the age of 40, spanning the gap between Graham McKenzie and Alec Bedser.

Bedser was the toast of English cricket when he devastated India in the first Test series after the war. But when England played at home to South Africa the next year, he struggled as Bill Edrich dominated batting and bowling.

Edrich had scored a double century against South Africa before the war, and against India at The Oval in 1946 he achieved his best Test figures of 4-68. Against South Africa in 1947, he topped both the batting and bowling averages, hitting two centuries and taking 16 cheap wickets, eight of them at Old Trafford, where he hit 191.

Edrich was small, but he approached batting and bowling with rare vigour. He could bowl just about as fast as anyone, hurling himself towards the batsman as though he intended his body rather than the ball to crash into the stumps.

On that 1947 tour the South African spearhead was Lindsay Tuckett, son of the Orange Free State toiler, Len Tuckett. At Old Trafford, Lindsay Tuckett, who had a 12-pace run-up and played nine Tests for the Springboks, was supported by the left-arm Jack Plimsoll of Western Province.

After the war, India searched for another Mahomed Nissar but, although no-one of his pace could be found, Dattaray Phadkar took 62 wickets in 31 Tests and his courageous batting and lively fast-medium bowling were features of the 1947-8 tour of Australia, where he opened with the more sedate Lala Armanath.

At the same time, England was preparing for the home Ashes series by taking on the West Indies in the Caribbean.

Gubby Allen, then 45, came out of retirement after most of England's key players, including Bedser, chose not to tour.

Predictably, Allen was forever breaking down, and in his absence another opening bowler, Ken Cranston, led the team.

England's attack relied on a combination derived from Cranston, Allen, Somerset's Maurice Tremlett and Nottinghamshire's Harold Butler.

The West Indies side was just as adventurous, trying the powerfully built Prior Jones, the aged Berkeley Gaskin, and Ernest

Cuan McCarthy took 0-47 in his Test debut.

74

"Foffie" Williams, who once hit Gary Sobers, then 14, in the jaw with a bouncer, strengthening the youngster's resolve.

John Trim and the bespectacled Lance Pierre were also used, and in the fourth Test a highly successful pairing was formed between Esmond Kentish and Hophnie Hobah Hines Johnson. The MCC did not win a match on tour.

Harold Butler had received his big break nearly 15 years before when Larwood's foot injury caused Butler's promotion to the Nottinghamshire team as Voce's opening partner. Tremlett had taken match figures of 8-86, in his debut against Middlesex in 1947, but he found the Calypsos more resolute.

At 37, Hines Johnson took 5-41 and 5-55 to give the West Indies victory by 10 wickets in his debut at Kingston, the West Indies taking the series 2-0. But the next season, when the West Indies travelled to India for the first series against that country, the West Indies relied on Prior Jones and the outstanding all-rounder Gerry Gomez in the first three Tests. Gomez also scored a century in the first match at New Delhi.

The fourth Test at Madras was the most absorbing. Weekes, chasing his sixth consecutive century, was run out at 90, and Phadkar, who took 7-159 on a lively pitch, tried to intimidate the tourists with the bouncer.

He was paid back with dividends by the West Indian fast men, Jones and John Trim. Mauled by the West Indians and Australia, England went to South Africa in 1948-9 pinning its hopes again on Bedser. The South Africans unveiled a new quick in Cuan McCarthy, of Natal.

At Durban, England needed only 128 to win the first Test. But McCarthy let fire in his debut. He took 6-43, and the match was anybody's with three balls left and England needing three runs to win. The inswing and seam bowler Cliff Gladwin, who preceded Les Jackson as Derbyshire's spearhead, scored the winning run off the last ball.

Finishing behind McCarthy in the wickets, 21 to 16, Bedser returned home to play Walter Hadlee's 1949 New Zealanders, forming a long association with Bailey, the Cambridge and Essex amateur and a man of similar pace and determination.

Against the bowling of Jack Cowie in his last series, Bailey averaged 73 with the bat and twice took six wickets in an innings. In Australia, his dour Test-saving batting earned him the nickname "Barnacle Bailey".

But, though he was no Botham, Miller or even Sam Loxton, who bowled as fast as he could and hit the ball hard for Australia in the 1950s, Bailey could chase the runs when he had to, and his energetic fast-medium bowling earned 7-34 against the West Indians at Sabina Park in 1953-54 and 7-44 against them at Lords four years later.

Frank Tyson remembered the cheekiness of Bailey playing great speed, playing deliberately forward to Lindwall's bouncers, making contact with the ball directly in front of his eyes and then moving the bat to one side to reveal an "engaging, innocent and irritating" smile.

Bailey's absence from the English attack after Lindwall broke his thumb in 1950-51 emphasised the lack of depth in English bowling.

Freddie Brown, the middle-aged skipper switched from leg-breaks to bowl medium pace, opening with Bedser at Sydney. John Warr, of Cambridge, backed them up, bowling 36 overs and finishing with 0-142.

He had to wait until the second innings of the next Test at Adelaide for his only Test wicket, the keeper Godfrey Evans taking a catch off Ian Johnson and the umpire asking about Warr's heart before raising his finger.

Australia was undisputed world cricket champion when it arrived in South Africa in 1949-50, but the Aussies did not always have an easy time of it, despite a resounding series triumph.

The drawn fourth Test at Johannesburg was the only match Australia did not win, partly because Michael Melle took 5-113 in his debut.

Some said Melle was as quick as Miller and Lindwall. The following year, he took 8-8 for Transvaal against Griqualand West, and at Launceston, against Tasmania in 1952-3, he took 9-22.

Cuan McCarthy had 11 catches dropped off his bowling in the 1949-50 Australian tour and was hoping for better luck with the 1951 South Africans to England, but his short bowling on a lively Old Trafford pitch may have cost South Africa the Test in a series in which he and Melle were as quick as anyone in the world and were well supported by the bespectacled, 40-year-old Geoff Chubb, who took 21 wickets in his only Test series.

The following year, McCarthy was called for throwing when playing against Worcester for Cambridge. His action had caused a good deal of controversy in the previous Test series, and less than two weeks before the umpire Paddy Corrall no-balled him, he knocked the 46-year-old Jim Langridge, of Sussex, unconscious.

The 1950 West Indian tour of England was marked by the spin of Ramhadin and Valentine, and it also saw the debut of Derek Shackleton, of Hampshire, who had taken five wickets in nine balls that season against Leicestershire but was unfortunate to enter the international arena against the in-form Worrell and Weekes.

His county career was far more impressive than his Test record — 18 wickets in seven Tests — and for 20 seasons from 1948 he took more than 100 wickets each year, a record almost impossible to top.

Shackleton was a medium-pacer with a 10-

metre, high-stepping run, a smooth action and a great length.

He took 8-4 for Hampshire against Somerset at Weston in 1955.

Ian Chappell recalled facing him 20 years after Shackleton entered the first-class game. For 20 overs, Shack kept sending them down right on the spot, never bowling a ball that Chappell could let go. Finally the bowler's composure cracked. He let one stray six inches outside leg stump.

"He was so upset," Chappell recalled, "that he apologised to me."

In 1951-2, John Goddard led the West Indies to Australia in what was seen as a world championship in the first series between the teams since they first met 21 years before.

The Windies had high hopes for Ramhadin and Valentine, who had destroyed England 18 months earlier. But they were also served brilliantly by their pace bowlers, particularly the part-timers Gomez and Worrell.

The bouncers of Lindwall and Miller swung the series, but at Adelaide the tourists won by six wickets after Worrell took 6-38.

At Melbourne, Trim took 5-34 but Bill Johnston and Doug Ring managed to save the game, and in the fifth Test Gomez took 7-55 and 3-58 in stifling heat.

While Gomez was doing his bit in Australia, Phadkar was scoring a century against England at Calcutta, where Kent's Fred Ridgway, who had taken four wickets in four balls skidding the ball through against Derbyshire the year before, took 4-83 in the best pace-bowling spell of what was a

Batting great Trevor Bailey was also adept with the ball.

frustrating series for the tourists. Although Phadkar and Buck Divecha opened the Indian bowling, the spin of Vinoo Mankad and Ghulam Ahmed was more worrying.

When the West Indians toured India in 1952-3, they brought with them another Barbadian,

Frank King, who took 17 wickets in the series.

Phadkar was supported by the inswing of Ram Ramchand and the medium pace of Vijay Hazare but, as usual, the spinners did most of the work.

When South Africa visited Australia in 1952-3, it was thought to have no chance; but it drew the series and its victory at Melbourne was its first over Australia in more than 40 years.

Melle and Jack Watkins opened efficiently in the first three Tests, and Eddie Fuller was brought in to partner Melle in the fourth, getting Morris with the score at two only to see Australia recover and make 530.

In the fifth Test, the selectors dumped Lindwall and Miller and brought in Noblet and the bulky young Ron Archer, whose back and knee problems cut his Test career to 19 appearances and 48 wickets from his fast-medium pace.

Fuller took eight wickets in that match and, despite a double century by Neil Harvey, South Africa squared the series.

The next season, Fuller gave ground to Neil Adcock as New Zealand cricket had its bravest hour on the lively Johannesburg wicket, where Adcock repeatedly struck heads and bodies as he and the seamer David Ironside both finished with eight wickets.

Two Tests later, at Johannesburg, Guy Overton, a speedster from Otago, had 3-1 off 13 balls. South Africa still won by nine wickets.

The best of New Zealand's bowlers on tour was Tall Tony MacGibbon, who took 22 wickets without managing five in an innings. He found success only after a pulled muscle made him operate off a shortened run.

Two years later, at Auckland, MacGibbon and Harry Cave helped bowl New Zealand to its first victory in Test matches — against the West Indies.

MacGibbon had some valuable pace support in the 1950s from such men as his heroic skipper, John Reid and John Hayes, who was decidedly sharp, toured England in 1949 and at Christchurch in '51-52 dismissed Worrell, Walcott and Gomez in eight balls.

Bob Blair was a good Kiwi quick bowler whose greatest feat came as a batsman at Johannesburg against Adcock. He was still playing first-class cricket in 1965.

Harry Cave was a sheep farmer and fighter who bowled big inswingers from a windmill action and who could be miserly — bowling 118 maidens out of 255 overs on a tour of India, and once taking 3-52 off 48 overs against a batting line-up of Graveney, May, Cowdrey, Hutton and Reggie Simpson.

New Zealand's great win over the Windies had come about despite some marvellous medium-pace bowling by Denis Atkinson, with 7-53 off 40 overs.

During the 1955 Australian tour to the Caribbean, Atkinson hit 219 at Bridgetown against Lindwall, Miller, Archer, Ian Johnson and Richie Benaud, then went out and bagged 5-56.

Tom Dewdeney, of Jamaica, made a good debut against the Australians in only his third first-class match; but he was disappointing in England in 1957, when Frank Worrell, who opened the batting with young Gary Sobers at Trent Bridge, carried his bat for 191 not out and then took 7-70 with his nippy fast-medium swing bowling in the next Test at Headingley.

When Pakistan toured the West Indies in 1957-8, Dewdeney supported Roy Gilchrist, along with Denis Atkinson's faster brother, Eric, and Jaswick Taylor, of Trinidad, who took 5-109 on debut.

Gilchrist and Wes Hall were terrifying in India the next season as local paceman Tiny Desai caused barely a ripple, despite some wholehearted efforts.

In 1959, the Indians also encountered terror against Trueman and Statham, although their fast-medium bowler Surendranath managed 16 cheap wickets in the series with his inswingers, with five wickets in an innings at Old Trafford and The Oval. Tiny Desai was not as successful but he took five at Lords.

India lost all five Tests, and the Englishmen were full of fire when they arrived to meet Wes Hall in 1959-60, Alan Moss, of Middlesex backing Trueman and Statham. Moss, on his second tour to the Caribbean, was fast enough at his peak to hit the sight screen at Sabina Park first bounce.

Wes Hall's opening partner was Chester Watson, of Jamaica, who was pushed to first change when the faster and more hostile Charlie Griffith made an inauspicious debut in the last Test.

Neil Adcock (1931-) and Peter Heine (1928-)

South African Muscle

Trevor Bailey, England's resourceful all-rounder who could seemingly bat for an eternity without so much as a single, was once in a particularly stoic mood facing the big Afrikaaner Peter Heine.

Gritting his teeth with frustration at such stonewalling, the South African snarled: "I want to hit you, Bailey. I want to hit you over the heart."

Heine once hit Jim Laker on the shoulder with a short ball, something the fast man found outrageously funny, asking sarcastically, "Have I hurt you?"

Peter Heine showed no mercy.

Laker remembered him hitting Peter Richardson in the head a couple of times, too, and Richardson being particularly careful to show no sign of pain. It would have acted like blood to sharks.

Peter Heine and Neil Adcock were a ferocious fast bowling combination for South Africa, taking 102 wickets in 13 Tests together and earning a place along-side the finest pace-bowling twosomes from any era.

Many have compared them to the partnership of Gregory and McDonald in the early 1920s. Like Gregory, Adcock was a friendly, likeable man. Like McDonald, Heine was a taciturn, often brooding man of dark menace.

Adcock made his Test debut against New Zealand in 1953-4, the same season in which he recorded his best first-class bowling of 13-65 for Transvaal against Orange Free State at Johannesburg.

In his second Test, at Ellis Park, he repeatedly struck the New Zealand batsmen to finish with match figures of 8-87 in another win for the South Africans, but one which inspired heroics from the tourists rarely matched in Test cricket.

On a lively, dangerous pitch, two batsmen retired hurt before scoring. Lawrie Miller left coughing blood and Bert Sutcliffe sustained a terrible blow behind the ear which caused him to faint twice in hospital.

In 25 minutes at the crease, John Reid took five thumping blows. Murray Chapple and Matt Poore were bowled off their chests.

All who faced Adcock could hardly imagine a more dangerous opponent.

Tall and pencil-slim, he had an action that was all balanced rhythm and revolved around a long, flowing approach to the crease and an easy action that placed little strain on his body. The master of the short ball, he could always obtain lift from just short of a length, and the New Zealanders who faced him in Jo'burg realised

that, although Adcock was a new boy, he would be around for a long time.

New Zealand's bravest moment in cricket came in the face of such fearsome hostility. Lawrie Miller returned to the wicket, and Sutcliffe came back at 6-81 with his head bandaged to play one of cricket's most defiant innings.

The left-hander, who 12 years later, at 41, would be flattened by Freddie Trueman, took the attack to the South Africans, slamming seven sixes in a score of 80 not out. Helping him add 33 in 10 minutes for the last wicket was New Zealand's pace bowler, Bob Blair, whose fiancee had just been killed in a train crash, and who marched to the crease as the crowd stood in silence.

It was fairytale stuff but Adcock was not about to let the New Zealanders off the hook, and in the second innings he took 5-43, smashing them out for 100 and another big South African victory.

The New Zealanders were to suffer against another big fast bowler on that tour, collapsing against the Orange Free State, where powerfully-built Peter Heine took 7-29.

Heine made his debut for South Africa at Lords on the 1955 tour of England and on the first day of the match took 5-60 as he and Trevor Goddard skittled England only to see Statham pay South Africa back in kind.

Adcock and Heine shared 14 wickets in the next Test, at Old Trafford, where South Africa won. England still managed to take the series 3-2.

The pair were in great form when England toured South Africa in 1956-7, taking with them Statham, Tyson and Bailey. In a drawn rubber, Adcock and Heine, supported by Goddard, shared 39 wickets.

With the record-breaking South African spinner, Hugh Tayfield, doing the damage in the second innings, Adcock and Heine (with 4-20 and 4-22, respectively) routed England in the first innings at Port Elizabeth to level the rubber.

Against Ian Craig's Australians in 1957-8, the pacy pair had some fine individual performances but could not prevent a 3-0 series win to the tourists. Adcock had his best Test performance of 6-43 in the drawn match at Durban, while Heine, who finished the series with 17 wickets at 19 each, took 6-58 in the drawn first Test at Johannesburg and 6-96 there three Tests later when Australia won by 10 wickets.

In the next Test, at Port Elizabeth, Adcock and Heine were both fired up even though the series had been decided. They turned on a terrible ordeal for the Australians, who needed only 68 runs to take the series 3-0.

In poor light and cool temperatures, they sent down seven vicious overs as Australia struggled to score.

In his first over Adcock gave Colin McDonald three straight bouncers that just missed his head. Both the umpire and the captain, Clive van Ryneveld, called for an end to the short-pitched bowling, so Adcock replied with yet another bouncer, even faster than the first three, and McDonald was caught at slip.

Australia still won by eight wickets.

Heine made a brief appearance against New Zealand in 1961-62 and retired with 58 wickets (25.08) in 14 Test matches.

Adcock's early career had been hampered by injuries and his love of the bouncer. But some time between that series against Australia and the 1960 South African tour of England, which Heine missed, he matured into a more complete fast man.

After Geoff Griffin had been thrown out of Test cricket at Lords because of his suspect action, Adcock, haunted by the memory of so many breakdowns but strengthened by special exercises and the knowledge that so much depended upon him, shouldered the responsibility of two fast bowlers. He took 108 first-class wickets on tour at just 14 each and in the Tests took 26 wickets at 22.57, including 6-65 at The Oval.

He retired as the first South African fast bowler to top 100 wickets, taking 104 at 21.10 in 26 Tests.

He became a popular radio commentator and, after moving to Australia, was appointed the coach of the NSW Sheffield Shield team for the 1989-90 series.

Neil Adcock matured after early days as a tearaway.

Alec Bedser
(1918-)

Old Faithful

In the years after World War Two, Alec Bedser virtually carried the English bowling attack alone on the massive shoulders that gave him surprising pace from a short, easy approach.

He was a huge man whose best years were probably spent in the Royal Air Force in World War Two but who was so dedicated and skilful as a fast-medium exponent that at 35 he had the best series of his career, taking 39 wickets against the 1953 Australian tourists.

From the time Test cricket resumed, Bedser was England's chief strike weapon through 14 Test series until he finally bowed to speed and youth, making way for Tyson, Statham and Trueman.

Just as Maurice Tate kept the opposition honest until Larwood developed into a human missile, Alec Bedser kept England competitive until faster men were found.

Until he was left out of the second Test in Australia in 1954-5, Bedser played in every post-War Ashes match. Yet, after Tyson's triumphs, he played only once more for England, against South Africa, before retiring.

He bowed out as the greatest Test wicket-taker until that time, with 236 victims in 51 matches for England at an average of 24.89.

Like Tate, Bedser was a man with big shoulders, feet, legs and a huge heart to match his torso. He had an economical run-up and an easy but brisk action and could derive surprising speed off the pitch, so that batsmen felt the ball gained momentum after landing. He left the field only once in his career, at Adelaide during a heatwave.

He practised his craft for hour after hour in the nets, putting a white handkerchief on the spot of ideal line and length and hitting the mark almost every time.

Bedser was so accurate that, despite his lively pace, he preferred his wicket-keepers, Godfrey Evans and Arthur McIntyre, to stand up to the stumps for him.

He joined Surrey with his twin brother, Eric, in 1938 and made his first-class debut against Oxford in 1939. It was not until after the war that he played his first Test, like Maurice Tate at an advanced age, nearly 28.

Bedser took 11 wickets each in the first two 1946 Tests against India, taking 7-49 in his first innings for England at Lords. In the second Test at Old Trafford, he took 7-52 after Dick Pollard, of Lancashire, took 5-24 in the first innings.

Bedser struggled through his first Australian summer later that year, opening the bowling with little support from the pre-war veterans, Bill Edrich and Bill Voce.

He took four wickets in a big New Zealand score on

the way home and struggled again against South Africa. But in the same year, 1947, he hit his best first-class score of 126 for Surrey against Somerset.

Against Arthur Morris, Syd Barnes, Bradman, and Hassett he was the best of the English bowlers in a losing Ashes series in 1948. But he was overshadowed by the bowling of Cuan McCarthy in South Africa in 1948-9, when England narrowly won the series 2-0.

Trevor Bailey twice took six-wicket hauls against the New Zealanders in 1949, leaving Bedser behind, but the big man kept on keeping on.

He managed 5-127 against the 1950 West Indians at Trent Bridge, opening with Derek Shackleton against the power of Weekes and Worrell, and finished the series with 11 wickets at 34.

By the time England toured Australia in 1950-1, Bedser was 32 with several arduous series and moderate returns behind him; but in a losing battle he managed 30 wickets at 16 in a remarkable display of consistency, having to operate in the third and fourth Tests without Bailey, whose thumb had been broken by Lindwall.

In five matches against the 1951 South African tourists, he repeated his Australian success with 30 wickets at 17, taking 7-58 in a 12-wicket haul at Old Trafford, helping England to a 3-1 series victory.

By 1952, the arrival of Fred Trueman told Bedser that his time at the top was short. England's bowlers were getting younger and faster. But before he left the international arena he was determined to put up a fight.

Backing Fiery Fred, he took 20 wickets at 14 each against the Indian tourists, beguiling all those who were still standing after Trueman's full frontal assaults. That same year, he took 8-18 bowling for Surrey against Nottinghamshire at The Oval.

While Trueman was away doing his national service in 1953, Bedser took the opportunity for the finest peformance of his career. With Fiery Fred, Brian Statham and young Frank Tyson all breathing down his neck, Bedser, then 35, broke Maurice Tate's Ashes record with 39 Australian wickets at just 17 apiece, number 39 coming up when he dismissed Arthur Morris at his beloved Oval for the 18th time in 20 Tests. England regained The Ashes after 19 years.

At Trent Bridge, Bedser followed 7-55 in the first innings with his best Test figures of 7-44 in the second; and in the same season on The Oval he took another 8-18 for Surrey against Warwickshire.

He took 10 cheap wickets against Pakistan the next year, but the Test debut of Tyson spelt his doom and, though both men struggled in Brisbane in 1954-5, Len Hutton preferred Tyson's raw speed to Bedser's reputation.

Just as Maurice Tate had done during Bodyline, the big medium-pacer watched from the dressing room as a typhoon devastated Australia.

Bedser took four wickets against South Africa the next season at Old Trafford in a match the Springboks won with minutes to spare and then retired, although he kept playing first-class cricket until 1960 and was a major figure along with Peter Loader in Surrey's remarkable run of county championships between 1952 and 1958.

In 1962, he became an England selector, chairing the panel from 1969 until 1982, in yet another record achievement.

Alec Bedser, big man with a big heart.
ABOVE: With twin brother Eric

Alan Davidson, Aussie stalwart of the '50s and '60s.

Alan Davidson
(1929-)

Big Swing And Big Hits

Alan Davidson spent the first half of his first-class career struggling for recognition and the last half as the finest opening bowler in the world.

He rose to Test status at a time when Australia had three of its greatest talents in Ray Lindwall, Keith Miller and Bill Johnston and at times it was tough even for him to hold down a place in the NSW side with Lindwall, Miller and another left-armer Alan Walker.

Davidson persevered and after a slow introduction to Test cricket became one of the finest left-arm fast bowlers the game has seen.

Don Tallon, the Australian wicket-keeper, said the burly Davo could be almost as quick as Lindwall, but most of the time he bowled fast-medium left-armers from over the wicket, aiming the ball on or just outside off stump and moving it both ways through the air and off the seam.

He took an easy run of 15 paces, and such was his ability to bring the ball back at the right-handed batsman that many were bowled not playing a shot, expecting the ball to continue its slant toward the slips.

Most of the time his immaculate action was accompanied by a hearty grunt of effort as he propelled his big frame, sometimes as much as 96 kilograms of it, toward the batsman.

Born at Lisarow, near the NSW resort town of Gosford, on June 14, 1929 Davidson started out bowling leg-breaks on a pitch he dug for himself out of a hillside. Like Ray Lindwall, he was also an exceptional rugby league talent who even late in his career trained with the Western Suburbs club in Sydney to maintain his strength and fitness.

A powerfully-built man of 180 centimetres, he moved to Sydney at 19 to pursue his cricket career and quickly found himself in a NSW side which had some of the finest fast bowlers in the world.

When Australia's best players were in South Africa in 1949-50, Bill Brown took an Australian B team to New Zealand which included the promising Davidson as well as such veterans as Don Tallon, Phil Ridings and Doug Ring.

Against Wairarapa, Davo took 10-29 off 81 balls and then hammered 157 in the kind of all-round performance that rekindled thoughts of the great South

Australian slow bowler, George Giffen. But such was the strength of Australian cricket at the time that Davo lost his place in the NSW team in 1951-2 and had to wait until Bill Johnston broke down in England to make his Test debut.

Even then the presence of Lindwall, Miller and Ron Archer in the Australian team meant his hands were rarely on the ball, and in five Tests in England he took just eight wickets. Opportunities were scarce.

By the end of the 1956 tour of England, Davo's third Ashes series, when he was 27, he was acknowledged as a master bowler. Yet he had played just 12 Tests and taken an unremarkable 16 wickets.

Then things started going his way. Bill Johnston was long gone, and Lindwall and Miller had recently retired. Suddenly the bit-part player was given the lead role.

For the next five years Alan Davidson proved himself to be one of the all-time great players, a left-arm speedster with few equals. In his next 32 Tests he took 170 wickets, and at 32 was still quick enough to record his best first-class figures, 7-31, for NSW against Western Australia in Perth.

Davo was given the new ball in South Africa in 1957-8 and immediately wickets began tumbling as though he had been storing them up in all the previous seasons of frustration.

After Ian Meckiff, his fellow left-hander, began his Test career brilliantly at Johannesburg, Davo followed with 6-34 in the first innings and finished the series with 25 wickets at 17.

He and Richie Benaud bowled Australia to victory at Port Elizabeth, Davo taking nine wickets.

He took 24 cheap wickets against the touring Englishmen the next season, far outgunning the likes of Statham, Trueman, Tyson and Loader, and at Brisbane his swing accounted for Peter Richardson, Willie Watson and Tom Graveney in one over with the score on seven.

He took 12 cheap wickets in Pakistan, where Benaud and Slasher Mackay stole the honours. In India Davidson was a daunting puzzle, taking 29 wickets at 15, his best Test figures of 7-93 coming at Kanpur.

In the tied Test at Brisbane's Gabba ground, Davo was the first man to score 100 runs (44 and 80) and take 10 wickets (5-135 and 6-87) in a Test match. The Australians were 6-92 against Wes Hall when Davidson joined Benaud, and the pair added 134 runs before Davidson was run out, setting up the unprecedented result.

He missed the thrilling fourth Test, at Adelaide, where Slasher Mackay held off Wes Hall. But in the other four matches, opening with Meckiff and Frank Misson he took 33 wickets at 18.54 with 6-53 in the second Test at Melbourne.

In England in 1961, Davidson took 5-42 at Lords partnering the debutant Graham McKenzie and finished the series with 23 wickets at 25.

With the Ashes in the balance at Old Trafford, he and McKenzie put together a blazing last-wicket partnership of 98 before the youngster was bowled, leaving

the left-arm veteran on 77 not out. David Allen, who had taken three wickets in 15 balls, suffered against Davo's bat, being hit for 20 in one over that included two searing off drives for six.

England was left to score 256 in four hours, and Ted Dexter led the run chase with 76 in 84 minutes. But Benaud took 5-12 in 25 balls and when Davo bowled Brian Statham, Australia kept The Ashes.

Davidson showed no sign of decline in his last series, even though he often limped during long spells and would be encouraged to persevere by a hand on the shoulder from Benaud and some kindly words of encouragement such as: "Just one more over, Al, pal".

Despite the limp and many hours spent on the massage table, Davidson again outshone Trueman, Statham and McKenzie with 6-75 at Melbourne and match figures of 9-79 at Sydney.

Davo hit a Colin Cowdrey full toss on to the roof of the old Brewongle Stand in what is still regarded as the biggest hit seen at the Sydney Cricket Ground. The next ball hit the wall at the back of the hill and was still going up on impact.

Davidson became a senior NSW cricket official and a national selector.

Fazal Mahmood
(1927-)
The Striking Cobra

Fazal Mahmood was known as the Alec Bedser of Pakistan, and many would see that as a huge compliment to the Englishman.

Though he was not nearly as big as Bedser, Fazal's methods were similar, his effect immense.

He was the best pace bowler produced by Pakistan until the arrival of Imran Khan, averaging more than four wickets a Test in a first-class career that lasted 20 years.

Like Bedser, Fazal was a master of fast-medium bowling, swinging the ball both ways and making it snake off the seam.

This green-eyed strongman was often unplayable on Pakistan's matting wickets. He was almost as formidable on turf.

He was the first Pakistan bowler to take 10 wickets against England, India, Australia and the West Indies, and his bearing on the fortunes of Pakistan cricket are reflected in his 12 for 99 at The Oval in 1954, which enabled Pakistan to beat England in its debut series — no mean effort, considering it took India 20 years and New Zealand nearly 50 to defeat the oldest rival.

Fazal and the two bowlers who gave him such great support, Khan Mohammad and Mahmood Hussain, all made their debut for Pakistan in the first Test series that country played — against India in 1952-3.

Fazal played for Northern India in the Ranji Trophy competition and would have toured with the India team

to Australia in 1947-8 but stood down, realising that the birth of a new nation, Pakistan, was imminent.

He bowled brilliantly in two series for Pakistan against Ceylon and against the touring MCC and as soon as his country entered the official Test arena, he stamped himself as one of the finest quick bowlers in cricket.

Khan Mohammad (born in 1928) took Pakistan's first wicket in Test cricket, bowling Pankaj Roy at Delhi in October, 1952. But he was injured soon after and Fazal and Hussain had to soldier on without him, India winning the series 2-1.

Fazal took 20 wickets at 26, with 5-52 and 7-42 at Lucknow, where Pakistan won by an innings thanks also to Nazar Mohammad, who batted throughout Pakistans innings for 124 not out, becoming the first player to be on the ground for an entire Test. Hussain finished the series with 12 wickets at 34.83.

Two years later, when the teams met in Pakistan, Khan Mohammad was fully fit for one of the few times in his career, and his performance

LEFT: Fazal Mahmood, who blazed the trail for Imran Khan. BELOW: His great partner Khan Mohammad.

The action of cricket's wild man, Roy Gilchrist.

showed just what he could do when he was free of strains and pains. His steady swing bowling dominated a series in which every match was drawn, Khan taking 22 at a little under 16, Fazal 15 wickets at 22 and Hussain 14 at 26.

Hussain (born 1932) was the quickest of the three pacemen, bowling big inswingers, but throughout his career he either wasted a lot of energy bowling leg theory or was used too much.

Against India in that second series he had early success with a spell of 6-67 in the first Test at Dacca, while in the fifth Test, at Karachi, Fazal took 5-49 and Khan 5-72 — their best bowling figures of the series.

At home to New Zealand in 1955-6, Khan and the spinner, Zulfiqar Ahmed, were largely responsible for a 2-0 victory in the three Test series, Khan taking 6-21 and then 2-20 off 30 overs on the soaked matting at Dacca to destroy the visitors for 70 in a match ruined by rain.

On their way home from being outfoxed by Jim Laker in England in 1956, the Australians were given another lesson on the matting at Karachi, where Fazal took 13 wickets to give Pakistan victory in the first duel between the two countries in what was to be a sad farewell for Keith Miller.

But the tricky trio of Pakistan did not always have teams in a state of confusion. They also found out the hard way that Test cricket can be cruel. In the West Indies in 1957-8, only Fazal had any success at all. Even that was moderate, his 20 wickets costing 38 each, even though only Gilchrist scored more victims.

In the third Test, at Kingston, Hussain broke down after just five deliveries and, with Nasim also injured, Fazal and Khan had to share the burden with Sobers and Hunte at their most aggressive.

Khan finished with 0-259 off 54 overs, Fazal 2-247 off 85.2. Sobers made 365 not out, the highest score in Test history, Hunte 260.

That was to be Khan's last series. He continued

playing in the Lancashire League and later became a professional cricketer in Canada. In 13 Tests, interrupted by injuries and appearances in the Lancashire League, he took a healthy 54 wickets at 23.92.

In 1958-9 as the skipper, Fazal, bowled Pakistan to revenge over the West Indians, who had sent Gilchrist home for his violence in India. Starting with a 10-wicket win on matting at Karachi, Fazal followed his fine bowling in that Test with 6-34 and 6-66 at Dacca, the West Indians collapsing in the first innings from 4-65 to all-out 76 as their last six batsmen failed to score.

Fazal captained Pakistan against Australia in 1959-60, but Benaud's men beat them on the mat at Dacca and on the turf at Lahore. The third, on matting at Karachi, was drawn.

In 1960-61, against India, Fazal was past his best in a series in which, all the matches were drawn because both teams were afraid of the furore defeat might cause in an unstable political world. But Fazal managed 5-26 at Calcutta, India being dismissed for 180, the only time in the series it made fewer than 400.

Hussain was Pakistan's best bowler overall, with 13 wickets at 38.69, taking 5-129 in the first Test, at Bombay.

Fazal was thought to have lost his penetration as a bowler and, after 10 Tests as captain for two wins and two losses, he was relieved of the job.

He played one Test against England at home in 1961-2, which also marked Hussain's retirement, and was flown over as a replacement for the 1962 tour of England but was a failure.

Hussain retired to become a senior Pakistan cricket administrator and manager of touring teams. In 27 Tests his pace and lift resulted in 68 wickets at 38.64.

Fazal began his first-class career with Northern India in 1943 and retired from the game in 1963. He played 34 Tests, took 139 wickets at 24.70, took five wickets in a Test innings 13 times, and took 10 wickets in a match four times.

Roy Gilchrist (1935-)

The Wild Man

Roy Gilchrist was cricket's premier wild man — a little coil of venom. After 13 Test matches in which he looked to be just the speedster the West Indies needed, Gilchrist was effectively banned for life from the international game. In subsequent years he was banned from the North Staffordshire League and the Lancashire League for fits of violent temper.

He was labelled a brute by a judge for burning his wife's face with an iron, and he was sent to prison for stabbing a cricket spectator.

Gilchrist was born into poverty on June 28, 1934, in Seaforth, Jamaica.

He had too much aggression and too little control of his own emotions. He was banned from Test cricket at 24, sent home from a tour of India in disgrace for constantly bowling beamers at the petrified batsmen.

There were public appeals to have him reinstated in the West Indies team, but Gerry Alexander and John Goddard, the West Indian hierarchy, believed him to be more trouble than he was worth. Despite the support of Frank Worrell and the great writer, C.L.R. James, Gilchrist, after 13 Tests and 57 wickets (26.68) never played for the West Indies again.

Gilchrist was just 170 centimetres and weighed 60 kilograms. But, like Harold Larwood, he was wiry and strong with long arms and a powerful action.

He bounded in off a 25-metre run-up and could generate ferocious speed, often accentuated by the fact that all too often the ball was sent for a spot between the batsman's eyes.

When Gilchrist arrived in England with Goddard's side in 1957, he was reckoned by team mates to be faster than the English kingpin, Brian Statham. Charlie Griffith, who replaced Gilchrist in the West Indies team, says that little Gilly was faster than both he and Wesley Hall.

But Gilchrist gave new meaning to what has been labelled "a fast bowler's temperament".

When he had a cricket ball in his hand and the wind at his back, he was an ominous proposition. When his temper was up, there was no telling what he might do.

Gilchrist opened the bowling with Frank Worrell in the first four Tests in England in 1957. Despite plenty of pace and plenty of well-aimed bouncers, he managed just 10 wickets at 46.6 each, his best bowling 4-115 at Lords, where England won by an innings thanks to the all-rounder, Trevor Bailey.

At home against Pakistan early in 1958, his performances were overshadowed by the batting of Sobers, Hunte, Walcott and Weekes. But he took more wickets than anyone else in the series, with 21 at 30.28, his best figures being 4-32 in the first innings of the drawn first Test at Bridgetown, where Pakistan made 657-8 following-on and Hanif Mohammad a tiresome 337.

Then it was off to India and the great crisis in his career. He played in four of the five Tests and took 26 wickets at 16.11.

In the third Test, at Calcutta, he took 3-18 off 23 overs in the first innings and then 6-55 in the second. Together with Rohan Kanhai (256), and his fellow century-makers, Sobers and Basil Butcher, Gilchrist gave the Windies victory by an innings and 336 runs.

The West Indians won the series 3-0 but from then on it was all downhill for Gilchrist. He was sent home before the Pakistan leg of the tour and Wes Hall took over his mantle of pace spearhead, becoming one of the game's finest ambassadors.

Sadly, Gilchrist became something else.

According to the writer, David Lemmon, Gilchrist had arrived in England in 1957 "untutored and barely literate."

"That his talent was wasted was due in some part to flaws in his own character, but also a lack of sympathy and understanding by some in positions of authority," he wrote.

In 1961, two years after the furore in India, Gilchrist was banned for life by the North Staffordshire League for constantly abusing umpires and finally for another misdemeanour.

Miffed at a batsman hitting the winning runs off his bowling, Gilchrist replied by fielding the ball and hurling it at the batsman's head.

Four years later, in August, 1965, while playing for Crompton in the Lancashire League, Gilchrist was firing away at the opening batsman, Derek Bickley, with Radcliffe 0-4 in reply to Crompton's 106.

Gilchrist began his second over in typical fashion —two beamers and a bouncer. But it was his fourth ball which caused all the consternation. Gilly came tearing in from his mark out near the boundary fence and kept on running. Past the umpire, past the crease and past the other opener, Bill McDonald.

He arrived at a point somewhere near the middle of the pitch and there, in full flight, took aim and hurled the ball fair at Bickley's head.

Bickley ducked, pulled himself together and then he and McDonald walked off, Gilchrist's team mates following a minute later.

After peace was restored and Bickley's heart rate was again approaching normal, he said: "I've never been so frightened in my life. When Gilchrist threw the ball, I just ran to square leg. I'll never again play on the same field as him."

One umpire, Bill Dixon, said Bickley had provoked the bowler by pointing at his chin and daring Gilchrist to "have a go". But he added that Gilchrist's actions were somewhat extreme.

Two years later, a Manchester judge labelled Gilchrist a brute for branding the face of his wife with an iron during an argument. Gilchrist pleaded guilty to causing his wife grievous bodily harm, leaving her with a permanent 10 centimetre scar.

Mrs Gilchrist told the court she was no longer afraid of her husband and that he was a good father to their four sons.

Placing Gilchrist on probation for three years, the judge said only the compassion and love of Gilchrist's wife had saved him from a long prison sentence.

"You are very fortunate in having a wife who is a good woman, very much better than you deserve," the judge said, "I hate to think English sport has descended so far that brutes are tolerated because they are good at games."

The warning was not enough to curb Gilchrist's temper, though. The following year he stabbed a fellow spectator at a match in Manchester.

He was sentenced to 18 months in prison.

Bill Johnston
(1922-)

The Smiling Assassin

Bill Johnston was the perfect foil for the fast-bowling combination of Ray Lindwall and Keith Miller.

He was a tall, gangly, left-arm swing bowler who, off a loping run of just 10 easy strides, could send down a shock bouncer quick enough to worry the best batsmen or change to spin bowling if the conditions prevailed.

Johnston was not as quick as his partners, and for much of his career he played in their shadows. But he was more successful, averaging four wickets a Test for 40 Tests between 1947 and 1955 and constantly taking more wickets than the faster men.

Born at Beeac, Western Victoria, he was a natural entertainer. A country boy with a droll sense of humour, he loved to take wickets almost as much as he loved to amuse crowds with what some might describe as batting.

All arms and legs and bounding good cheer, Johnston was a better batsmen than he made out to be but not quite so good as his average of 102 on the 1953 tour of England might suggest: batting at No. 11, he was not out 16 times in 17 innings. He summed up his tour performance with the quip "Class will always tell."

As a fast-medium left-arm bowler, though, there was nothing amusing about Johnston in the eyes of batsmen.

At 185 centimetres with long arms and long legs, he was so flexible that he often amused party guests by bending his feet up behind his head. He first came to Melbourne to make the grade as a left-arm spin bowler, but then World War Two came and he went off to do four years with the RAAF.

After the war, he found himself bowling left arm spinners in the nets to the former Test captain, Jack Ryder, then a Victorian selector, and, like Maurice Tate 25 years before, he slipped in a fast one to see what would happen.

Ryder convinced Johnston his future lay in swing bowling — and a great career was hatched.

Johnston's performances for Victoria made him a favourite for the 1946-7 Ashes series, in which Lindwall and Miller starred. But he was overlooked and had to wait until the next season, when the Indians came to Australia, for a place in the Test team.

Johnston began his career superbly with 16 wickets in four Tests at 11.37. Opening with Lindwall, he took 2-17 and 1-11 in his debut at Brisbane but had to play second fiddle to Ernie Toshack's memorable 5-2 and 6-29.

Naturally, Johnston was one of the first on the boat for the tour of England, and he and Lindwall both finished with 27 wickets in Bradman's victorious finale.

Johnston took 5-36 in his nine-wicket haul in the first Test, at Trent Bridge, to get the Australians off to a fine start that Bradman and Hassett finished. Wisden said no Australian had made a greater personal contribution to the playing success of that Ashes team.

The 1948 series was the first of five straight, in which Johnston would take more than 20 wickets — remarkable, considering he had two of the all-time greats competing for the new ball.

In South Africa in 1949-50, he overshadowed Lindwall and Miller with 23 wickets at 17.04 and a best of 6-44, the best performance by any of the Australian bowlers. This helped the tourists on their way to another 4-0 series triumph. In comparison, Lindwall took 12 wickets in four matches, Miller 17 in five.

Johnston was the best of the Australian bowlers again when England came to Australia in 1950-1, taking 22 wickets as Australia kept The Ashes, and he finished on top of the wickets when the West Indians came Down Under in 51-52, taking 23. His 6-62 in the Third Test at Adelaide came as the tourists scored their only win of the series.

At Melbourne in the

Bill Johnston, a master of pace, swing and spin.

fourth Test, the West Indians were poised to level the series, but Johnston and Doug Ring scampered to 38 runs as the West Indians panicked and Australia won by a single wicket to wrap up what might have been a tight contest, eventually emerging 4-1 champion.

Against South Africa in 1952-3, Johnston finished with 21 wickets and, even though Miller and Lindwall were bowling brilliantly, he had to do more than his share at Melbourne after the selectors left out the fast men and replaced them with Geoff Noblet and Ron Archer.

He finished with 6-152, and Australia lost the match, the South Africans levelling the series.

By the 1954-5 Ashes series, Johnston was having to bowl after Lindwall, Miller, Archer, Davidson and Benaud.

But he took more wickets than all of them, with 19 at 22.26, even though his 5-85 in Melbourne could not save a match in which Frank Tyson was as savage as his namesake, Mike.

Johnston took 100 Test wickets faster than anyone before him — in just four years and a few days — in a more sedate era when there was only one Test series a season.

Ray Lindwall
(1921-)

Silk And Fire

Freddie Trueman once said that if Tchaikovsky had been alive to see Raymond Russell Lindwall bowling for Australia, he would have been moved to compose a symphony to accompany the smooth acceleration, balance and power of the man.

Lindwall was all silky-smooth rhythm, easy strength and accuracy as an express speedster. He stood 178 centimetres with the strong upper body of the rugby league champion he might have been and with the kind of co-ordination that made most other fast bowlers look clumsy.

Lindwall did not run to the wicket so much as flow towards it, rolling along low before arching and skidding the ball through.

At 11, he and his brother, Jack, had sat on the Sydney Cricket Ground hill and watched Larwood taking 10 wickets in the face of Stan McCabe's defiance.

Although Larwood bowled so fast that the boys could not see the ball once it left his hand, young Ray was so impressed with the speed of the little English fast man that 20 years later Lindwall's 13-stride, 16-metre approach and low, wheeling delivery looked remarkably similar to that which frightened Australian batsmen during Bodyline.

Lindwall probably developed greater variety than Larwood, even if there was not much separating their pace. He was a master of accuracy, too, insisting that batsmen played at every ball he sent down, wasting little, and never giving the batsman time to relax.

When he first played for NSW, Lindwall achieved most of his movement away from the bat. But, while playing for Nelson in the Lancashire League in 1952, his fieldsmen helped him to develop a devastating inswinger as well by constantly dropping the slip catches.

Lindwall, born in Sydney on October 3, 1921, grew up in Hurstville, a southern Sydney suburb.

Such was the thrilling nature of Lindwall's duels with the likes of Len Hutton that he spawned thousands of imitators in hundreds of Australian parks. As well as the poetic rhythm of his bowling, he had a menacing bouncer that was a complete shock after a barrage of deliveries skidding through and difficult to sight.

He could cut and swing the ball both ways and was good enough as a batsmen to score centuries against England and the West Indies.

Lindwall could run 100 yards in 10.6 seconds and played a season with the St George rugby league club in Sydney as a goal-kicking fullback.

More than half of his wickets came without the help of fieldsmen, and in England in 1948, Bradman's last tour, Lindwall took 86 wickets — all but 18 of them without the help of anyone but the wicket-keeper.

He relied on deception as much as pace and he could send down the bouncer, slower ball and skidding yorker without any real change in his action. Despite the speed with which the ball could leap at a batsman's head, Lindwall caused only two serious injuries to batsmen in his career.

In later years, as fast bowlers began bouncing even the tamest batting bunnies, Lindwall would always recall his youth and his creed that if he had to bowl short to tail-enders then he should not be bowling at all.

In tandem with Keith Miller, Lindwall made Australian teams after the war invincible until England regained The Ashes with their victory at The Oval in 1953.

When Lindwall joined Miller in 1946, he was a veteran of campaigns in New Guinea and the Solomon Islands. He had a recurring illness which at first was thought to be malaria.

Lindwall recovered from chickenpox to take 7-63 in England's first innings in the final Test at Sydney in 1946-7 in a series Australia won 3-0.

At Melbourne, he scored a century in 115 minutes in only his fourth innings of Test cricket, confirming the batting potential he had shown as a 15-year-old when he scored 219 for Oatley juniors in 75 minutes in a Saturday morning competition and in the afternoon hit an unbeaten century in men's cricket with the Carlton Waratahs.

In 1947-8 at Adelaide, he took 7-38, the best figures of his career, and at The Oval in 1948 he snared 6-20 to wreck England for 52 in what was a great season for him. An experimental rule enabling the new ball to be taken after 55 overs won few supporters in England.

In South Africa, his 5-32 at Cape Town helped Australia to another 4-0 series win, when Lindwall broke the thumb of Trevor Bailey and took 15 wickets against the touring Englishmen in 1950-1, putting Australia on the way to another huge series victory, this time 4-1.

England's eight-wicket win in the last Test at Melbourne ended an Australian run of 24 Tests without defeat, a record for which Lindwall could take much of the credit.

He could not save Australia in England in 1953, although his 7-20 against Minor Counties at Stoke on Trent was a first-class best for him. In typical fashion, no fieldsmen were needed — six batsmen were bowled, one out lbw.

Lindwall managed only seven wickets in four Tests against Jim Laker's England in 1956, but on the way back to Australia he picked up 7-43 at Madras.

Trevor Bailey, perhaps pitying Lindwall limping in "Typhoon" Tyson's 1954-5 sweep through Australia, allowed the veteran fast bowler to rattle his stumps for his 100th against England.

But Lindwall, made of solid stuff, got over his limp and when recalled to the Australian team for the Adelaide Test of the 1958-9 series aged 37, repaid Bailey's charity by dismissing him for a pair of ducks when the teams met in Melbourne.

The last two Tests of that series gave Lindwall seven wickets, allowing him to pass Clarrie Grimmett's Australian Test record of 216. It also gave Australian fans a chance to see a model action at a time when controversy raged over the deliveries of Gordon Rorke and Ian Meckiff. By the time he saw out his Test career with four matches in India and Pakistan, Lindwall had 228 Test scalps from 61 matches at 23.03. He spent the last five years of his career as a fast-medium swing bowler.

The controversial action of Ian Meckiff.

Ian Meckiff (1935-) and Gordon Rorke (1938-)

Chucked Out

Ian Meckiff had been found guilty and sentenced to death.

The Test umpire, Col Egar, reluctantly volunteered to act as hangman and as he took off from the Vulture Street end of the Brisbane Cricket Ground the career of the Victorian left-arm speedster was killed off for good.

That is pretty much the way Dick Whitington saw the demise of Ian Meckiff, the most famous victim of the anti-throwing purge that dominated the international game in the 1960s just as it had done in the early years of the century.

Meckiff's left elbow had a permanent bend in it, and he had been a controversial figure in Australian teams since making his Test debut at Johannesburg with Ian Craig's side in 1957-8. The outcry over "chucking" usually increased with Meckiff's success

and in the summer of 1963-4, when he opened the bowling for Australia in the first Test against South Africa at Brisbane, officials started seeing him as a daunting problem.

Egar had passed Meckiff's action for several seasons and, despite the suspicions about his bowling, Meckiff had been called for throwing only twice in his career, both times in the previous season.

Eddie Barlow and Trevor Goddard opened the batting for South Africa and the Australian skipper, Richie Benaud, let McKenzie send down the first over before tossing the ball to Meckiff.

Egar no-balled the second, third, fifth and ninth deliveries and told Goddard that if he lost his wicket to Meckiff, he would no-ball the delivery retrospectively.

Dick Whitington watched Meckiff's over through binoculars and remarked later that even if he had never bowled with a straight elbow before, he delivered all 12 deliveries in the over immaculately and at only three-quarter pace.

Despite jeering from the crowd, Benaud would not give Meckiff a bowl from the other end under the other umpire, Lou Rowan, and Meckiff did not bowl again in the Test or in any other first-class match.

The controversy and furore his bowling had created in the preceding few years often made him ill. But at last it was over. Richie Benaud handed over the Australian captaincy to Bob Simpson.

Gordon Rorke's rare bowling style ended his career.

Don Bradman, chairman of Australian selectors, called the problem of throwing the most difficult cricket had faced, and many saw Meckiff as the scapegoat for the whole dilemma.

At the London conference on chucking in 1960, Australia was represented by Bradman and the president of the Australian Cricket Board, Bill Dowling, who told delegates he was appalled by the campaign to get Meckiff and another Australian fast bowler, Gordon Rorke, saying it was contrary to every principle of fair play that Meckiff should be condemned by the English without having appeared in their country.

The questions, suspicions and outright condemnation of Meckiff's bowling intensified after he took 6-38 in Australia's eight-wicket win in the second Test, at Melbourne, in 1958-9, when he bundled England out for 87 — its lowest total in Australia for 55 years, Meckiff finishing the season with 17 wickets from four matches at 17 each.

For much of his Test career Meckiff opened the Australian bowling with another left-hander, Alan Davidson. After a slow run-up, he attained sharp speed from double-jointed shoulders; and in 18 Tests he managed 45 wickets at 31.62. Ironically, as a fieldsman he had a poor throwing arm. Meckiff took 11 wickets in four Tests in his debut in South Africa, and his action was never questioned even when he took eight wickets, including 5-125 in the first Test, at Johannesburg.

He partnered Davidson again at home against England and provided his burly partner with fine support again touring India, taking 12 wickets at 33.

Because of the controversy fanned by the English press, Meckiff began working hard in the nets to change his action, throwing his front arm higher in the delivery stride.

He was chosen in two of the five Tests against the West Indies in 1960-1, and at Brisbane, the scene of the lowest ebb of his career three years later, he was involved in one of cricket's most stirring finishes, being run out by Joe Solomon on the second-last ball of the match, creating Test cricket's first tie.

Meckiff tore tendons in an ankle and missed the 1961 tour of England, but by the summer of 1963-4 he had recovered sufficiently to warrant a recall to the Australian team and the awful over in Brisbane. He should have stayed in bed.

Gordon Rorke was a blond 192-centimetre strong-man who could generate great pace because of his big shoulders and who became largely responsible for cricket's front-foot rule.

He had a rare and awesome action in which, in delivery, he could take the whole weight of his body on the outside of his right foot and slide several metres up the pitch toward the batsman.

Rorke released the ball metres closer to the batsman than they were accustomed to. He had been a none-too-successful spin bowler at high school, but Rorke made his Test debut at the age of 20 at Adelaide in the 1958-9 series against England, in which Lindwall had been recalled to open with Alan Davidson.

Rorke finished the match with five wickets, and Australia won comfortably.

When Colin Cowdrey was asked at the end of the third day's play why he was not playing forward to the young bowler, he said he was afraid Rorke would tread on his toes.

Rorke came into the Australian team because Meckiff was injured, and he could not have made his debut at a more controversial time.

Other members of the Australian team, Jim Burke and Keith Slater, bowled with suspect actions and South Australia had two controversial fast bowlers — Alan Hitchcox and Peter Trethewey, better known as Pitchcox and Trethrowey.

The English journalist Brian Chapman called Rorke a "honey of a chucker". But while he was at his peak it was Rorke's drag that created more problems for the batsmen.

Rorke and Meckiff both went on the tour of India and Pakistan in 1959-60. But Rorke came home early 16 kilograms lighter, ravaged by hepatitis. He never seemed to recover his great speed or the rhythm that had allowed him to bowl so fast.

In 1964, Rorke was only 26 but no longer good enough to play for NSW. He joined Ian Meckiff in a premature retirement.

Keith Miller
(1919-)

A Most Dashing Hero

Keith Ross Miller was a wartime fighter pilot who spent his cricketing career as a flannelled Errol Flynn, a dashing, handsome man who loved gambling and classical music.

Richie Benaud called him the game's greatest all-rounder, and Miller's commanding officer in the Royal Australian Air Force reckoned him to be "the bravest and most willing pilot under his command".

Miller would probably have earned millions from cricket had he been playing in the 1990s, such was his charisma and heroic standing.

He was born in the Melbourne suburb of Sunshine on November 28, 1919, the son of an engineer.

His friend, the cricketer and journalist Dick Whitington, said everything "Nugget" Miller did in life was spontaneous and unplanned.

Miller was the kind of man who rose to a challenge, who needed a Compton or Edrich to bowl at in order to perform at his best. He took no pleasure in bowling out "bunnies". One writer said he was the kind of cricketer who could crashland at 11am and join in a game of cricket at 12.

David Frith described Miller as a "man husky and handsome enough to have played d'Artagnan on the screen, an RAAF hero and one of the great bar emptiers in cricket history".

He was, in the administrative eye, intolerably extrovert, the eyes holding an amused and challenging glint beneath a thick, swept-back mane of black hair. A bowling study would show the athleticism of a man who could bowl the fastest ball of the day off four easy paces.

He was the kind of player who could turn a game with a few minutes of lusty hitting, who could ravage a batting side with a run-up that could start anywhere or could take catches at the slips, even though he often gave the impression of boredom in the field and sometimes seemed not so much interested in who was playing at Lords but more so in where his next hangover was coming from or what was running at Ascot.

Miller was immensely strong with a rhythmic action, likely to toss down a googly or two in between a pair of searing bouncers. More than once in his career he dropped the ball during his run-up but, rather than walk back to start again, he would merely gather the ball while trotting and take off from there.

"His bowling will always linger in my memory," wrote Frank Tyson. "A spring-heeled acceleration, short approach, and an eruptive high action over a ramrod front leg. To the man at the business end of the wicket, the run-up, action and grip suggested an outswinger; but it was all bluff and, Nugget was just as likely to produce anything from an inswinger to a wrong 'un. Keith Miller was unfathomable and ever unpredictable."

Tyson remembers seeing him play for the first time at the Old Trafford Victory Test of 1945, racing in to bowl with his mane of black hair "trailing like clouds of glory behind him". His batting, said the Englishman, was simply the rape of the bowler.

Miller made a career out of defying authority. He feuded with Bradman on the 1948 tour of England. With no challenge to be had, Miller allowed himself to be bowled first ball against Essex when Australia made 721. He refused to take the new ball against Jack Ikin, who was then on 99 playing for Lancashire, and at Lords Miller again refused to bowl and tossed the ball back to a skipper who knew full well that the all-rounder's back, injured in a fighter-plane crash, was playing up.

Miller repaid The Don by bouncing him in his testimonial game. Many blamed Bradman for Miller's original omission for the 1949-50 tour of South Africa, Nugget eventually being flown over after Bill Johnston was involved in a car accident.

Officialdom and Miller's own image saw to it that Miller never captained Australia, but he did fill in at Kingston, Jamaica, on the 1955 tour of the West Indies after Ian Johnson had been hurt by a bouncer. Nugget led his team to a nine-wicket victory.

Richie Benaud, no mean leader himself, rated Nugget the best skipper he played under and said no-one was better at summing up a player's weaknesses.

Miller fell in love with horse racing when he was a boy and remembers crying when he realised he was too big to become a jockey. Between the ages of 16 and 18 he grew from 150 centimetres to 180 centimetres, hitting 185 centimetres and 86 kilograms in his cricketing prime.

His first job was as a clerk in an oil company, and he was a promising Australian rules footballer with St Kilda as well as a Victorian batsman when Clarrie Grimmett, the champion leg-break bowler of the 1920s, advised him to give more time to his bowling.

That was at the outbreak of World War Two. Like Jack Gregory, Miller made his reputation as a mighty all-rounder in the Victory Tests, among his performances a lusty 185 in 165 minutes for a Dominions XI against England at Lords.

Miller made his Test debut with Ray Lindwall against New Zealand in 1946 and in his first Test against England, in the summer of 1946-7, he hit 79 runs, including the longest six seen at the Gabba ground, and took 7-60 bowling fast and slow on a sticky wicket.

Had he not been burdened with the role of pace-bowling spearhead, Miller might have had one of the highest batting averages in Test cricket.

In 55 Tests, many of them played with a bad back and in advancing years, Miller snared 170 wickets at 22.97, hit seven centuries, and averaged 36.97 with the bat. Miller could occasionally bowl faster than his partner, Lindwall, but his mood and pace often depended on how he had spent the previous evening.

Even though Miller was never a spiteful man, Len Hutton said he never felt physically safe against the big Australian.

Denis Compton, who became both Miller's great friend and respected adversary — Miller named one of his sons after the gallant English batsman — was more wary of Nugget than of Lindwall, especially if his old drinking mate had a hangover and was in a sour mood.

At Adelaide in 1955, after Frank Tyson had cut loose, the Englishmen needed a mere 94 in their second innings to win the match and secure the Ashes. As Australia took the field, Miller was asked who would win. "I haven't a clue," he growled, "but somebody's in for a nasty half-hour".

In 20 balls, he fired out Bill Edrich, Len Hutton and Colin Cowdrey and, while fielding at extra cover, took a magnificent catch to dismiss Peter May. But his shoulder was damaged in the process, and victory evaporated.

In the West Indies later that year, he had the kind of success he had enjoyed in his first series against England nearly 10 years before.

He opened the series with his highest Test score of 147, at Kingston, scored 137 at Bridgetown in the fourth Test, and in the next match scored 109 and took 6-107. All-up, he scored 439 runs at 73 and took 20 wickets at 32.

By the time of the 1956 tour of England, Miller was nearly 37, but, even though his pace was cut considerably, he was still Australia's best bowler as his team tried to survive the efforts of Laker and Lock.

Miller hit 281 not out, his highest first-class score, against Leicestershire, and in the Tests he took 21 wickets at 22, including 5-72 and 5-80 in Australia's 185-run win at Lords, after the NSW fast bowler, Pat Crawford, broke down after 29 balls. Though hampered by his suspect back, Miller bowled 70 overs.

He came out of retirement in 1959 to play for Nottinghamshire against Cambridge University, a team which included a youngster named Henry Blofeld, and Miller scored an unbeaten century in 125 minutes in the second innings to enter the record books as a batsman who made a century in his county debut.

Interestingly Miller had also scored a century in his Sheffield Shield debut, hitting 181 for Victoria against Tasmania at the MCG 22 years before.

Miller was always marvellous company. He never forgot a name and he was always a compelling storyteller, filling almost as many bars in retirement as he had emptied in his playing peak.

RIGHT: Miller the magnificent, a larger than life hero.

Brian Statham
(1930-)

The Hungry Whippet

As nightmares go, Brian Statham was a hell of a nice guy.

Though without a vindictive bone in his body, this spare-framed genial Lancastrian created torment wherever he played, taking more than 250 Test wickets and proving that even in a craft demanding aggression, nice guys do not always finish last.

He was plagued by sore feet and bloody toes from the pounding they took in the delivery stride, and sometimes he bowled with a bloody sock protruding from a hole in his boot, cut to relieve the painful pressure.

Statham was such a nice guy that did he not bowl short to the tail-enders and sometimes would warn batsmen when the short ball was coming.

Vic Marks, the Test off-spinner of the 1980s, recalled a story about Statham bowling against Easton McMorris in Jamaica and how the batsman was proving difficult by continually thrusting his front foot down the wicket.

"Statham quietly informed him that he would have to bowl a couple of bouncers if he continued with this policy. McMorris ignored the warning and was soon hit painfully in the ribs and taken to hospital regretting his error of judgement."

According to Frank Tyson, "Even when he pared a layer of skin off the Adam's apples of his more accomplished opponents, he gave the impression of taking part in an impersonal scientific experiment, the sole object of which was their dismissal."

Tyson remembers Staham hitting the Northhamptonshire opener Waddie Reynolds squarely between the eyes on a green Old Trafford wicket and having never seen a more worried man than Statham or a more relieved one when Reynolds recovered.

Bowling uphill into the wind off a 17-pace run-up and driving the batsmen to distraction with deliveries that were sometimes criticised for being too accurate, Statham was the perfect foil for the more fiery Trueman and Tyson, even though he was to play more Tests than both of them.

Statham did not enjoy a great deal of luck throughout his career. His accuracy resulted in many deliveries that beat the edge repeatedly or shaved the stumps without dislodging the bails.

Sometimes he had trouble controlling his swing, but his stock ball was the off-cutter — he called it the "nip-backer" — darting in from outside off-stump to rap the pads or the stumps.

He was double-jointed in the shoulders and had an extended joint in the elbow, which not only gave rise to some suggestions that he threw, but was also largely responsible for his great pace. He was not belligerent or boastful like Trueman, but he was just as tough and tireless, his deliveries tending more often than not to skid at the stumps rather than leap at the throat.

He was a fine outfielder with a strong throw, and as a left-handed bat he was a useful tail-ender, his fighting knocks in Sydney in 1954-5 contributing to England's 38-run victory in the wake of Australia's brush with Tysonitis.

Statham made his first-class debut for Lancashire in 1950 on his 20th birthday, against Kent at Old Trafford. His coach, Harry Makepeace, groomed him as the county's answer to the long-serving Dick Pollard. Fifteen years later, he succeeded Ken Grieves as the county captain.

In the winter of his debut season, after performances that included five wickets for five runs against Somerset, he was flown to Australia to strengthen the touring English team, and he made his Test debut in New Zealand, his first Test wicket being that of the master batsman Bert Sutcliffe at Christchurch.

On the 1954-5 tour of Australia, he was the perfect partner for the ferocity of Tyson, taking 18 wickets at 28 with his nagging line, length and nip-backer.

Some saw his 5-60 in the first innings at Melbourne as the result of Tyson firing down the cannon shot at the other end just as Gubby Allen had benefited during Bodyline by the speed and fire of Larwood.

But, according to Tyson, Statham deserved many accolades.

"The accuracy often produced wickets for (Statham's) bowling partners rather than for himself," Tyson wrote. "Batsmen driven to desperation by their inability to score off him frequently took unwarranted risks against the bowler at the other end, and paid the price."

Statham was at his peak in the mid-1950s. After partnering Tyson to such great effect in Australia, he picnicked in New Zealand with spells of 4-24, 1-30, 4-28 and a burst of 3-9 as England destroyed the Kiwis for 26. He took 12 wickets at 7.58 in the two matches.

That northern summer, he took his best Test figures of 7-39 against South Africa at Lords when he and Trueman went tag team against the visiting big guns, Adcock and Heine. The tourists needed only 183 to win, but against Statham's unwavering line and length they made only 111.

Jackie McGlew was out to Statham twice for a duck, and Trueman's main contribution was to smash the visiting skipper, Jack Cheetham, on the elbow, forcing him to retire hurt.

In 1957, Statham achieved his best first-class figures, 8-34 for Lancashire against Warwickshire at Coventry, and in Melbourne in 1958-9 he took 7-57, only to see England collapse against Davidson and Meckiff.

In 1960, Statham took 27 wickets at 18 to top the bowling averages against South Africa, and at Lords he claimed 6-63 and 5-34. It was the only time Statham, for all his persistence, managed more than nine wickets in a Test. But, sadly, the performance was overshadowed by the hat-trick and then the throwing contro

Brian Statham, naggingly accurate in line and length.

versy surrounding South Africa's Geoff Griffin. Statham bowled well at home against Australia and Pakistan in 1961 and 1962, but his form fell off in the summer of 1962-3, when he captured only 13 wickets in five Tests touring Australia.

But, after he took 15 wickets in a match against Leicestershire in 1964 he was recalled to the England side in 1965 for the third and final Test against South Africa, England needing victory to level the series.

Statham, then 35, and his Lancashire partner, Ken Higgs, bowled beautifully, Statham taking 5-40 in the

first innings. His fifth wicket — Tiger Lance, lbw for 69 — brought him to the 250 mark in Test cricket. Heavy rain prevented an England victory in the last match between the two nations.

Statham captained Lancashire from 1965-7 and retired the next season. In his last match, a benefit for Ken Higgs at Old Trafford, he took 6-34. Yorkshire scored only 61 runs. In his 19 years with Lancashire, Statham took more than 100 wickets in a season 13 times, did the hat-trick three times and twice took 15 wickets in a first-class match.

Fred Trueman
(1930-)

Fiery Fred

Freddie Trueman's great ambition in life was to be the finest fast bowler "that ever drew breath".

He was the first bowler to take more than 300 Test wickets, an express man with one of the finest actions ever and the control of a medium-pacer. With pigeon toes, thick legs, big hips, a huge chest, pasty face and thick, jet-black hair, Trueman in full flight was one of cricket's greatest sights.

He was a man of temper and hostility on the field. A shipping company once named a trawler after Fiery Fred and, perhaps appropriately, it blew up in the North Sea. Yet away from the field he was a man of great mirth who turned his anecdotes into amusing books and a sometimes hilarious cabaret act.

He once estimated that his brushes with authority cost him 35 appearances for England and more than 100 wickets. Many of the stories told about his deeds and misdeeds are probably fiction, yet, given his ready wit and defiance of authority, they all seem plausible.

In 1952, for instance, when he terrorised the Indian batsmen into submission in his debut, he is said to have attended a dinner in honour of the touring team and asked a high-ranking Indian diplomat to "Pass the salt, Gunga Din".

Trueman denied even being at the same table and once summed up his reputation by remarking: "I hear things about myself I'd never have dreamt of in a million years, and I don't reckon to be short on imagination."

Trueman was a larger-than-life character throughout 20 years of first-class cricket until 1969, bringing spirit to every match he played. In 67 Tests he took 307 wickets at 21.57, and he probably would have topped 400 had he not fallen foul of the selectors.

Born at Stainton, Yorkshire, he possessed a rhythmical run-up and a classical side-on action.

He was first spotted in 1948 by the Yorkshire slow-bowling legend, Wilfred Rhodes.

He already had a good outswinger and bouncer, but he was wild. He became a first-class cricketer after graduating from the coal pits via some valuable tuition from the grand old Yorkshireman, Bill Bowes, who would recall that much of the youngster's bluster stemmed from an inferiority complex.

Bluster was something on which Fred was never short. In his book *Ball of Fire*, he wrote: "Godfrey Evans has been quoted as saying he thought Frank Tyson was faster than me. But how can he be so sure? I am only certain of one thing, that I bowled faster over a longer period than anyone else on earth."

That he may have done. But part of his rare talent was that he made periodic appearances in opposition

dressing rooms to warn his rivals of what they faced against him and he could quickly sum up a batsman's weaknesses.

At 178 centimetres and heavily built, he was thought to have the ideal frame for a quick man, all muscular co-ordination with a powerful trunk and thick legs to keep him going all day.

He had a sensational debut in the 1952 series against India at Headingley, where in the second innings he and Bedser gave the tourists the worst start in Test-cricket history, making them wallow at four wickets down for nought, three of them falling to Fiery Fred.

The new speedster took eight wickets at Lords, and on a greasy pitch at Old Trafford finished with his best Test figures, 8-31. England won the first three Tests and would have won the fourth, in which Trueman and Bedser both took five wickets in the first innings, only to be beaten by rain before they could force the follow-on.

Trueman had revitalised English cricket for the first time since World War Two, and at last the Englishmen had someone to match Lindwall and Miller. The Indian batsmen were clearly scared of the newcomer, and in four matches he had 29 wickets at 13 each. He was also a gifted fieldsman at short leg.

When Hassett's Australians arrived in England in 1953, Trueman was seen as the logical match-winner for the home side. But Fred spent most of the summer doing national service with the Royal Air Force and it was not until after four drawn Tests that he was sooled into the visitors at The Oval.

He had Arthur Morris dropped by Compton in the first over and had to wait until his third spell for his first Ashes scalp, when Neil Harvey top-edged a bouncer to Hutton. Trueman finished with 4-86, and Laker and Lock sealed The Ashes in the second innings.

Trueman was the toast of English cricket by them, but on the 1953-4 Caribbean tour the toast got burnt. He feuded with Hutton, and West Indian crowds were not happy when he broke Grand Old George Headley's arm and hit Wilfred Ferguson in the face.

Trueman struggled through three Tests and had his good-conduct bonus withdrawn. He did not play in any of the remaining 11 Tests under Hutton's captaincy, he missed 12 of the next 15 Tests under Peter May, and he had to wait five years before touring again with England.

He played one Test against South Africa in 1955 and two against Australia in 1956. At the Leeds Test that year, Gubby Allen made him bowl at a handerkerchief in the nets and, watched by a big crowd, Trueman was understandably embarrassed and uncomfortable about his public trial.

He was left out of the tour to South Africa. After years of drought, the selectors, now blessed with a plethora of pacemen in Statham, Bedser, Peter Loader, Les Jackson, Trevor Bailey, Alan Moss, Fred Ridgway and the fastest of them all, Tyson, felt they could afford to do without a gifted but outspoken problem.

In 1957, Trueman reduced his long run-up to 18 paces and bowled well after recovering from the strained

Colin Cowdrey hugs Trueman after Fred's 300th Test wicket.

side that had plagued him since 1954. With Tyson in decline, he seized the moment to reappear as England's spearhead, forming a relationship with Brian Statham that prospered on and off the field. They were every bit as feared as their contemporaries Adcock and Heine and Hall and Griffith.

Trueman's 22 wickets at home against the West Indians in 1957 helped England win the series, and the next year he knocked the 20-year-old New Zealander John Sparling senseless. After a good season against the Kiwis, he became a regular in the English side at the age of 27.

Fred took his 100th Test wicket in New Zealand in 1959, his 200th in 1962, and his 300th in 1964.

His 21 wickets in the Caribbean against Wes Hall in 1959-60 helped England to a series win, as did his 25 wickets against South Africa at home in 1960.

Australia kept The Ashes in 1961, but Trueman took 20 cheap wickets, 11 of them for just 88 runs at Headingley, where England levelled the series.

At one stage he bowled 27 deliveries that took five wickets for no runs as Australia went from 2-99 to all out for 120.

Three years later on the same ground Peter Burge and Wally Grout hammered him to the boundary after baiting him to bowl a succession of wayward bouncers.

His 22 wickets at 20 against Pakistan came after he and Les Coldwell both grabbed six-wicket hauls at Lords. England won the series 4-0.

More than 10 years had gone by since Fred's dynamic debut against India, but at 32, after a successful tour of Australia and New Zealand, he had his best series. Stung by unfavourable comparisons with Wes Hall and Charlie Griffith, Fiery Fred roared into the 1963 West Indians, taking 34 wickets — two more than the fearsome Griffith — in a series England's batsmen still managed to lose.

At Edgbaston, he had match figures of 12-119, including 7-44 in the second innings against a batting line-up that included Hunte, Kanhai, Butcher, Sobers and Worrell, as he bowled England to its only victory in a 3-1 defeat. He claimed the last six Windies wickets for four runs off 24 balls as they were all out for 91.

At Lords, he took 11 wickets in a match in which any of four results were still possible with two balls remaining. Basil Butcher was the only batsman to handle the accuracy of Trueman and the much slower Derek Shackleton.

At The Oval, Trueman was injured in the second innings of the last Test when England needed victory to square the series. Against Shackleton and Statham, the West Indians won comfortably.

In that same series, he hit his highest first-class score, 104 for Yorkshire against Northamptonshire.

Fiery Fred was on his way out against the Australians in 1964 and, despite 5-48 at Lords, he was dropped after the third Test at Headingley when his career tally stood at 297 Test victims.

Trueman returned for the fifth Test, at The Oval, and dismissed Redpath and McKenzie with successive balls to go to 299. Unfortunately for the record book, a hat-trick triple century was not on. But when Neil Hawke edged a catch to Colin Cowdrey in the slips, a lot of Yorkshiremen had a tear in their eye.

It was the first time anyone had taken 300 Test wickets.

Fred did not go quietly. He played his last series against New Zealand the following year and flattened the 41-year-old Bert Sutcliffe with a bouncer.

He continued to play first-class cricket until 1969, leading Yorkshire to an innings defeat against the 1968 Australians and turning out in a few one-day games for Derbyshire.

Asked whether anyone else would take 300 Test wickets, he remarked that if they did they would be "bloody tired".

Frank Tyson
(1930-)

The Typhoon

At his bat-breaking best, Frank Tyson was a prematurely balding man of 24, a scholar who quoted Shakespeare, who perceived cricket as drama and saw in the angst and fury of fast bowling the colourful turbulence of Van Gogh.

In his own art form, Tyson was something of a grand master, who gave up what could have been a long, illustrious Test career for one brief season in which he bowled as fast, perhaps faster, than anyone ever.

Cricket, to him, was a pursuit which should "uplift, gratify and stimulate intellectually as well as sensually".

Richie Benaud says he has never seen anyone bowl quicker than Tyson did during his assault on Australia in the summer of 1954-5 when Tyson roared in with his long-striding charge, pounced with his long, straining final leap, scared the wits out of Australia's best batsmen, and won The Ashes for England.

Tyson came along at a period when Fred Trueman and Brian Statham were already established. Though such glorious fast bowlers surrounded him, he is probably remembered with Harold Larwood as the most terrifying quick man England has produced.

He was destined for big things right from his very first delivery in county cricket, playing for Northamptonshire under the guidance of Freddie Brown in 1952. Tyson came pounding in off his 35 metre run up, leapt into the delivery stride and bowled a ball that travelled so fast and swung so much that it rocketed into the slips cordon, which immediately jumped back another five metres.

Tyson was born in Lancashire, but the county rejected him and Tyson went to Northamptonshire to become its big gun.

He wrote: "To bowl quick is to revel in the glad animal action, to thrill in physical prowess and to enjoy a certain sneaking feeling of superiority over the other mortals who play the game. No batsman likes quick bowling, and this knowledge gives one a sense of omnipotence."

In Wellington, New Zealand, Tyson and Statham were once clocked at just under 144km/h but it is certain that going flat out Tyson was much quicker than that.

He did little with the ball, but it was travelling so quick that pace was all he needed.

RIGHT: The terrifying Frank "Typhoon" Tyson.

Against the Australian tourists in 1953 he was bowling express pace, but no-one expected the carnage of the following Ashes series in Australia. The English captain, Len Hutton, was convinced speed would win, and he decided to use the fast youngster as his pace spearhead in preference to Fred Trueman.

Tyson would be the man to gain revenge for all England had suffered against Lindwall and Miller.

Tyson made his English debut in the fourth Test at The Oval against Pakistan in 1954, taking 4-35 on a day that favoured swing bowling and in a team that included Statham and Loader. But Fazal Mahmood took 12 wickets and England suffered a stunning setback.

In Brisbane for the first Test against Australia, Tyson struggled to find his rhythm, and Arthur Morris and Neil Harvey helped themselves to big centuries. Tyson was quick enough but after just 29 overs he had the galling figures of 1-160, bowling behind Bedser and Statham.

England dropped 12 catches and lost by an innings.

Before the second Test began in Sydney, Tyson bowled with savage pace and good control against Victoria and by the time England arrived in Sydney he had shortened his run from 35 metres to 25. He had found perfection.

Bowling with the wind at his back, The Typhoon took 4-45, including the wicket of Ray Lindwall, sent ducking for cover from a bouncer.

When it was Tyson's turn to bat, Lindwall bounced him and Tyson turned his head only to be hit squarely on the back of the skull. He was carried from the field with a lump visible from over a hundred metres but he came back to bat again and in the second innings took 6-85.

Only Neil Harvey made more than 16, his 92 not out emphasising his courage. Tyson shattered the stumps four times, and England won by 38.

In Melbourne on a poor pitch, Australia needed 240 to win but in front of 60,000 people expecting a close, tough struggle, it could only make 111. Tyson took his best Test figures of 7-27 (6 for 16 off his last 51 balls), and a brilliant leg-side catch by Godfrey Evans to dismiss Harvey was the turning point.

Australia lost its last eight wickets for 36 runs in an hour and 20 minutes.

England won the fourth Test, at Adelaide, to secure The Ashes, Tyson taking six wickets and, although the fifth Test was rained out, Hutton asked Tyson to bowl off just six paces to try for a result. The Typhoon was still quick enough to knock the bat from the hands of Keith Miller.

England won The Ashes for the first time in Australia since Harold Larwood had caused similar chaos more than two decades earlier.

Tyson rarely bowled as fast again, but he did have some thunder left.

On the way home England stopped off in New Zealand for two Tests, which they won easily. Tyson had figures of 4-16 at Dunedin, and at Auckland England's 246 was enough for an innings victory, the Kiwis making a record low score of 26 in their second innings, Tyson taking 2-10, Statham 3-9, Appleyard 4-

Tyson cowed Australia's best.

7 and Wardle 1-0. That English summer at Trent Bridge, Tyson took 6-28 (5-5 from 45 balls) and then in Port Elizabeth, South Africa, the next season he took 6-40 as Adcock, Heine and Tayfield squared the series for South Africa.

Bowling against Surrey on the normally docile Oval wicket in 1957, Tyson took 8-60, his best first-class figures, and followed up with 5-52 in the second innings. According to Wisden, nearly half the runs scored off Tyson came from the edge of the bat.

But by the time of Tyson's second tour to Australia in 1958-9, some of his pace and strength had left him. He took just three wickets for 193 runs in two matches. At Adelaide, Tyson, Trueman and Statham played their only match together. But by then Tyson's excessive style had taken its toll, and he finished the first innings with a disappointing 1-100.

Tyson retired from first-class cricket in 1960 after 17 Tests and 76 wickets at 18.56.

Realising he was no longer express, he refused to settle for anything less. "The coming of guile to a quick bowler," he once said, "can be like the advance of creeping paralysis of the body."

He moved to Melbourne, where he became a teacher, headmaster and renowned cricket coach whose pupils included an Australian captain, Graham Yallop.

He writes erudite books, profound articles and essays and is a stimulating commentator.

Neil Harvey Rates The Bowlers

Frank Tyson and Wes Hall were the two fastest bowlers I ever faced but Ray Lindwall was simply the best. Ray certainly wasn't the quickest bowler of my era be he was still very fast and with that beautiful round-arm action he had great control. His yorker was magnificent.

Together with Keith Miller, Ray formed a truly lethal combination and players such as Len Hutton probably still have nightmares from their battles with the two Australians. When he let himself go flat out, Keith was faster than Ray but of course the back injury he suffered in World War II often curtailed the fire.

There wasn't a great deal between Tyson and Hall when it came to pace, though Hall was always at a disadvantage in the '50s being without a regular opening partner. Both were express, so quick that they didn't need to swing the ball or move it around a great deal to get their wickets. They just beat guys with speed.

Brian Statham was another like that. He and Tyson formed a tremendous partnership in Australia in 1954-55. Statham relied on speed and great accuracy. He tended to skid the ball through and that made his bouncer so much more dangerous and effective. Of every 10 balls he sent down the batsman had to play at nine.

Freddie Trueman was the best of the English fast bowlers I played against. He was only a fraction behind Tyson in speed but he had more fast bowling skills and he was one of the few pacemen who could keep going for years, getting wickets in every country.

Fred was the first guy to hit 300 Test wickets and he did it in an age when Test matches were a lot less frequent than they are today. He had it all — he was fiery, he had a menacing bouncer and he could swing and seam the ball around.

Another fast bowler with similar talent was Neil Adcock. I would rate the big South African as one of the top four or five quick men of my day. Together with Peter Heine, Adcock formed a truly ferocious partnership. They were both giants — Adcock a wiry 193 centimetres and Heine 196 centimetres. Heine was the more belligerent and he gave me plenty of bruises. Like Frank Tyson, he tended to rely on sheer pace while Adcock had a great deal more guile and in the long run was a lot more difficult to play.

Alan Davidson was the best swinger of the ball I ever encountered and he had a great career after years of struggling to find a place. One of the men who kept him out of Test teams for a long time was Bill Johnston, another great left-arm swinger who could really play havoc with his variation. I still remember the look on Keith Miller's face after Bill trundled up to the wicket in a Sheffield Shield game and sent down a shock bouncer that knocked off Keith's cap.

Alec Bedser was the best bowler of his type I've seen. He bowled at about the same pace as Terry Alderman and could do freakish things with his inswinger and then turn to sharp legcutters when the shine had gone.

I never encountered Fazal Mahmoud on turf but he bowled Australia out on matting for 80 in Karachi in '56 and at Dacca in '59 he was making the ball talk.

THE 1960s

A Hurricane
Gathers Force

South Africa had developed by the end of the 1960s into the most powerful cricket team in the world. But the decade had begun rather less successfully for it. At Lords in 1960, Geoff Griffin, a fair-haired paceman, was called for throwing 11 times by the umpire, Frank Lee, in England's only innings, a remarkable innings in which Griffin took 4-87 including the hat-trick.

An accident at school had left Griffin with a permanent bend in an elbow and, after being called against the MCC, Nottinghamshire and Hampshire, he sought the advice of Alf Gover in a three-day stint at the old paceman's coaching school, but in vain.

Griffin's hat-trick was overshadowed by the throwing controversy. After England claimed an innings win soon after lunch on the fourth day thanks to Statham and Alan Moss, Griffin was no-balled four times in five balls during an exhibition match.

In frustration he switched to bowl an underarm lob, but the umpire no-balled him again for not notifying the change.

Griffin was the first visiting bowler to be no-balled for throwing in England and, although he saw out the tour, he did not bowl again. Only the previous season, he had been the most successful paceman in South Africa's Currie Cup; but he never played Test cricket again, and his first-class career finished in 1962, by which time he was playing primarily as a batsman with Rhodesia, now Zimbabwe.

The controversy surrounding Griffin made South Africa's wet summer in England even more miserable and, although Neil Adcock performed splendidly, supported in three Tests by the fast-medium Jim Pothecary, of Western Province, the tourists lost an unhappy series 3-0.

The issue of chucking dominated cricket in the early 1960s, with continued whisperings about the bowling of Ian Meckiff and Charlie Griffith. Griffin, the West Indian Conrad Stayers, Derbyshire's Harold Rhodes and Hampshire's David "Butch" White had all been called for throwing.

Rhodes was called six times while bowling against Griffin's South Africans at Derby. Later, he was called for throwing in other matches. After a great deal of negotiation and trials, the MCC ruled that Rhodes had a "hyper-extended" arm and he was officially cleared of throwing eight years later. But he did not play for England again.

In 1960, Butch White, Hampshire's earnest trier, was also called for throwing; but he managed two Tests in Pakistan a year later. White could send down inswingers at a moderate pace and then shoot in an express delivery that would rocket off the seam toward the slips.

Throughout the late 1950s and early 1960s, South Africa had been well served by the left-handed all-rounder Trevor Goddard, who was one of South Africa's few success stories on the

Wes Hall, spearhead of the Windies' attack.

The controversial Geoff Griffin

bowling mate from Natal, Pat Trimborn.

McKenzie had to carry the Australian bowling almost single-handed on that tour, but he did have the support of the big, strong Dave Renneberg from the Balmain club in Sydney who took 11 wickets at 48 and managed 5-97 at Johannesburg.

Renneberg once bowled with a gale behind him against the Queenslander Peter Burge, and hit the stumps before Burge had even finished his backlift. He took 5-39 against the 1967-68 Indians at Adelaide.

Against England in 1964-5, South Africa faced Ian Thomson, who failed to perform as he had done for Sussex, where he was considered the best medium-pacer since Maurice Tate, taking 10-49 (15-75 in the match) against Warwickshire. Supporting the South Africans was Mike Macaulay, a left-arm seamer who failed to win a Test in England the next season, though he did do the hat-trick against Kent.

Australia searched in the 1960s for a reliable partner for McKenzie. Big Frank Misson played five Tests, Colin Guest one, Des Hoare one, Renneberg eight and Graham Corling five in England in 1964. Ron Gaunt had a good tour of England in 1961, but he played only three Tests in his career, taking seven wickets with his fast medium pace.

Misson opened the bowling with Des Hoare against the West Indies at Adelaide in the match in which Lance Gibbs did the hat-trick and with Alan Davidson at Melbourne, where 90,000 people saw the second day's play.

Before the second coming of Charlie Griffith after a poor start to his Test career, the West Indies attack centred on Wes Hall, Frank Worrell and the left-arm pace of Gary Sobers, who could also turn to spin, or do anything else he liked for that matter.

Sobers was the master of late movement in the air and using the crease for variation, having left Barbados in 1958 to learn all about swing and seam bowling at Radcliffe, England.

Later, the Windies found Lester King, who took five wickets in his debut against India, and Richard "Prof" Edwards, who had a fine tour of New Zealand after the Windies had lost in Australia in 68-9.

But he was left out of the team to tour

tour, with 17 inexpensive wickets and 99 runs at The Oval.

Goddard had earlier given great support to the Adcock-Heine combination and he was later joined by pig farmer Eddie Barlow, a bespectacled all-rounder with a habit of breaking big partnerships. Both men bowled fast-medium pace, and at times both opened the batting and the bowling.

Known as Bunter because of his eyesight and solid frame, Barlow could see no further than the end of his bike when he was at school. But there was nothing lazy about him. Louis Duffus wrote that he had more influence over the spirit of South African cricket than anyone.

Trevor Goddard was a non-drinker and non-smoker who kept in great physical condition.

Free of the restrictions of captaincy, Goddard took 26 wickets at 16 and averaged 33 with the bat against the 1966-7 Australians, taking 6-53 at Johannesburg. By the end of the season South Africa had the world's best attack — Pollock, Procter, Goddard, Barlow and Procter's seam-

England, his job being taken over variously by Vanburn Holder, John Shepherd and Grayson Shillingford. Peter Allan, Laurie Mayne, Eric Freeman and Allan Connolly were all touted as the ideal partners for Graham McKenzie in later years, Allan taking 10-61 for Queensland against Victoria in 1965-6.

England in the 1960s first had Trueman and Statham and then John Snow. But many of its potential heroes suffered injuries. Alan Ward made his debut against New Zealand in 1969 but between then and 1976, when he played against the West Indies, he appeared in just five Tests.

In 1973, his Derbyshire captain ordered him from the field when he would not start an afternoon spell. David Larter, a 197 centimetre speedster from Northamptonshire, had a spectacular action but was always breaking down, as was John Price, the strongly-built Middlesex quick who took 40 wickets in 15 Tests. Larter took a 19-metre run which he covered in just 10 strides.

Len Coldwell topped the bowling averages against Pakistan in 1962, taking 6-85 in his debut at Lords with his inswingers from a whippy action. But he did not perform as well in Australia. He and Jack Flavell, one of England's fastest bowlers, helped bowl Worcester to two successive championships.

Bob Cottam took 9-25 for Hampshire against Lancashire in 1965 and played four Tests in India and Pakistan.

The 194-centimetre Rhodesian, Godfrey "Goofy" Lawrence played in only one series for South Africa; but it was a good one. He took 28 wickets at 18 each backing the debutant Peter Pollock against New Zealand in 1961-2. His 8-53 at Johannesburg remains the best figures for a South African pace bowler.

He and Pollock were also supported by Ken Walter in two Tests.

The New Zealand attack was led by Frank Cameron, a lean schoolteacher who had been overshadowed by Guy Overton at Dunedin. At Perth on the way to South Africa, Cameron had taken 7-27, emulating Overton's feat of seven years earlier.

Cameron, 29, took to his first Test series with the enthusiasm of a teenager.

At Cape Town, Syd Burke took 11 wickets from a marathon 81 overs (6-128 and 5-68) in his debut, but he was dropped for the return of Neil Adcock and played in only one more Test, in which he went wicketless.

RIGHT: Injury-prone David Larter

Gary Bartlett bowled with great pace for New Zealand, and 12th man Peter Pollock remembered his skipper Jackie McGlew fuming over his bouncers, demanding the recall of Adcock and Heine to sort out the visitors.

"Gary Bartlett was quick," wrote Pollock, "That he was a chucker was undeniable, but no umpire had the guts to call him.

"This also annoyed Jackie McGlew, especially after his experiences in England the previous year when Geoff Griffin was hounded out of the game."

Bartlett was probably the fastest bowler produced by New Zealand, and big things were expected of him. He was rushed into Test cricket and over bowled, so that, in the words of Dick Brittenden, "He became one of the most disappointing and disappointed cricketers New Zealand cricket has known. Disappointing only in that such magnificent material was misused and largely wasted."

Bartlett's delivery stride was spectacular, his

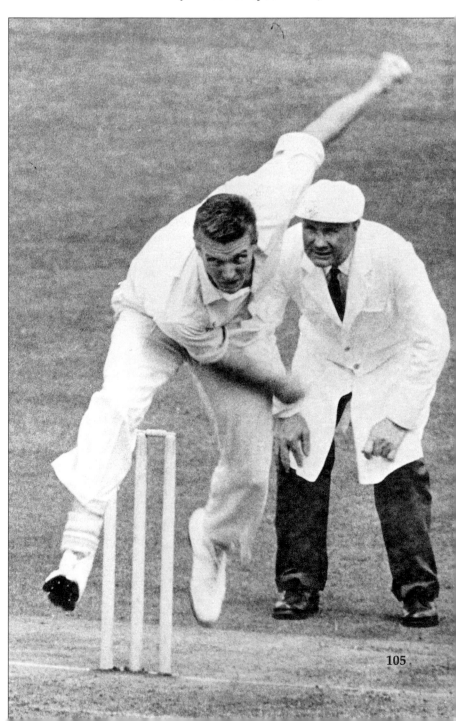

left foot rising to chest height as he rocked back and his powerful right hand almost touching the grass behind him.

"Inevitably," wrote Brittenden, "he had back trouble, shin touble, foot trouble and no-ball trouble . . . But the cruellest blow was the spread of ugly stories that he was 'psycho' — that his injuries were largely figments of his imagination."

Bartlett's greatest performance was his 6-38 against India at Christchurch in 1967-8.

One of India's new ball bowlers through the 1960s was Rusi Surti, who played 26 Tests and took 42 wickets and had several productive seasons with Queensland as a much-respected all-rounder with a hat-trick to his credit.

Surti gave three chances on 99 in New Zealand and was picked up on the third, the only time he went close to a Test hundred.

In Australia in 1967-8, Surti bowled brilliant left-arm swing, supported in Adelaide by the stocky little Abid Ali, who could never repeat his 6-55.

In the Australian summer of 1963-4, the South Africans dominated batting and bowling but could only draw the series, the aggression of Peter Pollock and the swing of Rhodesian Joe Partridge, who took 7-91 at Sydney, being highlights.

Partridge was a bespectacled bank official who once took 7-9 for Rhodesia against Border and who made his Test debut at 31. He and Pollock took 25 wickets each in the series and were supported by newcomer Clive Halse.

Trevor Goddard averaged 65 with the bat and grabbed 5-60 at Adelaide, where Barlow, who averaged 75, hit 201, 47 not out and took 3-6 off five overs to bowl Australia out.

Against England in 1965 South Africa confronted Statham, Larter and Ken Higgs. Tom Cartwright was a reliable medium pacer in county cricket but was not quite quick enough for the Tests, though he did take 6-94 at Trent Bridge with the ball wobbling through the air.

In Australia in 1965-6, Jeff Jones, the left-handed paceman from Wales, plagued by an elbow injury, led the attack with David Brown, Barry Knight also doing his bit. Jones once hit Rohan Kanhai over the heart and gave Terry Jarvis a cut on the face that needed 14 stitches. He took 8-11 for Glamorgan against Leicestershire in 1965, but his career was cut short by injury.

In New Zealand on the way home, Ken Higgs took 17 wickets at 9.34 each, including 4-5 in the first Test, at Christchurch. Higgs, a mighty fast-medium bowler, was part of at least two memorable batting partnerships. In 1977, when he was 40, he and the 45-year-old Ray Illingworth rescued Leicestershire from Nottinghamshire, adding 228 for the last wicket after the side had been 9-45.

In 1966, against the Windies at The Oval, he and John Snow put on 128 for the last wicket to help England to an innings victory.

Higgs really had two careers, the first with Lancashire between 1958 and 1969, when he also played 15 Tests, and the second with Leicestershire, where he was a revered veteran, becoming skipper in 1979.

Eric Freeman was an Australian fast-medium bowler between 1967 and 1970, when he played 11 Tests touring England, India and South Africa, where that country's master batsmen blasted him.

Freeman was a huge hitter and a South Australian Aussie rules player, like Neil Hawke, his occasional opening partner.

One of the best Australians never to play test cricket was Ian Brayshaw, the medium-pace wizard from Western Australia. In 1967, this personable seam-and-swing bowler took 10-44 against Victoria at Perth.

Charlie Griffith (1938-)

Big And Mean

When Charlie Griffith and Wes Hall arrived in England for the 1963 Test series, Ian Wooldridge likened them to two huge hired assassins set for a bloodbath.

Griffith was always the more overtly menacing. One hundred and eighty-five centimetres and more powerfully built than his lithe partner, Griffith had a suspect action and a reputation for not caring too much where the ball landed.

Before the third Test between the West Indies and India in March, 1962, Nari Contractor ducked into a short one from Griffith at Bridgetown and was flattened by a blow to the back of the skull, which fractured. He bled profusely from the nose, and it was feared for many hours that Contractor might die. He recovered, but he never again played international cricket.

Many of the Indians believed Griffith threw the ball when he strived for extra pace and later in the same match, after Contractor had been carried off to hospital, Griffith was called for throwing.

At that stage of his career the big lumbering bull of West Indian cricket had played only one Test in something of a disastrous debut, relegating Chester Watson to first change for the fifth Test against England, at Port of Spain, in 1960. Griffith took the wicket of Geoff Pullar in the first innings, but it was his only success of the match against 102 runs.

Like Jeff Thomson, a man of similar speed and fearsome reputation, Griffith would recover from an inauspicious beginning to become a major fast bowling force for several years.

Born on December 14, 1938, in the rum territory of St Lucy, Barbados, Griffith began his cricket career as a right-arm off-spinner but changed to pace bowling after filling a gap in his club side and taking 7-1 with his new style.

Griffith was a clean-living but volatile fast bowler whose stormy temper created plenty of headlines. His action caused a great deal of concern.

He sauntered rather than ran to the crease over a 19 metre approach but once there he harnessed his massive body into a giant spring and from an open-chested delivery stride brought his arm over low, skidding the ball through and making it awkward for the batsman to dodge the frequent bouncers.

Griffith always seemed to save his best for England, and he was the master of cricket's old one-two, the searing throat-high bouncer to rattle the batsman's composure followed by the express-paced yorker to rattle the stumps and often send them cartwheeling.

He made his first-class debut for Barbados against Peter May's English tourists in the 1959-60 Caribbean series, and he earned a Test spot because of his performance in helping Barbados to an upset win by dismissing Colin Cowdrey, Mike Smith and May in two overs and then dislodging Ken Barrington soon after.

In England in 1963, he took 8-23 and 5-35 against Gloucestershire and, partnering Hall, he took 5-91 against England at Lords, 6-36 at Headingley and 6-71 at The Oval, which allowed the Windies to win the match and the series 3-1.

Griffith finished the series with 32 wickets at 16.21, twice as many wickets as Hall took from the other end. Many of the Englishmen, including Fred Trueman, queried the legality of Griffith's action, however.

His bowling came under constant fire from the likes of Richie Benaud when Australia visited the Caribbean in 1964-5, when, in a series the Windies took 2-1, he captured 15 wickets at 32 including 6-46 in the final Test at Port of Spain, which Australia won.

In the second Test, Griffith hit O'Neill with a bouncer, causing Benaud and other journalists to condemn Griffith's action, condemnation which seemed to be well supported by photos of the big man bowling with a bent arm.

The next season, in England, he was called for the second and final time of his career — by Arthur Fagg in the match between the Windies and Brian Statham's Lancashire at Old Trafford.

That same season he gave young Derek Underwood a fiery welcome to Test cricket when he gave

The ferocious Charlie Griffith.

107

England's No. 11 batsman a spate of bouncers at Trent Bridge before one finally hit the youngster in the teeth.

But Griffith seemed to have lost much of his effectiveness in the wake of the controversy over his action, accusations which Sobers claimed attacked the fast man "sideways like so many angry crabs, never straight so that we could face up to them".

Griffith failed to produce the form of his previous tour and finished a series dominated by Gary Sobers with 14 wickets at 31, sometimes being relegated to first change so Sobers could open the bowling with his left-arm swingers.

He took 5-69 against the English tourists at Port of Spain the following year but was then in decline and failed to impress much after that as Sobers and John Snow jousted for control.

In Australia in 1968-9, he played in three Tests, taking eight expensive wickets. In the fourth Test at Adelaide, with Australia chasing 360 and going for them with relish, he ran out Ian Redpath backing up and aroused the kind of crowd reaction once reserved there for Douglas Jardine.

The match finished in a draw, but the West Indians were poised for victory until the final ball.

In the next Test, Redpath, who had made 99 in his first Test four years earlier, survived a flurry of bouncers from Griffith to score his first Test hundred and, despite some of the old fire from Griffith and Hall, Australia won by 382 to take out the series.

Griffith retired from Test cricket with 94 wickets from 28 matches at 28.54 each.

Wes Hall
(1937-)

Teeth Flashing, Crucifix Flying

For those lucky enough to see Wes Hall at his peak, he came to represent the epitome of fast bowling.

A hundred and eighty-five centimetres with a magnificent physique, he had a run-up that began somewhere near the boundary and he would bound to the wicket, until the thundering, cartwheel of his action made the batsman jump.

His popularity with crowds stemmed from his marvellous athleticism and from the fact he played in so many exciting matches with teeth flashing, gold crucifix flying, shirt tails trailing like a cape.

One of them was in the tied Test at Brisbane, when Frank Worrell told him, "Whatever you do, don't bowl a no-ball."

Soon after, at Adelaide, he was the man pounding away at Slasher Mackay and the last man in, Lindsay Kline, as they held out for more than an hour and 40 minutes to force a draw.

At Lords in 1963, Big Wes broke Colin Cowdrey's arm earlier in the match and bowled the final over, his 40th of the innings, in another thrilling draw.

With nine down, the last man in, David Allen, had to see out Hall's fastest deliveries with two balls left and six runs needed. Cowdrey, at the other end with his broken arm, wondered how he would play the bouncer one-handed.

Not that Wes was likely to drop the ball in short to a one-armed batsman even if a Test series hinged on the balance.

Against younger batsmen Wes occasionally took it a little easier, as he did when bowling for Queensland against young Doug Walters, who was making his debut for NSW. Walters did not receive a single bouncer from the tall West Indian but the Queensland keeper, Wally Grout, had a fractured jaw trying to take a fast one down leg side.

Wes was born in Christchurch, Barbados, on September 12, 1937, and began playing cricket as a wicket-keeper/batsman on the beaches near Bridgetown where Charlie Griffith would also build his muscles running in the soft sand.

At 11 he broke both ankles while horseriding and throughout his career had to wear a specially-made broadfitting boot. As a boy he promised himself that if he failed to make it at cricket, he would make it as a jockey. But, like Keith Miller, who once had similar aspirations, Wesley Hall became a giant, physically and statistically. In 48 Tests he took 192 wickets, at 26.38.

Hall toured England with the 1957 West Indians but did not play a Test. He was only a last-minute choice to tour India and Pakistan in 1958-9, after Worrell withdrew from the side. Hall was preferred to Jaswick Taylor as the opening partner for Roy Gilchrist.

He and Gilchrist, physical opposites but both tremendously fast, formed a deadly combination. Hall finished with 30 wickets from five Tests at 17.66, with 6-50 and 5-76 at Kanpur.

Even after Gilchrist was sent home in disgrace, Hall was devastating, taking 16 wickets in three matches at 18 each, including the first West Indian hat-trick — at Lahore, where Fazal, who virtually won the series for Pakistan, was strangely ineffective.

Against Trueman and Statham in the 1959-60 series, Hall bowled as though he were trying to prove himself the world's fastest bowler. He took 22 wickets (at 31) compared to Trueman's 21 but at Port of Spain in the second Test, where Hall and Chester Watson were warned for persistent bouncers, Fiery Fred's 5-35 helped England win the match and the series.

Big Wes took 7-69 in the third Test at Kingston and 6-90 in the fourth at Georgetown before joining Charlie Griffith, an unimpressive debutant, in the fifth Test, again at Port of Spain.

At Brisbane in 1960, Hall had scored 50 and 18 and had taken eight wickets in the match going into the last over.

At one stage, Hall had Australia at 6-92 before Davidson and Benaud put on 134. Going into his last eight-ball over, Australia needed six runs; and the resulting few minutes were among the most eventful

Time stands still: the end of the famous tied Test between the West Indies and Australia.

cricket has seen. The first ball went for a leg bye. The second had Benaud caught behind. The fourth was snatched for a bye even though it went to the keeper. The fifth resulted in another run after Big Wes dropped a skied hook shot from Grout.

Meckiff hit the sixth ball toward the boundary, and Grout was run out by a perfect throw from Conrad Hunte when the batsmen turned for a third and winning run. The scores were dead level. Two balls left. The crowd sweated. Kline and Meckiff drew deep breaths. Hall walked back to his mark, way out in the distance and turned on his heel to charge in again.

Kline, the last man in, hit the seventh ball toward square leg. Meckiff took off to scamper the winning run a second time; but Joe Solomon hit the wicket from side on and Test cricket had its first Tie.

The excitement created one of the finest Test series seen in Australia and gave the game a much-needed injection of excitement right around the world.

Hall finished the series with 21 wickets at 29 and proved to be such a crowd-pleaser that the Queenslanders, chasing the Sheffield Shield they had never won, signed him up for the next three seasons, and, though he could not win them their coveted prize, he set a Queensland record of 43 wickets in his first season there. Later, he played for Accrington in the Lancashire League.

He was the best bowler in the 1961-2 series against India, helping his team to a 5-0 victory with 27 wickets at under-16 each, including 6-49 at Kingston.

He took 16 wickets in the Tests in England in 1963. On the same tour, he hit his best first-class total, 102 not out against Cambridge, and took his best first-class bowling figures, 7-51 against Glamorgan at Swansea.

In 1964-5, a series that was anti-climatic after the great 1960-1 series, Hall took nine wickets at Kingston to bowl the West Indies to their first victory over Australia in the Caribbean.

In 1968, he showed brave defence to help Gary Sobers save the first Test against England in Trinidad.

Although he was in decline by the time of the 1968-9 return series in Australia, he recovered from an eye injury to bound in with the same old fire in the fifth Test, at Sydney.

But dropped catches cost the Windies dearly, Lawry made 151, Redpath 132, and Doug Walters was hardly away from the crease with 242 and 103, Australia winning by nearly 400 runs.

After one Test against New Zealand in 1969, in which his only wicket was that of the young Glenn Turner, Big Wes hung up those broad boots.

He became a coach in Trinidad, a senior West Indian cricket official, and a senator in the Barbados Parliament.

Neil Hawke (1939-)
and
Alan Connolly
(1939-)

Faithful Servants

Neil Hawke, once a strapping crowd favourite with a handsome head and impressive physique, returned to Australia in 1980 after an 11-year absence, had a game of golf with some friends, ate a packet of peanuts and spent the next two years on life-support systems hovering close to death.

He became a medical guinea pig. His liver, kidneys, stomach and bowel, cut into pieces, ceased to function and for three months he survived only with the help of a respirator, taking oxygen through a hole in his throat.

His heart often stopped functioning. One black day it stopped beating 12 times. He spent 10 months in intensive care.

Hawke, the man's man of cricket in the 1960s, had suffered a blockage of the bowel after eating the nuts, complications had set in during surgery, and an infec-

tion rapidly spread throughout his body.

On what doctors thought would be his death bed, the former Australian opening bowler received more than 1000 letters of support and the people of Adelaide donated $30,000 for his medical bills through a radio appeal.

Hawke says his fiancee, Beverley Holmes, whom he would later marry, was the person who kept him going.

Hawke was a champion footballer, who stood 182 centimetres and weighed 186 kilograms and who was chosen to play both cricket and Australian rules for South Australia.

Born at Cheltenham, South Australia, on June 27, 1939 he had two moderate seasons for the State before taking 12 wickets against Western Australia in Perth in 1961-2, which, combined with 5-71 against New Zealand and 6-130 against England in 1962-3, led to his Australian debut that year against England in the fifth Test, Alan Davidson's last.

Despite his athleticism, Hawke possessed an ungainly crab-like run-up and chest-on bowling action. But he could swing the ball both ways, particularly in at the right-handed batsmen. After playing for South Australia, Western Australia and Tasmania and in 27 Tests Hawke declared Test captain Bill Lawry a dictator and quit Australia to marry an English girl and follow Ted McDonald and Learie Constantine in playing for Nelson in the Lancashire League. His 91 Test wickets cost 29.42 each.

Hawke picked up the wickets of the Reverend David Sheppard and Fred Titmus in his debut. In the second Test against South Africa the following season, Hawke was joined by the big Victorian, Alan Connolly, a fast-medium bowler who had started his career as a fast man but cut down his pace for the sake of accuracy and swing. Connolly made the Australian pace bowling trio led by Graham McKenzie, formidable in both size and ability. Connolly had made his debut against South Africa at Brisbane, having to shoulder much of the bowling burden after Ian Meckiff had been thrown out of the game.

Connolly, born on June 29, 1939, in Skipton, Victoria, was the kind of player Bill Lawry says would keep going until there was blood in his boots. He first played for Victoria at the age of 20, and by the time he retired 11 years later he had taken 330 wickets at 27 each for the State.

The first pairing of Connolly and Hawke resulted in an eight-wicket Australian victory after Lawry had scored 157 and the three quicks shared 13 wickets.

In four Tests in that drawn series, Hawke took 14 wickets at 33.78, his best of 6-139 not being good enough to stop huge scoring by Barlow and Pollock, that gave the visitors a 10-wicket victory at Adelaide.

Connolly did not have such a fine debut, with just six wickets at 44 each, and for the next few years, while Hawke soared, Connolly struggled to make a reputation internationally.

Hawke found English conditions ideal for his swing and was a marvellous support bowler to McKenzie, finishing with 18 wickets at 28 and taking 6-47 in the drawn fifth Test at The Oval and 5-75 at Headingley to help Australia win the series.

Despite the presence of Wes Hall and Charlie Griffith, he was the most successful bowler from either side in the Caribbean in 1964-5. But his 24 wickets at 22 were overshadowed by a series win to the West Indians, the controversy over Charlie Griffith's action, and the McKenzie bouncer that put Jackie Hendricks in hospital.

In the next season, against England, Hawke took 7-105 at Sydney. But England still won by an innings, even though he and McKenzie squared the series in Adelaide.

In the years that Hawke had been touring the world with great success, Alan Connolly had been waiting for his opportunity. Late in his career, he finally arrived as an accurate and clever pace bowler.

In the first Test against India in 1967-8, Connolly and Dave Renneberg helped bowl India out and Australia won by 146.

Connolly then overshadowed McKenzie in England, taking 23 wickets, more than any other bowler in the series.

He took 5-72 at Headingley, where Cowdrey and Lawry were injured and Jarman and Graveney captained their countries. At The Oval, he bagged 4-

65; but England squared the series.

Connolly bowled so well that Middlesex signed him to a three-year contract, though he would play only two seasons because of back trouble.

In the next three series against the West Indies, India and South Africa, Connolly took 57 wickets; and in the second last Test of his career, the final match South Africa played, he took a Test best of 6-47 off 28.2 overs at Port Elizabeth in 1970, even though Australia still lost by 323. In a series Australia lost 4-0 he took 20 wickets at 26. McKenzie, in comparison, took just one wicket for 333.

He was overlooked for most of the Test series against England in 1970-1 and quit.

After a mediocre beginning to his career, he played 29 Tests and took 102 wickets at 29.23.

The resolute Alan Connolly.

Graham McKenzie (1941-)

Garth

Over 180 centimetres and with a husky frame that earned him the nickname Garth, after a muscular cartoon hero, Graham McKenzie did not have a mean bone in his body.

He bowled fast-medium off a relaxed run-up of nine strides which culminated in a textbook action and wheel of his big shoulders that could generate speed and sufficient lift to put Jackie Hendricks in hospital and break Geoff Boycott's forearm.

Graham McKenzie, strong and persistent.

Born on June 24, 1941, Garth played for Western Australia, Leicestershire and Transvaal and in 60 Tests for Australia took 246 wickets at 26.96.

He may not have had the overt anger of a Lillee or Trueman but McKenzie achieved remarkable feats for Australian cricket, usually without the assistance of a genuine fast man at the other end.

Born in Cottlesloe, Western Australia, he had a father and uncle who both played for Western Australia. He made his debut for the State in 1959-60 at 18, making a name for himself the next year when bowling to Frank Worrell in the nets at Perth.

As a boy he was a champion all-round athlete who first played top cricket in Perth as a batsman and did not concentrate on bowling until being dropped to his club seconds.

He made his Test debut as the team baby at Lords in 1961, taking 5-37 in the second innings and at Old Trafford, batting at No. 11, he helped Australia retain The Ashes with a 98-run partnership with Davidson.

Before he retired, the gentle giant toured England, South Africa, India, Pakistan and the West Indies, setting records as the youngest bowler to take 100, 150 and 200 Test wickets and bridging generations, bowling early in his career with Alan Davidson and finishing his career in the era of Dennis Lillee.

In the home series of 1962-3 against England, he took 20 wickets at 31 supporting Davo. But he struggled in the drawn series against South Africa the following season when Pollock and Partridge took all the bowling honours.

But in 1964, making his second tour of England at the tender age of 23, he blossomed in the English drizzle, combining with Neil Hawke to win the series with victory at Headingley.

At Old Trafford, where Bobby Simpson made 311 and Ken Barrington 256, McKenzie never faltered in a marathon 7-153.

He finished the series with 29 wickets at 22.55 and even though Freddie Trueman passed the 300 mark, Garth emerged as the bowler of the series.

He bowled well on the way home against India and Pakistan and, ironically, in 1964-5 in a series of ill-will and hostility in the West Indies, it was the languid McKenzie who caused the most serious injuries at a time when West Indies paceman Charlie Griffith was being hounded as a chucker.

At Bridgetown, where Australia needed victory to have any chance of levelling the series, he hit the opposition keeper Hendricks in the head with a short ball and the tall Jamaican's life hung in the balance.

Graham McKenzie, Aussie stalwart.

Australia lost the series 2-1, but McKenzie's 5-33 in the final Test at Port of Spain helped Australia to a face saving victory.

McKenzie always seemed to need a psychological spur to add to the strength of his broad back and big shoulders.

He was dropped from the Australian team after the third Test against England in 1965-6 and replaced by a Queenslander, Peter Allan. But before the fourth Test began Allan broke down and McKenzie was determined not to let his opportunity pass. He bowled some magnificent outswingers at Adelaide to take 6-48 in a series that ended 1-all.

Faced with the opposition of Pollock and Procter in South Africa in 1966-7, McKenzie still took 24 wickets at 26 without a great deal of support.

When he shot out South Africa for 199 with a burst of 5-46 in the first innings of the series at Johannesburg, the Australians took heart for a great series ahead. But the batting of Denis Lindsay and Graeme Pollock helped dash their hopes.

Often overbowled because of his great physique and stamina, McKenzie also suffered some scandalous barbs from selectors. Against India in 1967-8 he had 13 wickets in the first two Tests, including 7-66 and 3-65 in the second at Melbourne when the Australian selectors decided to rest him and give some other fast bowlers a chance. The move ultimately cost McKenzie the Australian Test record of dismissals, which at the time was 248 held by Richie Benaud.

Despite the setbacks, he still had his mind on the job against the 1968-9 West Indians, led by the two ageing warhorses, Hall and Griffith. Garth's 8-71, his best Test figures, at Melbourne helped level the series Australia would eventually win 3-1.

In 1969, McKenzie joined Leicestershire and played for it over the next seven seasons as an all-rounder, taking 465 wickets and helping the side to its first county championship in 1975, his last season there.

But by the age of 29 his critics claimed he was over the hill as a Test spearhead. He had a fine tour of India in 1969-70, taking 21 cheap wickets, but he took only one wicket for 333 runs on tour of South Africa.

He bowled in the first three Tests against the Englishmen in 1970-1 but was dropped from the team two wickets short of Benaud's record to make way for another West Australian quick bowler, Dennis Lillee.

Between the sixth and seventh Tests McKenzie fractured the arm of England's chief run-getter, Geoff Boycott, in a one-day game between the MCC and WA. Hopes were raised that he could make a record-breaking comeback partnering his young fan, Lillee, for the deciding match of the series at Sydney. But the selectors chose Tony Dell instead. England won The Ashes.

At 29, Graham McKenzie was finished as a Test bowler, having taken five or more wickets in an innings 16 times.

He bobbed up as a piece of nostalgia in World Series Cricket in 1977 and then went to live in South Africa, the homeland of his wife. At 45, he rekindled some fine memories bowling against the rebel Australians in 1986.

Dick Motz (1940-) and Bruce Taylor (1943-)

Carrying The Load

Dick Motz and Bruce Taylor were a pair of lively medium-pacers who shouldered much of New Zealand's bowling throughout the 1960s, becoming the first Kiwis to top 100 Test wickets.

Motz was occasionally very fast and always deadly accurate and tireless, even though he did not always have the best of luck, once going through an entire season with Canterbury when not one slips catch was held off his bowling.

Motz made his first-class debut for Canterbury in 1957 at 17 when the Test bowler, Tony MacGibbon, was injured and although he was unknown at Lancaster Park it wasn't long before he had 3-9 and was never again left out of the side.

Motz battled against a weight problem all his life and had to work harder than most fast bowlers. But until a back injury forced his retirement at the age of 29 he was a key figure in his country's development as a Test nation.

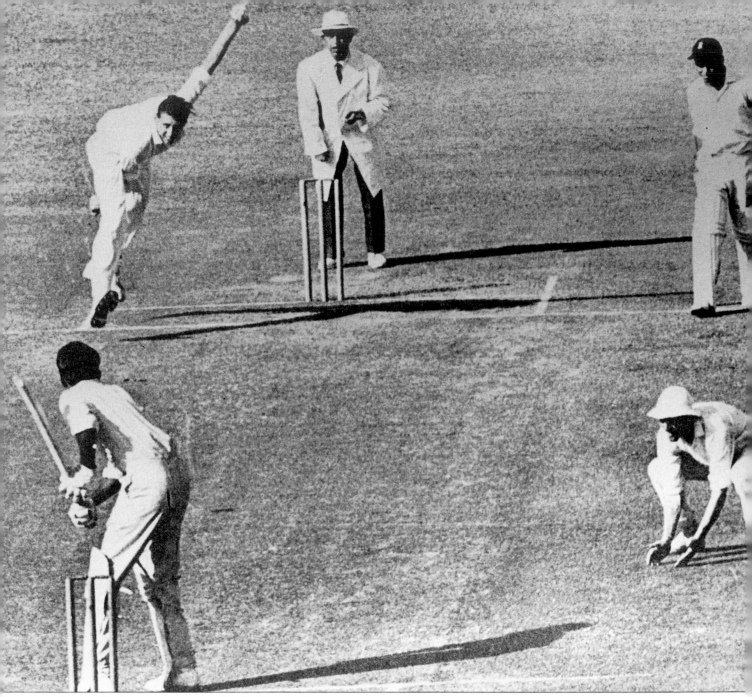

Bruce Taylor, spectacular Kiwi all-rounder.

Motz was twice chosen to play against Australia in non-Test matches in 1959-60, and on the Test tour of South Africa in 1961-2, where at one stage he collapsed from exhaustion, he took 81 first-class wickets at 18 runs each.

Nineteen of the wickets were in New Zealand's most successful Test series to that time.

Motz was a fierce hitter of sixes, throwing all his considerable beef behind the bat, once hitting 65 in 52 minutes against Dennis Silk's 1960-61 MCC side, and in the same series hammering three sixes off an over from David Allen.

Against Otago in 1967-8, he scored his only first-class century. It was the innings of a master, the fastest hundred in New Zealand cricket.

Against an attack led by the wily and frugal leg break bowler Jack Alabaster, Motz made 103 off 63 deliveries in 53 minutes, including seven sixes and eight fours.

Early in his career, Motz earned comparisons with New Zealand's great paceman of the 1930s Jack Cowie, even though he never really had the same mastery of the outswinger as The Bull. Nevertheless, with significant pace and a prodigious off-cutter, Motz, bowling for Canterbury against the Australian tourists in 1965-6, took 6-24 with a spell of 26 deliveries that saw him remove Brian Booth, Ken Cunningham, Norm O'Neill, Peter Burge and Paul Sheahan.

Two years later at Christchurch, he took 6-63, helping New Zealand to its first victory over India. The following season, he bagged 6-69 at the Basin Reserve, Wellington, against the West Indians, winning the Windsor Cup as New Zealand's outstanding bowler for the third straight season.

When he had Phil Sharpe leg before at The Oval in 1969, he became the first New Zealand bowler to reach 100 Test wickets.

Even with his suspect back, he managed to hammer 73 not out against Lancashire on the penultimate county match of the tour. When his team mates left England for India and Pakistan, Motz left for home, leaving cricket for good.

In 1964-5, Motz was joined in the New Zealand team by the tall right-arm fast-medium bowler and left-handed bat, Bruce Taylor, after Gary Bartlett had been ruled out.

Taylor, who first played for Canterbury two years earlier as a 20-year-old, was, like Motz, a quick bowler with a love of big scoring. He made a spectacular start to his career at Calcutta, scoring 105 in 158 minutes in a big partnership with Bert Sutcliffe, and then taking 5-86.

In the next Test, at Bombay, he took 5-26; but he could not do the same damage in the giant Indian second innings. At Rawalpindi, in his debut against Pakistan, he blasted 76 in 88 minutes.

The greatest knock of his career came when New Zealand, floundering at 6-152 against the West Indies at Eden Park, Auckland, in 1969, called on him for some much-needed heroics.

Against an attack that included the ageing Wes Hall, Richard Edwards, Gary Sobers, David Holford and Lance Gibbs, he cracked a half-century in 30 minutes and brought up his century in 86 minutes — at the time the fifth-fastest in Test history — with a six off Edwards.

Three years later, against the West Indians at Bridgetown, he took full advantage of a lively wicket to record figures of 7-74.

Taylor retired in 1973 but made a comeback to New Zealand cricket six years later.

His 111 Test wickets at 26.60 came from 30 matches. Dick Motz played 32 Tests, and took 100 wickets at 31.48.

Dick Motz specialised in belting sixes.

Peter Pollock
(1941-)

High And Mighty

In the first Test at Lords in the 1965 series between England and South Africa, Peter Pollock (left) hit John Edrich in the head with a bouncer and put the gutsy little left-hander in hospital.

All Geoff Boycott could say by means of consolation when gazing upon the injury was that the lump was so big it looked like half the ball was still in there.

Peter Pollock was Neil Adcock's successor as the premier paceman in South Africa. Tall, blond and strapping, he took a long straight approach to the wicket, running with the ball held at his side and delivering it at great pace after a high leap and high side-on action that could produce alarming movement away from the bat.

In England in 1965, Pollock's aggressive fast bowling was the deciding factor in the last Test series played between the two countries. He took 20 wickets in the three Tests at 18 runs each, 10 of them (5-53 and 5-34) coming at Trent Bridge in the second Test, in which he bowled the tourists to a 1-0 lead that would determine the series. In the same match his younger brother, Graeme, a left-handed batsman who could have been magnificent in any era, hit 125 and 59.

Not that England did not have its chances for victory. At Lords, England needed 191 in 235 minutes but, after Pollock changed the shape of Edrich's head, the home team was never in the race.

Pollock, born on June 30, 1941, made his first-class debut for Eastern Province at the age of 17. In 1961, he toured England with the Fezelas, which included most of South Africa's top young players. He made his Test debut against New Zealand in 1961-2, taking 6-38, in his debut at Durban.

Pollock finished the series on top of the bowling averages with 17 at 17.58 each and, even though he was overshadowed by the one-series wonder, Goofy Lawrence, Pollock would be around for a lot longer.

The following season, Pollock recorded his best first-class figures, 7-19 against Western Province at Port Elizabeth, and in Australia in 1963-4 he and Joe Partridge, a bespectacled swing bowler, had spectacular results in a drawn series, taking 25 wickets each.

Pollock took 6-95 in the first Test, at Brisbane, but had the headlines stolen away by Ian Meckiff's one-over swansong and in the second Test at Melbourne Australia hit their 136 for victory without drama after Pollock damaged a hamstring.

In New Zealand, Pollock and Partridge were just as impressive but, although they were backed by batsmen who made plenty of runs, all three matches were drawn, Pollock taking 15 wickets, including 6-47 at Wellington. The arrival of Mike Procter for the 1966-7 home series against Australia seemed to shock Pollock as much as it did the batsmen under Bobby Simpson.

Pollock had been disappointing against the English tourists in 1964-5, and Pollock's mantle of South Africa's top fast bowler was stolen. Yet he still bowled tremendously fast and, with Procter, formed the most lethal combination in world cricket.

Because of South Africa's isolation in the cricketing world, three years went by before Pollock had another chance to prove he had some fire left in his powerful frame. He finished his Test career supporting Procter again but this time with more success — 15 wickets in four Tests at 17 runs each with 5-39 at Johannesburg, where South Africa won by 307.

In 28 Tests, Pollock had taken 116 wickets at 24.18.

South Africa's politics prevented him from a much longer and varied international career.

In April, 1971, at the Newlands Ground in Cape Town, where a team was being picked for an aborted tour of Australia, he and Graeme walked off the field after the first ball had been bowled — in a protest against apartheid and the Government's declaration that non-whites would not be chosen for the tour.

Pollock retired from first-class cricket the following year. Only Hugh Tayfield and Trevor Goddard took more wickets for South Africa.

Mike Procter
(1946-)

Breaking All The Rules

Mike Procter's fast bowling worked on the simplest of physical equations: the faster he ran to the wicket, the faster he bowled. Unfortunately for Australian Test batsmen and the unfortunates of English county cricket, Procter was a very fast runner.

The chunky South African did not have much grace or rhythm or any semblence of what the purists call style. But, with his physique and toughness he did not need to. His delivery was based all on arm-and-shoulder action, a charging sprint to the crease and a whirlwind chest-on catapult with his right arm whizzing over in a blur.

Procter's arm action was so quick that he released the ball fractionally before his left foot landed, giving the impression that he bowled off the wrong foot.

He hardly left a mark at the crease, because, unlike most pacemen, he did not derive any speed from a slammed-down front foot. Because of his awkward action and his sharp pace, the batsman was never quite sure when or where to expect the ball to land, even though most of the time Procter's action resulted in booming inswingers that had a habit of knocking stumps from the ground or bruising shinbones.

Such was the stress on his body that Procter was

Mike Procter had little grace or rhythm but got results.

given only a few years in cricket before he broke down. Yet his action did not destroy him; it made him strong.

The more he bowled, the fitter and faster he became, and the more resilient were his bones and muscles. For many years he was such a driving force with bat and ball for Gloucestershire that the county became known across the cricketing world as Proctershire.

But for the perilous mix of sport and politics, Procter might have become the greatest all-rounder in Test cricket.

In 1970-71, he joined C.B. Fry and Bradman in the record books by scoring six consecutive first-class hundreds; and twice in the 1970s he scored a hundred and a hat-trick in matches for Gloucestershire. His run

of centuries were all made for Rhodesia and the last century, 254 against Western Province and Salisbury, stands as his highest total in first-class cricket.

In 1971, Procter scored 1786 runs for Gloucestershire, and in 1972-3 he achieved his best first-class bowling performance of 9-71, for Rhodesia against Transvaal at Bulawayo.

He always regarded himself as a better batsman than fast bowler, and many will remember him as a powerful hitter in the mould of Jessop and Botham.

Yet in his brief Test career — seven matches against Australia — it was his freakish pace from such an action that added new chapters to the textbook.

At a little under 180 centimetres and with the bull

neck and barrel chest of a rugby hooker, Procter developed strength and stamina to bowl fast all day long.

Born on September 15, 1946, in Durban, Procter was a brilliant schoolboy batsman and vice-captain of the South African schoolboys who toured England in 1963. He did not start bowling fast until his second-last year at school.

Fortunately, his coaches did not try to change a bowling style that gained results.

Occasionally during his county career he could turn to off-spinners when the pitch warranted it or when his knees rebelled against the constant pounding of his fast-bowler's approach.

Procter joined Gloucestershire in 1965 and made his Test debut at the age of 20 in South Africa's home series of 1966-7, in which Peter van der Merwe's men smashed the Australians 3-1.

Procter came into the team for the third Test before his hometown crowd at Durban and was an instant success, taking 3-27 and 4-71 in Australia's eight-wicket victory, Procter's first scalp being the visiting skipper Bobby Simpson.

Procter took six wickets in the next Test, at Johannesburg, including 4-32, and he finished with a series tally of 15 from three matches at 17.53 each.

By the time Australia was in South Africa again —

this time under Bill Lawry in 1969-70 — there was no stopping Procter or the South Africans. Procter charged at the Australians and ran right over them, 26 batsmen succumbing to his pace and aggression in four Tests at just 13.57 for each wicket. South Africa won the series 4-0, Procter taking as many wickets as Peter Pollock and Eddie Barlow together against a team that boasted such class players as Bill Lawry, Keith Stackpole, Ian Chappell, Ian Redpath, Doug Walters and Paul Sheahan. South Africa's smallest winning margin was 170 runs.

Procter summed up the series with his best Test performance of 6-73 at Port Elizabeth.

Despite a knee operation that caused him to miss the beginning of the 1976 English season, Procter could still bowl with great speed and fire as the 1970s closed, and he became one of Kerry Packer's touring trumps in Australia.

Captaining Gloucestershire in a Benson and Hedges semi-final against Hampshire in 1977, Procter took four wickets in five balls at Southampton, including the hat-trick, in dismissing the cream of Hants batting — Gordon Greenidge, Barry Richards, Jesty and Rice.

It was yet another memorable performance to add to his three county hat-tricks, nearly 22,000 runs in first-class cricket (average 36) and 1407 wickets at 19.36.

John Snow, stormy petrel of England sides of the '60s.

John Snow
(1941-)

Rebel With Applause

John Snow once described fast bowlers as the men who really win Test matches, the players most likely to get the breakthrough or bowl a side out on good wickets or bad.

Apart from providing the most exciting sight in cricket, they gave the game a sense of urgency. They wanted to "slice the batting side open and watch it bleed".

John Snow, the abominable snowman of English

cricket for more than a decade, did more than his share of slaughtering.

The son of a vicar, Dr W. Sinclair Snow, he was born at Peopleton, Worcestershire, on October 13, 1941, and educated at Christ's Hospital.

He was a fast bowler put together with the minimum of materials, all skin and sinew, yet his wiry frame could unleash deliveries of genuine express speed and on his day he could destroy the world's best batting line-ups.

When he made his debut as a batsman for Sussex in 1961, he had close-cropped hair and, in the words of one writer, the head of a gladiator. By the time he retired after World Series Cricket, he had a bushy mop, an autobiography behind him called *Cricket Rebel* and two volumes of published poetry.

He played 49 Tests, took 202 wickets (26.66) and made enemies of various captains and some in the heirarchy of English cricket.

Snow did not have the classical action of a Lillee or Hall, but he had magnificent rhythm and could generate great speed from a fairly short run that finished in long measured strides, the coiling of his body and the final whip of his torso that from a high, slightly chest-on action startled batsmen with speed.

Snow made the most of his 182 centimetres, stretching as high on his toes as he could at the moment of release.

Snow joined Sussex as a batsman, but he bowled so quick and with such movement that anyone who saw him firing away in his limited opportunities knew he could become a great fast bowler.

His progress through first-class cricket was not rapid and he did not become a Sussex regular until 1964. But the next season he took over 100 wickets for Sussex and made his Test debut at Lords against New Zealand, in what was Fred Trueman's last match.

Against the West Indians at home in 1966, Snow took a modest 12 wickets at 37.58 in the last three Tests, his most significant contribution being an unbeaten 59 at The Oval in a last wicket partnership of 128 with his pace-bowling partner, Ken Higgs.

At home against India the following year, he took 10 wickets at 26 in a series dominated by Ray Illingworth and Geoff Boycott.

But later that year, after more than half a decade as a first-class cricketer, Snow finally hit his straps and became the fast bowler England had been waiting for since the decline of Statham and Trueman. On tour of the Caribbean in 1967-68 he played four Tests and took 27 wickets at 18.66, including 7-49 in his Caribbean debut at Kingston; 5-86 in the next Test, at Bridgetown; and in the fifth Test, at Georgetown, he took Gary Sobers's first ball, just as he had done at The Oval in 1966, to finish with 10 wickets in the match, including 6-60.

Backed by David Brown again, Snow took 17 wickets at just under 30 against the Australians in 1968, but his best series came on the controversial Ashes tour of Australia in 1970-1.

In six Tests, Snow took 31 wickets, 24 of them top-line batsmen. He finished off the fourth Test, at Syd-

ney, with 7-40, his best Test figures, fellow quicks Peter Lever and Bob Willis taking spectacular catches and England winning by 299 runs.

Graham McKenzie, playing his last Test, had to leave the field with blood streaming from his face after being hit by a Snow delivery that climbed after pitching on a good length.

In the fifth Test, at Melbourne, Snow had given the young wrist spinner, Kerry O'Keeffe, a tough time with the bouncer. In the seventh Test, again at Sydney, where England needed a draw to win The Ashes, he hit the leg-spinner, Terry Jenner, in the head with what he called "a bad ball" — a short delivery the batsmen ducked straight into.

Snow's shock bouncer was a difficult weapon to counter at any time but, bowling it around the wicket, it became almost impossible to fend off.

Illingworth, the English skipper, had moved in from mid-wicket to forward short leg for the ball aimed at the armpit, just the sort of delivery that had made Jenner jump in the first Test, at Brisbane.

The umpire, Lou Rowan, cautioned Snow for intimidatory bowling — and the pair clashed. When Snow went off to field at long leg, in front of the notorious Paddington Hill, a drunken spectator reached over the fence to grapple with him and the fast bowler was showered with beer cans.

Illingworth led his team from the field and the umpires warned the Englishmen that the game would be forfeited and The Ashes — very much in England's grasp — also forfeited.

In the second innings, Australia needed only 223 to win, and Snow had been put in hospital after first bowling Ken Eastwood for a duck and then breaking the index finger of his bowling hand in trying to catch a hook shot from Keith Stackpole at fine leg.

Even without him, the Englishmen won by 62 runs, taking The Ashes 2-0.

Snow was embroiled in controversy again that English summer. Playing in two Tests, he could not prevent Venkat, Chandrasekhar and Bishen Bedi winning India's first match and series in England, though he did score his highest Test total of 73 in the first Test, at Lords.

It was in that match that Snow knocked Gavaskar off his feet as the Indian was trying for a quick single. Snow was ordered to apologise, and he was left out of the team for the Old Trafford Test as punishment.

He never again toured with England, and he gained a reputation for being moody and obstinate.

But he was the answer to Dennis Lillee and Bob Massie during the 1972 campaign against Australia, taking 24 wickets at 23 and helping England to draw the series at 2-all to retain The Ashes he had won for them 18 months before.

No-one will ever know what he might have done in stemming the fury of Lillee and Thomson during the tribulations of England's next encounter with the Aussies. Certainly there were plenty calling for his selection, ever mindful of the way many prominent Australian batsmen had flinched against his short stuff in the previous two series.

Barry Richards
Rates The Bowlers

In the late 1960s South Africa was blessed with two exceptional fast bowlers — Peter Pollock and Mike Procter. When the ball is coming at you at 160 kilometres per hour it's difficult to make comparisons, but I'd say Procky was just that little quicker.

Both guys were tremendously strong and were very different. Mike stood around 180 centimetres and even though he didn't really bowl off the wrong foot as some people thought, his action was certainly ungainly. But he generated great pace and had a devastating inswinger. Even though he couldn't swing the ball away much, he tended to vary his deliveries by rolling the seam the other way so that after a spate of inswingers the batsman would be met by a very fast delivery going straight ahead.

Peter Pollock stood around 188 centimetres and was the master of the away swinger. His action was certainly a lot more classical than Procky's.

One of the great fast bowlers of the 1960s was John Snow. He could be very quick, but the best thing about his bowling was that he gave it so much thought. He had a marvellous economy of action and the ability to rise to any occasion. He continually pitched the ball on the seam and the ball moving sideways off the wicket is a lot more difficult to counter than the ball swinging through the air.

The fastest bowling I ever faced was from Michael Holding in the 1970s, but on his day Gary Sobers, often under-rated as a fast man because of his other talents, could be deadly. Gary had a terrifying bouncer and his left-arm bowling, combined with great variation, often made him unplayable.

A man who was also extremely quick at the end of the '60s was Alan Ward from Derbyshire, though injuries really hurt his career. Young Bob Willis was also knocking at the door then and I also had a high opinion of Warwickshire's David Brown and the fast West Australian Laurie Mayne.

Dennis Lillee was a real tearaway at the same period and even though I managed a triple century against him playing for South Australia, he gave me plenty of anxious moments.

Lillee, of course, idolised Graham McKenzie, who was simply a fantastic bowler, although his final visit to South Africa was something of a disaster. "Garth" wasn't up there with Procky or Holding in terms of speed but he had the incredible ability to generate real pace off an easy, economical action. He was a great swinger of the ball away from the right-hander.

When McKenzie failed in South Africa, Alan Connolly, who was nowhere near Garth's pace, took over. Although he wasn't likely to beat anyone with speed, I remember the Test at Port Elizabeth when we were 4-300 or so and cruising to a huge score. But Al came out in overcast conditions and blitzed us, taking 6-47 with his bounce and swing.

Alan Connolly and Neil Hawke served Australia well. Hawke bowled with an ungainly crab-like action but, unlike Mike Procter, he could swing the ball both ways. Compared to the fast men, his pace was only gentle, but the art of fast bowling involves a lot more than sheer speed.

Facing Lillee was the sternest test for any batsman

THE 1970s

Blood On
The Pitch

When the selectors chose to write off Graham McKenzie at the start of the 1970s, their decision left Australia without a recognised Test spearhead. Alan "Froggy" Thomson had become a favourite with Victorian fans because of his curious "wrong foot" windmill bowling style, but his enthusiasm and will to win were not enough to compensate for a lack of real pace when he tried to match it with John Snow in 1970-71.

Dennis Lillee was clearly the brightest fast-bowling prospect in Australia since McKenzie himself a decade earlier, but he had a variety of partners before teaming with Bob Massie for a brief and spectacular fling and with Jeff Thomson for a later and even more fruitful partnership.

Ross Duncan and the Hampshire-born Tony Dell were both tried as opening bowlers, and the enthusiastic Sydneysider David Colley, who had been coached by Barry Knight and took a hat-trick in his first-grade debut at 15, backed Lillee and Massie in England in 1972, though he had more results with his powerful hitting than with the swinging ball.

When Lillee broke down with stress fractures in the Caribbean in 1972-3, Australia's batsmen were still able to flourish against a transitory West Indian line-up, and his absence was compensated for by the emergence of Max Walker and the South Australian quick, Jeff Hammond, who took 15 wickets in the Tests.

Hammond had made his debut for South Australia at the age of 19 and toured England in 1972, though he could not get a Test because of Lillee and Massie. He still managed 6-15 against Minor Counties at Stoke, beating the batsmen with pace. But he broke a foot and suffered back troubles that hampered him throughout his career, restricting his Test appearances to just five.

In the same way many fine fast bowlers were kept out of the Australian team by Lindwall, Miller and Johnston 20 years before, Alan Hurst, a Victorian with a spectacular follow-through, had to bide his time in the mid-1970s when Lillee, Thomson, Walker and Gilmour were at their peaks

English critics reckoned Hurst was as fast at Lillee when the two toured England in 1975, but it was Lillee who did the bowling in the Tests. Back injuries kept Hurst quiet until the 1978-9 season when Lillee, Thomson, Max Walker, Len Pascoe, Gary Gilmour, Mick Malone and Wayne Prior all defected to Kerry Packer's World Series Cricket.

Backing Rodney Hogg, Hurst had a good deal of success against England and Pakistan that season, taking 40 wickets in eight Tests, including 5-28 against England at Sydney, and doing the hat-trick in a one-day match against Western Australia in Perth.

Lillee's absence from the 1977 tour of England allowed Mick Malone, a clever West Australian swing bowler with a long, curved run, to show some of his talents.

Malone, who could give away fewer runs than overs bowled in one-day matches, made his Test debut at The Oval with the series already lost, taking 5-63. After two years with World Series, where he had to fight hard to get a game, he had some success with Lancashire.

The Packer defections allowed a number of fast bowlers, who might otherwise have remained buried by better-known heroes, to rise to the green-and-gold cap. When Bob Simpson was recalled to lead Australia against the 1977-8 Indians, he had at his disposal J.B. "Sam" Gannon, a left-arm fast-medium bowler from Western Australia who had made his Sheffield Shield debut 11 years earlier but had dropped out of big cricket after the 1972-3 series because there were too many better players around. In a great moment of good timing, he made a comeback just as Australia was looking for pacemen, and finished with 11 wickets in three Tests, coming on behind Thomson and Wayne Clark.

For the final Test of the series Australia used Ian Callen, a tall, stylish part-time model from Victoria whose high arm action and whippy deliveries owed a lot to the advice of John Snow. Callen took six wickets in the match, which Australia won to take the series.

Like Callen, Perth's Wayne Clark was another whose career was curtailed by back problems. He had a relaxed run to the wicket and a powerful shoulder action like Graham McKenzie. He had a vicious bouncer that created doubts over the fairness of the action in the Caribbean in 1978, though he was finally cleared. In 10 Tests he took 44 wickets at 29.

The controversy over his bowling style was a ripple compared with the resignation of the contracted Packer players from the West Indies team that season and the riot over the dismissal of Vanburn Holder at Kingston.

The locals had been at full strength for the first two Tests which the Windies took easily, but the axeing of three Packer players caused a walkout and the formation of a new side, spearheaded by Sylvester Clarke, Holder and Norbert Phillip.

At Port of Spain, Holder who had given long and meritorious service to the West Indies from a trekking run-up, took 6-28 against Australia to set up a series win in his last hurrah.

By the time of the Packer players' return, the West Indies had enough fast bowlers to fill a Test XI just with quickos, but it was not quite the case

at the start of the decade when Griffith and Hall had retired.

In 1970-71, the West Indians were struggling, and India managed to beat the Calypsos in a series for the first time, despite their own moderate pace attack of Solkar and Abid Ali and the success of the West Indian off-break bowler, Jack Noreiga. Sobers was again the best of the West Indian quicks, even though he had enough on his mind batting against the turning ball of Venkat and Bedi.

In the early part of the decade, the West Indian attack was led by Holder, John Shepherd, the medium-pacers of Clive Lloyd, the supremely athletic Keith Boyce and the solid Uton Dowe, who was so erratic against the 1972-3 Australians that his Jamaican fans invented a new cricket commandment: "Dowe shalt not bowl".

By the time the West Indians arrived in England in 1973 Sobers, their best quick bowler, was 37 and aware his side no longer had the power it had a decade earlier. The tourists had not won a Test match in four years and had not beaten England since 1966.

But in the first Test, at The Oval, Keith Boyce came of age, scoring 72 and then flailing the ball down at a good pace to take 5-70 and 6-77. The Windies won by 158.

Boyce had become the quickest West Indian bowler of the day and his team mates rejoiced, unaware that within three years a batallion of fast bowlers, all quicker than him, would emerge to dominate international cricket. Boyce played for Essex between 1966 and 1977, where much of his best cricket was displayed, particularly in the one-day game.

He scored a 58-minute century and had the double of 113 and 12-73 against Leicestershire at Chelmsford in 1975. In the same year, he took four cheap wickets and hammered the bowling for a while to ensure a remarkable West Indian triumph in the World Cup. In 21 Tests he took 60 wickets at 30 each.

Sobers, who had been recalled to the team for such an important tour, still opened the bowling for the first two Tests but by the third and final match, which the Windies won by an innings and 226 runs, Boyce, Holder and the left-arm all-rounder Bernard Julien were doing a good-enough job to let him rest. For a time Julien was spoken of as another Sobers, but he failed to live up to the promise.

Three years later in England, Wayne Daniel, like Holder a big, powerful but friendly Barbadian, was part of the West Indian attack that tested the heart of Dennis Amiss as he defied his critics to hit a double century against the fastest bowling in the world.

Daniel, known as the Black Pearl, had a long, bounding run and spectacular cart-wheeling action not unlike that of Wes Hall. He had made his debut for the West Indians against India in

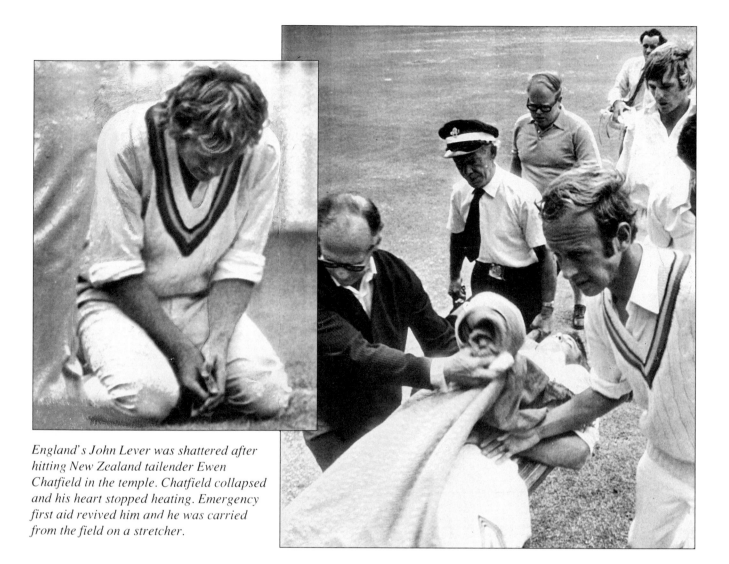

England's John Lever was shattered after hitting New Zealand tailender Ewen Chatfield in the temple. Chatfield collapsed and his heart stopped beating. Emergency first aid revived him and he was carried from the field on a stretcher.

1975-6 when the visiting opening bowlers, the capable, bouncing, little Madan Lal and Mohinder Armanath looked like stone throwers against heavy artillery.

Madan Lal had his best series against England in 1982, when he took 5-23 partnering Kapil Dev to beat Keith Fletcher's Englishmen at Bombay, giving India the series.

Daniel was on the verge of greatness in the mid-70s, but a back injury forced him to miss the home series against Pakistan and by the time he had recovered, Joel Garner and Colin Croft had a foothold in the team and Sylvester Clarke and Malcolm Marshall were on the rise. But he remained consistently quick, if a little straight and predictable, for the West Indies and Middlesex, helping it share the county championship in 1977 and partnering the tall, brilliant South African Vintcent van der Bijl to victory there in 1980.

The West Indies had a fast-bowling attack to petrify English batsmen from 1976, when Mike Selvey, often outstanding in county cricket, could do little to thwart them with his own pace. But at the start of the decade, England, led by its Snow blizzard, had a pretty ferocious line-up itself.

Snow led England to The Ashes triumph in 1970-1, when his sidemen included Ken

Shuttleworth, with a long, curved run-up and an action reminiscent of Trueman's, the pacy Peter Lever, and, for the last four Tests, the gangling Bob Willis, flown to Australia to replace the injured Alan Ward.

Lever was hampered late in his career by back trouble, but he still took 6-38 at Melbourne in the 1974-5 series when England was paid back for Bodyline. Lever opened the Lancashire bowling with Shuttleworth and was quick enough to take 7-84 against the Rest Of The World in 1970.

He had also bowled well against India in 1971, supported at times by Richard Hutton, son of Sir Len and an all-rounder who could swing and cut the ball brilliantly.

It was a great irony that after the punishment England took from Lillee and Thomson in Australia, one of its bowlers would cause an injury that came close to being Test cricket's first death.

On Sunday, February 23, 1975, at Eden Park, Auckland, the Kiwis were on the verge of an innings defeat when Ewen Chatfield, a 24-year-old medium-fast bowler and No. 11 batsman from Wellington, defied the English pace attack.

Lever, then 34, had hit Greg Chappell on the jaw at Melbourne and bounced Terry Jenner in

Brisbane. He dug a ball in short. It hit Chatfield's glove and slammed into his temple.

Chatfield staggered and collapsed moaning, legs twitching, face turning purple. His heart stopped beating.

An ambulanceman gave him mouth to mouth as Lever fell to his knees and wept.

Chatfield recovered consciousness an hour later in hospital and said he wanted to get back on the cricket field as soon as he could. Five days after his brush with death, he watched a subdued Lever bowling at Christchurch.

The fact that Chatfield recovered to top 100 wickets for New Zealand said as much for his courage as it did for his love of the game.

The injury to Chatfield recalled another to Graeme Watson, himself a lively fast-medium bowler, who was hit on the nose by a full toss from Tony Greig in a match between Australia and The World in 1972. Watson lay in intensive care for days and received 40 pints of blood in 14 blood transfusions, eventually ignoring surgeons' advice never to play again.

Melbourne's Centenary Test of 1977 was a fitting tribute to the history of the game, emphasising the courage of batsmen against the hostility of pace. With his jaw wired after a Bob Willis bouncer, Rick McCosker came out in the second innings and hooked John Lever for four. Derek Randall, hit on the head by a Lillee bouncer, merely rubbed the sore spot and got back to his nervous, fidgety way, hitting 174 and almost swinging the game which Australia won by 45 runs, the same margin as the first Test 100 years before.

John Lever had made his England debut against India a couple of months earlier, scoring 53 and taking 7-46 at Madras, amid claims he used vaseline to help his left-arm inswing. Lever bowled a lively medium pace off a run up that would have exhausted Wesley Hall.

During that series the

Keith Boyce, Mr Reliable for the West Indies.

Indians let the quick bowler, Karsan Ghavri, bowl slow at Bombay; and he took four of his 5-33 with left arm spinners. But, opening with Kapil Dev against the West Indies in 1978-9, he bowled fast, taking 27 wickets in six Tests to overshadow Kapil and make a bigger impact than any of the tourists, including Clarke, Phillip, Holder and Malcolm Marshall.

New Zealand lost four out of six Tests against India and Pakistan in 1976-7, but Lance Cairns took 5-55 at Madras. Four years later, he picked up 5-33 when the sides met in New Zealand.

Cairns was a handy chest-on medium-pacer, usually at first or second change, and his immense scoring potential packed many a one-day fixture.

The 1979-80 series between New Zealand and the West Indies was one of bitterness and controversy, but the New Zealand bowlers performed splendidly. Richard Hadlee and his left-arm opening partner, Glenn Troup, shared 37 wickets in the three matches, Cairns taking 12, and all three grabbing six-wicket hauls.

The Kiwis had managed to draw all five Tests aginst the Windies back in 1971-2 when Bruce Taylor was backed by the long-haired Murray Webb and the broad shouldered Bob Cunis, the wrong-footed rugby five- eighth with the chest-on action and dicky knees.

By the late 1970s, Imran Khan had emerged as Pakistan's best bowler since Fazal Mahmood and he was getting better with every series. As an 18-year-old on the 1971 England tour he played very much in the shadow of the menacing Asif Masood, whose driving run began with an amusing stutter at the beginning. Pakistan might have won at Headingley after Saleem Altaf put a broom through the tail, but rain preserved England's lead.

Sikhander Bakht, who once broke Mike Brearley's arm, had proved himself a better proposition than Liaquat Ali as the support to Imran and Sarfraz. He developed his pace from a fast approach and an action that was all long arms and legs.

Sikhander had a fine season against New Zealand in 1978-9 and a better one with 24 wickets in India the following season, when he and a pacy club player from England, Ehteshamuddin, proved more than competent back-ups to Imran. Sikhander took 8-69 at New Delhi.

In 1970, South African Test cricket came to an end, killing any chance Transvaal's Chaka Watson had of playing in the ultimate cricket challenge. Later in the decade, two South African quicks, Van der Bijl, and the faster and more menacing blond giant Garth Le Roux with a slinging action and hyped as a "sex bomb" in World Series Cricket, suggested the country might still have dominated the game in the 1970s.

Colin Croft (1953 -)

The Bomber

Colin "Bomber" Croft was in a bad mood. He had just taken 16 cheap wickets in the West Indies series win over Australia, and, like all his team mates, he was tired, jaded and eager to get home. But there was still a tour of New Zealand to get through. When the West Indies arrived in the land of the Long White Cloud in the summer of 1979-80, dark clouds of trouble were brewing.

An 11-wicket haul by Richard Hadlee in the first Test, at Dunedin, and a loss to the Kiwis by one wicket did nothing to bring out their ivory smiles. The mood among the West Indians was malevolent, Hadlee calling it the sour summer, the most bitter and controversial he had played in.

After one unsuccessful appeal Michael Holding had acted totally out of character by kicking over the stumps, and by the time the second Test, at Dunedin, began, Colin Croft, all 192 centimetres of premeditated mayhem, was about to crack.

On the third day of the match, Howarth and Hadlee had made centuries as the West Indian appeals were constantly refused. The visitors locked themselves in the dressing-room protesting against the decisions. When they emerged 12 minutes later some of the team showed apathy in the field, and Colin Croft showed his fury.

"As a fast bowler," said Hadlee, "I can understand (Croft's) frustrations. He was at boiling point. But he over-reacted in a manner that lacked self-control and brought the game into disrepute."

What Croft did was to straighten his long run-up and as he roared in to send down one of his vicious short balls, he seemed to be aiming more for the umpire, Fred Goodall, than the batsman or stumps at the other end.

Sure enough, Croft hit the umpire with his shoulder. "Had this been a soccer or rugby match," Hadlee said, "the player involved would have been sent off and possibly banned for life. Clive Lloyd appeared to show a complete lack of interest and responsibility in defusing a highly explosive situation."

The hit on Goodall was just one example of the anger Colin Croft could generate. As part of a phalanx of regular West Indian speedsters that included Andy Roberts, Michael Holding, Joel Garner and Malcolm Marshall, he contributed pace and hostility, bowling with a chest-on action after a long-striding run and delivering ferocious inswingers and off-cutters.

Born on March 15, 1953, Croft made his debut for Guyana at 19. He had the misfortune of bowling to Jamaica's Lawrence Rowe in a run-scoring mood. Croft's 0-75 from 15 overs was enough to convince him he belonged not on the cricket fields of Georgetown but in a shrimping fleet as a professional fisherman. But after studying to become a sailing

Colin Croft, menacing, angry and an umpire's nightmare.

master in Trinidad, he began playing cricket again, bowling his club side to a championship in Trinidad. He played for Guyana again in 1976 and the following year bowled fast and straight enough to make his Test debut after injuries to Michael Holding and Wayne Daniel.

Playing in the first Test against Pakistan at Bridgetown in 1976-7, Croft opened the bowling with Andy Roberts and was supported by Vanburn Holder and another Test debutant, Joel Garner. The Bomber had immediate success with seven wickets in a drawn match in which both teams scored big totals.

But in the second Test, at Port of Spain, he was unplayable, taking 8-29, the best Test figures ever by a West Indian fast bowler, snared from 18.5 overs against a batting line-up which included Mustaq and Sadiq Mohammad, Majid and Imran Khan, Asif Iqbal and Wasim Raja.

The Windies won by six wickets, and by end of

the season Croft had taken 33 Pakistan wickets at 20 each, powering his side to a 2-1 victory in the series.

His size, strength and pace always meant he had an effect on a Test. After his deeds and misdeeds in Australia and New Zealand, he took 24 wickets in four Tests against England in 1980-1 as he and Garner shared the old ball behind Roberts, Holding and Marshall. In a one-day game at St Vincent he took six English wickets for 15.

Croft was an immediate hit after joining Lancashire in 1978, and he was a rebel first with the Kerry Packer brand of cricket and then with the West Indian tourists to South Africa who were banned for life from Test cricket.

Croft's Test career finished after 27 matches for the West Indies and 125 wickets at 23.30.

After he had finished his commitments in South Africa, Croft went to live with his family in the United States, working as a commercial pilot.

Geoff Arnold, Mike Hendrick, Chris Old

Three Craftsmen

During the 1970s, England uncovered three tall fast-medium bowlers with classical actions who could do disappearing acts with the ball on cloudy days but came to curse clear skies and sunshine.

Geoff Arnold, Chris Old and Mike Hendrick were three master craftsmen who lacked express pace but were hazardous to a batsman's reputation on a green wicket.

Arnold, born in 1944, was known as "Orse" throughout his career and made his debut for Surrey at the age of 19. Four years later, he scored a half century and took 5-58 against Pakistan at The Oval in his Test debut. When the wicket suited him, he had a superb outswinger and could make the ball move either way off the seam. He lost effectiveness away from English pitches but did take 6-45 at New Delhi in ideal conditions for fast-medium bowling. He suffered badly from injuries and runs of bad luck, once having three successive slips catches dropped off him against the 1972 Australians.

But he was an eager and successful support to John Snow, finishing with 13 wickets at 21 each as England retained the Ashes despite the swing of Massie and the pace of Lillee.

Arnold took 17 wickets at 17 in India later that year with his 6-45 in the first Test but India won the next two matches and the series despite some fine bowling from Tony Greig and Chris Old, born 1948, to wreck India at Calcutta. Known throughout his career as "Chilly", C. Old was from a well-known Yorkshire sporting family with a brother who played rugby union for England. In India he took 15 wickets at 25, showing little side-effects from knee operations in 1970 and 1971.

Although he was initially a right-arm fast bowler it was as a fast-medium swinger that Old achieved most success and selection in 46 Tests. He scored a 37-minute century for Yorkshire against a beaten and

LEFT: Mike Hendrick and (ABOVE) Chris Old, master craftsmen.

bowed Warwickshire at Birmingham in 1977, his second 50 coming up in just nine minutes.

Old's great value to English cricket lay in his ability to move the ball towards the slips or make it dart back towards the pads and stumps off the seam.

Orse and Chilly had an excellent series against New Zealand in 1973, backing Snow and bowling their side to an innings victory at Headingley.

Against the Windies that year in a losing series, Arnold opened with a different partner each time - Snow, Old and Willis - but finished the summer with a healthy 31 Test wickets.

Mike Hendrick, born 1948, first played for Derbyshire in 1969, when Alan Ward was all the rage. He made his Test debut against the 1974 Indians, partnering Arnold and Old in what was a marvellous season for the trio.

England won all three matches and, after Bob Willis had shaken the tourists in the first Test, the three medium-pacers cleaned up.

Hendrick's first Test wicket came with his third ball against India at Old Trafford, and he followed up with 4-28 in the Third Test at Edgbaston. In the second Test, at Lords, Old took 5-21, Arnold 4-19 and India was all-out for 42.

Hendrick developed his strength largely through the efforts of the England physiotherapist Bernard Thomas, after he had snapped a hamstring when running in to bowl his first over at Melbourne the following season. From then, Thomas oversaw a conditioning program that would keep the Derbyshire destroyer on top.

Against the 1977 Australians, Hendrick provided valuable support to the rampant Willis and the eager debutant Botham.

Hendrick's stock ball was delivered on a good length with the seam upright, so it would usually move toward the slips and cut either way on landing.

Most of the time the bowler was unsure what the ball would do when it pitched, making it doubly difficult for the batsman to decipher his deliveries.

He took 14 wickets in that series, including eight at Headingley, where Boycott staged his 100th first-class century to perfection for his loyal Leeds supporters.

In 1978 in New Zealand, Old and Hendrick backed Willis to perfection, Old taking 6-54 from 30 overs. But Hadlee and Collinge crushed the English batsmen for a historic Kiwi victory.

With Imran and Sarfraz absent, there was no saviour for Pakistan when Chilly blew out seven of its batsmen for 50 runs at Edgbaston a few months later and England won by an innings. Included in his great spell were four wickets in five balls.

The next season Hendrick, though no threat to Rodney Hogg's record, managed 19 wickets at fewer than 16 runs each when the English bowlers outclassed some uninspired Australian batting for a 5-1 series victory.

In the next season, against India, Hendrick and Botham were just too much for the tourists to handle.

Hendrick fell just short of 100 wickets for England but Old took 143 in 46 Tests and Arnold 115 in 34,

Joel Garner
(1952-)

The Big Bird

Joel Garner's best delivery was the yorker, largely because he sent it down from such a great height that on some grounds the ball started out from way above the sight screen.

At 200 centimetres, Garner was the tallest Test bowler of any note and though he may have been known as "Big Bird" after the loveable Sesame Street character, there was nothing particularly amusing about him when he was bowling.

Dennis Lillee once said Garner was unlike any other bowler he had experienced, partly because he was so tall and partly because he was so much more relentless. His stock ball rose from a good length to attack the rib cage and he bowled fewer loose deliveries than any other fast bowler in the game.

"Garner seems to be breathing down your neck even as he starts his run," Lillee said. "And when he reaches the bowling crease, 22 yards seems more like a dozen."

Garner may not have been as quick as the West Indian speedsters he partnered, but he made up for that with accuracy that made him consistently difficult to play. He was a surprisingly agile man for his size, and he could leap for gully catches with all the high-flying manouvres of a basketball champion or bowl all day, ball after ball forcing the batsman to leap on to the back foot and fend off the lifting deliveries. Occasionally the yorker would spear in from a height of almost three metres to bite at the toes.

Garner was born in Christchurch, Barbados, on December 16, 1952, and early in his career received coaching from Seymour Nurse, Wes Hall and Charlie Griffith, whom he credits with teaching him not to round-arm the ball but to exploit his great height.

Places in the Barbadian team were so keenly sought that despite his promise Garner had to wait until he was 23 to play first-class cricket, and then only because Vanburn Holder and Keith Boyce were trying to stave off a West Indian defeat in Australia.

He made his Test debut the following season with Colin Croft in the first Test against Pakistan at his native Bridgetown and, although he did not have the immediate success of his fellow debutant, Garner still bowled well enough to take 25 wickets at fewer than 28 in the series, though never more than four in any innings.

Garner had two good matches against Australia the next season in the Caribbean before becoming one of

"Big Bird" Joel Garner at full stretch in the first Test against England at Edgbaston in 1984

130

Joel Garner had height, speed and a superb technique.

the best players in World Series Cricket. He played a few matches with Somerset in 1977 and 1978 and then joined the county full-time in 1979, partnering Viv Richards and Ian Botham in giving the team some major successes, particularly in one-day games, until an acrimonious split in 1986.

It was in limited-overs competition that Garner first made his big impression in England. His 5-38 helped the West Indies beat England in the 1979 World Cup final at Lords after Viv Richards had made 138 not out.

England's openers, Brearley and Boycott, began with a century stand; but with Garner firing they slumped from 2-183 to all-out 194.

Garner's final 11 balls brought him five wickets for four runs with Gooch, Gower and Larkin all clean-bowled in one over.

A couple of months later at Lords Garner took 6-29 against Northamptonshire in the Gillette Cup final though another smashing century by Richards denied Garner the Man Of The Match award.

In 1981 and 1982, Somerset won the Benson and Hedges Cup with Garner taking 5-14 against Surrey and 3-13 against Notts. In 1983, his 2-15 off nine overs helped the county beat Kent for the NatWest Trophy.

In 1979-80, Garner took 28 wickets in Australia and New Zealand combining with Holding, Roberts, Croft and the medium-pacer Collis King to form perhaps the best West Indian attack ever.

At Auckland, his best Test figures of 6-56 could not save a fiery series for the West Indies; but he bowled

better than anyone else and took 26 wickets at 14 each in England in 1980, though with such a pace battery to share the scalps he never took more than four in an innings.

He finished with 10 wickets from four matches against England in the Caribbean in 1980-1 but was a mighty force in the two subsequent "Blackwashes" of 1984 and in his last series, 1985-6, when he took 29 and 27 wickets respectively, as the West Indies won 10 straight matches.

At Edgbaston in 1984, he took nine wickets; but his 5-55 in the second innings was the only time in 20 innings in those two series that Garner would take more than five wickets.

Still, his 29 wickets cost fewer than 19 runs each; and he and Marshall, more than a head shorter than the big man, formed a ferocious combination of contrasts, and Garner's 27 wickets in his final series cost only 16 each.

Garner's best Test season was in the home series against Australia in 1983-4 against the Australians under Kim Hughes, who never could get used to his alarming lift. Garner's 31 wickets at 17 were a major reason for the West Indian 3-0 triumph over a side boasting such players as Hughes, Border, Hookes, Lawson, Hogg and Alderman.

The wickets kept tumbling for the big man, who hardly seemed to stray off line once. He took 6-75 in the first Test at Georgetown; 6-60 in the second, at Port of Spain; and 5-63 in the fourth at St Johns.

Richard Collinge (1946-)

The Rock

When big Richard Collinge slammed down a savage inswinger that sent Geoff Boycott back to the pavilion for one, England had begun its dramatic decline and New Zealand was on its way to a historic first victory over the country that spawned cricket.

Collinge picked up Boycott, the stand-in captain, twice in that first Test of the 1977-8 series at Wellington, England crumbled to be all out for 64 in its second innings, and New Zealand won by 72 runs in the 48th match between the two countries.

Collinge took 3-42 and 3-45 and, although Richard Hadlee received most of the accolades, there was no prouder man on the field than the 190-centimetre left-arm speedster, who had given almost half his life to New Zealand cricket.

Collinge was a menacing prospect, and few fast bowlers have looked such a threat as him. A giant who pounded in off a long run and bowled with a vigorous action that involved both arms stretching heavenwards, Collinge was not as quick as he looked. He relied more on generous swing than sheer speed.

Richard Collinge, not quite as fierce as he looked.

An accountant, he was a dedicated family man who in later years was a reluctant tourist, once coming home early from the 1971-2 tour of the West Indies because one of his children was sick.

The doyen of New Zealand cricket writers, Dick Brittenden, recalled Collinge as a doting father to his twins. He spent a great deal of time shopping for baby clothes.

"It was an odd and touching sight-this huge young man, a menace with a new ball and one who inevitably made his bat seem like a toy, trudging off with loads of infant gear."

Collinge became a first-class cricketer in 1963-4 and, after taking 7-56 for Central Districts against Otago in Glenn Turner's second representative match, he made his Test debut as an 18-year-old the following season, against Pakistan.

In a low-scoring series in which all three matches were drawn, Collinge took 15 wickets at 24 each, bowling with Dick Motz and Frank Cameron and dismissing Hanif Mohammad each time.

He played sporadically for New Zealand over the next few years. At Lords in 1965, when Fred Trueman played his last Test and John Snow his first, Collinge took 4-85.

Four years later, Collinge was selected for the tour of England, India and Pakistan but, after a fair start it became a disaster, many saying that he lacked the killer instinct.

When he was 23, Collinge's career seemed to be sliding downhill. He played only one match for Central Districts in 1969-70 against Australia, but he showed his fighting qualities the next year and in 1971-2 he took 10 wickets in the match for Wellington against Canterbury and went to the West Indies with Graham Dowling's team.

Against Pakistan in 1972-3 Collinge's most important contribution to the series was an unbeaten 68 at Auckland made with Brian Hastings in a world-record last-wicket stand of 151.

On the 1973 tour of England, Collinge, partnered well by Dayle Hadlee, made up for his poor showing there four years earlier, topping the Test averages (including 5-74 at Headingley) and taking three times as many wickets (51 at 21.9) as he had done on the previous tour.

When the Englishmen made a reciprocal visit to New Zealand, Collinge was the best bowler from either side, with 17 wickets at 25.65.

Bowling well against India in 1975-6 Collinge took 5-23 in a one-day game at Christchurch and 6-63 in the Test match there. But, as was the case for much of his later career, the big man's best was overshadowed by Richard Hadlee — in this case 11 wickets at Wellington which saved the series for New Zealand.

On the tour of India and Pakistan in 1976, Collinge, who toured there three times without great success, was left out of the team for the final tour match with his tally on 99 Test wickets.

The 100th came, and when Collinge retired after 35 Tests, his tally stood at 116 wickets at 29.25 each. At that time he was New Zealand's greatest wicket-taker.

Rodney Hogg, a no-frills wicket-taker.

Rodney Hogg
(1951-)

Late Bloomer

Rodney Hogg was often portrayed by the Australian media as a genuine ocker hero, a Pom-hater who was all fire and tunnel-visioned aggression.

Yet he was a shrewd head on old shoulders who matriculated in pure and advanced mathematics, physics and economics.

He was often portrayed as sullen, moody and obstinate, and his own captains as well as the opposition batsmen had to treat him with the utmost caution. Most of the time he kept the media at arm's length, choosing to reveal his true self only on the cricket pitch, where for a few fierce overs at a time he could be the most devastating bowler in the world.

There was little complexity about Hogg's bowling. He sent the ball fast and straight, aiming to hit the wickets nearly every time he ran in. He hardly ever moved the ball through the air, but he could bring it back off the seam.

Yet he bowled fast enough and straight enough to break a Test-bowling record of nearly 60 years in his debut series.

Rodney Hogg earned his green-and-gold cap when he was chosen to help fill the vacuum left by World Series Cricket.

Playing for South Australia against England in 1978-9, Hogg took six wickets, dismissing Geoff Boycott twice in the space of 16 deliveries and claiming the scalp of Clive Radley by hitting him with a bouncer that had the double effect of bruising his head and making him tread on his stumps.

Rodney Malcolm Hogg, born on March 5, 1951, was no teenage tearaway when he joined the Australian team and set about tearing the English batting apart.

He was pushing 28 and had been forced to move from his native Victoria to South Australia to play first-class cricket. That he became the most talked-about fast bowler in the world in his debut season still ranks as one of cricket's most amazing feats.

Hogg first made it big playing for the Northcote club in Melbourne, sending down his first delivery wide of the stumps. His club captain, Bill Lawry, told him that if four of the next seven deliveries were not at the stumps he would be taken off. For the remainder of his career Hogg seemed to bowl with the threat still ringing in his ears.

He became a deadly accurate fast bowler whose occasional loose deliveries often picked up wickets as the batsmen lashed away at the rare opportunities he presented. Hogg could not win selection in the Victorian Sheffield Shield side, and contemplated a move to NSW, one which he abandoned when the State hired one of the fastest guns in the world, Andy Roberts.

In the 1975-6 Shield season, Hogg made his first-class debut, taking seven wickets against the Victorians, who had snubbed him, and two years later his 6-80 made him a Test candidate. The following year, his fire against the English tourists elevated him to Test cricket.

He was an immediate hit. Hogg's bowling was all power and aggression, derived from a stooped over, steadily accelerating approach to the wicket.

The delivery climaxed the last few thrusting strides and Hogg threw his whole body toward the batsman, with a mixture of bouncers, off-cutters and rapid straight balls. Like Roy Gilchrist, he was occasionally accused of deliberately bowling beamers.

Against the 1978-9 English tourists, Hogg took 40 wickets in the first five Tests and finished the series with 41 at just 12.85 — a record for an Australia in Ashes cricket, eclipsing the 36 taken by Arthur Mailey in five matches (though he only bowled in four) back in 1920-21. It also broke the previous best for a series in Australia, 38 wickets by Maurice Tate in 1924-5.

Hogg took 6-74 in his first Test innings at Brisbane, took 10 wickets in the next Test at Perth and 10 more in the third at Melbourne.

But Australia's batting ranks, depleted by the Packer defections, could not support him sufficiently and despite what should have been a series-winning effort, England won 5-1.

Hogg feuded with his skipper, Graham Yallop, and once asked to meet him at the back of the Adelaide pavilion. "And it wasn't to play tennis," Yallop later wrote.

A couple of months later, Hogg smashed his stumps with his bat after being run out for leaving his crease in the first Test against Pakistan. In India the next season he kicked out a stump after being repeatedly no-balled and he had an icy relationship with his new captain, Kim Hughes.

Despite the return of the WSC players to establishment cricket, Hogg retained his place and took 10 cheap wickets against New Zealand in 1980-1, helping Australia win 2-0 in the face of Richard Hadlee's guile.

Like Geoff Lawson, Hogg was often one of the walking wounded in England in 1981, and he played in only two Tests, suffering from a degeneration of spinal discs, though, according to Jack Pollard, "He was probably fortunate not to be sent home after complaining of injuries doctors could not diagnose."

He missed the following season in Australia because of his back problems.

Hogg bowled well supporting Lawson against the Englishmen in 1982-3 but, like the rest of Australia's pace battery, he was disappointing in the West Indies the following season, though his 6-77 in the third Test at Bridgetown, was, along with the batting of Allan Border, one of the few highlights for the tourists.

By 1985, Hogg was 34 with 38 Tests behind him and 123 wickets at 28.47. Most critics believed he was at the end of the road as a fast bowler; yet with Kim Hughes's rebel team in South Africa he sometimes bowled with the pace and hostility from that summer of England's discontent seven years before.

Gary Gilmour and Geoff Dymock

'Gary Glitter' And The Quiet One

Gary Gilmour and Geoff Dymock were a pair of left-arm fast-medium bowlers who made their debut for Australia during the 1973-4 home series against New Zealand and then went their separate ways, taking valuable wickets in international cricket.

Gilmour was the more spectacular, a quicker bowler with a penchant for hitting sixes, his success more immediate and his decline more alarming.

Dymock was an honest toiler, a man far removed from the hyperbole of cricket in the late 1970s, who bowled his left-arm seamers and swingers with a minimum of fuss no matter how successful he was.

Gary John Gilmour, dubbed "Gary Glitter" after the flamboyant pop star by the English press, was often described as the new Alan Davidson when making a name for himself as a junior cricketer in Newcastle.

Born on June 26, 1951 he first received rave reviews as a teenager, hammering 58 in 52 minutes for

Geoff Dymock, the honest toiler.

Newcastle against the touring West Indians. He made a remarkable first-class debut for NSW against South Australia in 1971-2, coming in at 6-48 and hammering a century between lunch and tea.

Bowling with an effortless action which could generate sharp pace and pronounced swing both ways, Gilmour took four wickets in four balls the next season for Western Suburbs in the Sydney first-grade grand final.

In December, 1973, at Melbourne he made his Test debut against the touring New Zealanders, batting at No. 9, hammering 52 in 69 minutes, and then taking 4-75, opening the bowling with Tony Dell in Australia's innings victory.

He took another four wickets in the next Test at Sydney, in which he opened with Max Walker and then both made way for the Australian selectors to try the opening combination of Alan Hurst and Dymock at Adelaide, Dymock taking 2-44 and 5-58 and Australia again winning by an innings.

Geoff Dymock was born on July 21, 1945, in Maryborough, Queensland, and throughout his career was the kind of cricketing gentleman of whom Gubby Allen would have approved.

A maths teacher, he suffered for many years by being posted to remote areas where Queensland selectors could not see him in action.

He played for Milnrow in the Lancashire League in 1970 and 1971, and also appeared for the Worcestershire Second XI, making his first-class debut for Queensland in 1971-2 at the late age of 26.

After his initial success with the Australia team he found a Test spot hard to come by, because of the performances of Lillee, Thomson, Walker and Gilmour.

But in 1977, contemplating retirement at the age of 32, he earned a trip to England with the Australian team and was only one of four players not signed to World

Series Cricket. The absence of Australia's best pacemen then afforded him the opportunity of showing his skills more frequently in the Test arena.

As Dymock got older he seemed to bowl better, developing an inswinger to go with his natural movement away from the right-handed bat.

Because of the performances by Hogg and Hurst,

On his day Gary Gilmour could be devastating.

136

Dymock struggled to find a permanent place in the Australian team for the 1978-9 series against England and Pakistan.

But he earned a tour to India and Pakistan the next season and performed well, taking 24 wickets in a six-Test series, which served as India's first series win over Australia.

Operating with Hogg at Kanpur, where Australia lost by 153 runs, Dymock took 5-99 and 7-67.

Against England in the post-Packer series of 1979-80, Dymock had arrived as a Test bowler. Rejected by WSC, he was now good enough to partner Lillee and Pascoe taking 17 wickets in three matches at 15 each including 6-34 in the first Test which set up a hat-trick of Australian victories and where only Boycott, who batted through the England innings to make 99 not out, could defy him.

In the same summer, Dymock was the best of Australia's bowlers, taking 11 wickets at 26 against the West Indies, even though Australia lost the series 2-0.

A few weeks before Dymock retired as Queensland's greatest wicket-taker, he scored 101 not out, his only first-class century. Dymock took 309 wickets for Queensland at 27.53 and in 21 Tests took 78 wickets at 26.91.

Although Dymock had played in the shadow of Gary Gilmour early in his career, he was to enjoy greater longevity.

After his initial successes against New Zealand in 1973-4, Gilmour took 5-64 against the Kiwis at Auckland to square the return series in New Zealand that same season.

In England in 1975, he was rarely off the back pages, taking 6-14 in a World Cup semi-final against England, 5-48 in the losing final against the West Indies and hitting 102 in 75 minutes against Sussex with five sixes and two fours off seven consecutive deliveries.

He was finally rewarded with a Test match at Headingley, where he took 6-85 and 3-72 to thumb his nose at the selectors who had waited until the third Test to try him.

In the Australian summer that year, he bowled splendidly against the Windies, swinging the ball around to take 20 wickets at 20, with a best of 5-34 in the last match at Melbourne.

In 1976-7 his decline began. He fractured his right heel but, not wanting to lose his place in the Australian team, he kept bowling and, like Bob Massie a few years earlier, he suddenly lost his ability to swing the ball, an ability he would never really recover.

He scored 101 against New Zealand at Christchurch in February, 1977, but was left at home when the selectors took Geoff Dymock to England in 1977.

He was chosen for World Series Cricket but his heel injury, increasing weight, a dissatisfaction with the increasing professionalism of the game and the loss of the swinging delivery kept him out of the spotlight.

After two years with the Packer troupe he failed to regain a place in the NSW side and drifted back to Newcastle to spend time fishing and to see out his days, like Bill Voce, as a slow bowler.

Michael Holding
(1954-)

Whispering Death

It was often said Michael Holding was so light on his feet that he could run in soft snow and not leave any marks on the ground.

He was so graceful that he earned the nickname of "Whispering Death" because Test umpires often could not hear him approaching as he strode out on a run-up that was one of cricket's most beautiful sights. Many batsmen could not see the ball as it whistled past their ears or crashed into their stumps.

Many times during his career, Holding's deliveries were clocked at above 90 miles an hour (more than 144km/h), but for the Englishmen who faced him at Barbados in 1981 he may have bowled the fastest spell ever in Test cricket.

In one searing over against Geoff Boycott, Holding beat the Yorkshireman for pace five times and then smashed his stumps with his sixth delivery.

Don Mosey, of the British Broadcasting Corporation, remembers Clive Lloyd had deduced early in the series that Boycott could be unsettled by great pace from around the wicket. He instructed Holding, who had assumed Thomson's mantle as the world's fastest bowler, to go flat-out at Boycott from the first ball of the innings.

"No looseners, no sighters, just sheer blinding pace," Mosey recalled. "The result was an over which will long be remembered by everyone who saw it. Players who were with Frank Tyson in Australia in 1954 — men like Len Hutton, Johnny Wardle, Bob Appleyard and Trevor Bailey — have told me that the Typhoon's bowling in Melbourne was the fastest from anyone in the history of the game.

"All one can say is that if it was faster than Michael Holding's at the Bridgetown Oval on March 14, 1981, it is possible to feel a rare sympathy for Australian batsmen."

Holding delivered to Geoff Boycott an over of such scorching ferocity that the greatest defensive batsmen of his day (and many another day) was scarcely able to lay a bat on the ball before his stumps were shattered.

Bowling to Botham, the other player Lloyd believed was capable of swinging the match, Holding had such quiet menace that after the fourth delivery, Botham hurled down his bat, walked away to a sort of short gully position and glared down the pitch, plainly nonplussed by it all.

Boycott was out to Holding in the second innings, this time for one, the West Indies won by 298 runs and took the series 2-0. Holding finished with 17 wickets at 18.52.

Born in Kingston, Jamaica on February 16, 1954, Holding showed such potential as a hurdler, high-jumper and 400m runner at Kingston College that there was talk of him earning an athletics scholarship to the

United States and perhaps emulating Don Quarrie, Jamaica's Olympic gold medallist.

But Holding's father was a former president of Jamaica's Melbourne Cricket Club, and it was as a fast bowler that the youngster really made a name for himself.

At 190 centimetres and with a lithe, wiry frame, he developed his pace from a long, smooth run-up that was all floating strides and a head held regally high.

His approach was too athletic to be called menacing, but his majestic action resulted in terrifying speed, even though most of the time it looked like Holding

was hardly extending himself. As Clayton Goodwin once remarked, if batsmen had the time to appreciate their own predicament against him, they would have been overwhelmed by the beauty of the action which had brought about their own destruction.

Holding first played for Jamaica in the 1972-3 series and as a teenager he bowled Ian Redpath three times in two matches against the touring Australians. He was chosen to tour Australia backing Andy Roberts in 1975-6, but he was nowhere near as accurate as he was fast. He made his Test debut at Brisbane, taking 0-81 and 0-46. In the whole series his 10 Test wickets cost 61 runs each, and at Sydney he showed his immaturity by sitting on the turf and refusing to bowl after an appeal against Ian Chappell was turned down.

It was a rare act of petulance from a speedster who made friends with even those who cowered against him on the field, and, apart from an incident at Dunedin five years later when he kicked down the stumps on a bitter tour of New Zealand, Holding's copybook was gold-star material.

Before long his fast bowling was, too. When he retired after taking 16 cheap wickets in the West Indies' 5-0 defeat of England in 1985-6, Holding had played 60 Tests and captured 249 wickets at 23.68 in a 13-year career that had also seen him opening the attack in a few matches for Lancashire, Derbyshire and Tasmania.

Within a few months of that blooding time in Australia, Holding was being compared to Thomson in terms of pace and to Charles Manson in terms of menace.

Opening the attack with Wayne Daniel, Whispering Death won the home series against India with a violent spell of fast bowling on his home turf, Sabina Park, Kingston, battering the tourists with a display of hostility they had never seen.

Persistent bouncers on an unpredictable pitch devastated the Indians. In the first innings, Vishwanath's hand was broken and Gaekwad was so alarmed at Holding's speed that he began backing away as soon as Holding began his run-up.

Repeatedly struck, Gaekwad was finally put in hospital for two days after being hit in the ear, and Patel retired to have stitches put in his mouth.

Bishen Bedi, protesting against the West Indian tactics, declared the Indian innings closed at 6-306 to protect himself and Chandrasekhar from any finger-breaking the pace battery had in mind.

After hitting 55 with the bat, Holding tore back into the Indians in their second innings, and, after Mohinder Armanath seemed to be steering his side to some sort of recovery at 2-97, three wickets fell without a run being scored. At 5-97, Bedi again declared, five of his team going into the scorebook as absent hurt. Some of them were probably absent through justifiable fear.

LEFT and RIGHT: The lethal Michael Holding

The West Indians needed only 13 runs to wrap up a controversial series 2-1 and Michael Holding with 19 wickets at 20 each had arrived as a rare fast bowling talent.

His reputation would be consolidated when the West Indians visited England in 1976, beginning more than a decade of domination that had its roots in a phalanx of fast men.

On a lifeless wicket at The Oval, Holding gave one of the finest displays of pace bowling seen in England, taking 14 wickets (8-92, 6-57) in a match in which Dennis Amiss, whose head had been slashed by Holding while playing for the MCC at Lords, played one of his finest innings, 203, against phenomenal odds. In the same match Viv Richards cracked 291 and the West Indies took the series 3-0.

Realising there was little assistance in the wicket, Holding merely bowled as fast as he could, straight at the stumps, beating most of his victims with speed through the air. As the first West Indian to take more than 12 wickets in a match, Holding finished the series with 28 wickets at less than 13 runs each.

In the next few years he, like all the Windies quicks, had to share wickets around. But sometimes he could rule a series all by himself, taking 24 wickets at 14 in the drawn three-Test series in Australia in 1981-2. In India in 1983-4 he took 30 wickets, even though Malcolm Marshall had overtaken him as the world's fastest bowler.

Against Australia in 1984-5, when operating often off a short run-up and relegated to the role of supporting Marshall and Garner, he took 6-21 off just 35 deliveries at Perth to set up a series victory. In reply to 416, Australia was all out for 76, its lowest total against the West Indies.

Dennis Lillee, who once described his opposition number as "so gentle and unwarlike", remembered an earlier series when Holding had been bowling to the tough, little West Australian opening bat, Bruce Laird, who was struck two eye-watering blows to the groin.

After the second blow had doubled Laird over in agony and apprehension, Holding sauntered down the wicket to make sure the batsman was still coherent.

When he saw that, despite his voice changing, Laird had set his jaw firmly for a big innings, Holding drawled: "Sorry, Bruce, but have you had any children?"

"Yes, two," answered the little opener, grim-faced.

"That's good," said Holding as he walked away, smiling.

Bob Massie
(1947-)

Miracle At Lords

Bob Massie once told the young cricketers of Australia that the first rule of swing bowling was not to bowl too fast.

"On the 1972-3 West Australian tour of the eastern States I continually found myself so worried about not getting a wicket that I tried to put too much into my bowling," he wrote, "Consequently, I lost my length, line and swing. The wickets didn't come, and by the end of the day's play the scoreboard nearly always told a pretty sorry tale for me. A swing bowler must let the ball do the work for him. Put too much into it, and you're dead."

A few months after he penned those lines, Bob Massie's career was dead too. His rise and fall as a record-breaking pace bowler was one of the most astonishing in cricket.

Within 18 months of cricket's finest debut performance — indeed one of the finest bowling performances in the history of the game — Bob Massie had been dropped from his State team. Frustrated at his inability to swing the ball he tried to bowl too fast.

Massie made his Test debut, opening with Dennis Lillee, at Lords in the second Test against England in 1972. He took 8-84 in the first innings and 8-53 in the second. The English fast bowlers, John Snow and John Price, could only drool with envy.

The "Massiecre" ranks as the finest Test bowling

Bob Massie had one golden series.

140

by an Australian. Only Jim Laker (19) and Sydney Barnes (17) have taken more wickets in a match.

Massie bowled magnificently in conditions that were perfect for swing bowling, with low cloud cover and high humidity. Coming around the wicket, he confounded the English batsmen with his late movement away from the bat, having three victims caught in the first innings and all eight in the second.

His accuracy and swing were helped also by the aggression of Lillee, who took the other four wickets, at the other end as well as the support of the NSW all-rounder, David Colley, who probably never bowled faster.

Massie managed to land quite a few of his fast-medium deliveries on the Lord's Ridge, the sharp rise in the pitch just short of a good length. But most of his wickets came through his ability to make the ball play hide and seek and destroy.

Rumours that the young West Australian used lip salve or sunburn oil to preserve the shine on the ball and keep it swinging were hotly denied, but suggestions by some of the players and the press that Massie would never be able to repeat his success were more than justified. He played just five more times for Australia and disappeared from the big time as dramatically as he had arrived.

Born in the Perth suburb of Subiaco on April 14, 1947, he made his debut for Western Australia in 1965-6 without taking a wicket. In fact, though Massie would take five wickets in an innings on six occasions for Australian teams, he was never able to do it for WA.

Playing in the Scottish League two years before he performed his magic at Lords, Massie had failed to win a contract with Northamptonshire after taking just three wickets in two Second XI games.

But in Australia in the early 1970s he blossomed as a medium-pacer, forming with Lillee what many saw as a combination that might one day rival that of Lindwall and Miller.

Against the Rest Of The World in 1971-2, he took 7-76, including a spell of 6-27 in 11 overs which earned him a trip to England. After Lords, Massie took only seven wickets in the next three Tests as Lillee went on to establish an Australian record in Ashes cricket. Back home, Massie took eight wickets in two Tests against Pakistan to finish his Test career, less than a year after it began.

His inability to take wickets on the tour of the Caribbean, where Max Walker and Jeff Hammond did all the work, was put down to the thin atmosphere in that part of the world. But in reality Massie had lost his rhythm and swing and would find it again only in fleeting moments.

Massie lost his place in the West Australian team in the 1973-4 season and realised his glory days were past him.

Young Dennis Lillee with Bob Massie.

Dennis Lillee
(1949-)

King Of Kings

When Greg Chappell snapped up a slips catch off Larry Gomes at the Melbourne Cricket Ground two days after Christmas in 1981, the band played Waltzing Matilda, the vast crowd stood to salute, and Dennis Lillee brushed a tear from his eye.

The man who had literally broken his back bowling fast for Australia nearly a decade before, had snared his 310th wicket in Test cricket, topping the world record of Lance Gibbs. By the end of the innings he had 7-83, his best Test figures.

Lillee had been a symbol of Australian strength and pluck ever since he had toiled for hours to take the wicket of John Edrich on his debut in Adelaide in 1971. The fact that Lillee had come back from the cricketing dead to rise again with real speed and fire to rival Sydney Barnes as the world's greatest bowler, spoke volumes for his character and determination.

On his own admission, it seemed he and controversy went together like a meat pie and sauce. He was driven by a hatred for batsmen and a loathing for what they could do to him.

During the days when Kerry Packer owned the World Series, Dennis Lillee ushered in a new way of marketing the game.

"It was deemed good television," wrote Patrick Murphy, "to see Lillee endorse a certain product on screen between overs then cut back to the play to see if

Dennis Lillee, arguably the best of all time.

burning eyes and a way of finding out weaknesses even the batsman did not know existed, he would sprint in along that precise, driving, approach over 19 paces, leap high and long and then explode with his classical action. Often he would then wheel around, glaring back at the umpire, daring him not to raise his finger.

Lillee retired from Test cricket when his back had done enough. He was nearly 34, and in 70 Test matches during a career interrupted by a broken back and a stint as one of Packer's World Series Cricket superstars, he took 355 wickets at 23.92.

The most famous Australian cricketer since Don Bradman, Lillee united chanting crowds behind him as though they were at British soccer games spoiling for a fight.

Born on July 18, 1949 in Subiaco, a Perth suburb, on the 101st anniversary of the birth of W. G. Grace, he learned to bowl on his father's front lawn, starting his run-up at the next-door neighbour's place.

Playing for Western Australia against England, Lillee knocked the cap from Geoff Boycott's head with a bouncer and was seen as a way of fighting English fire in the form of John Snow. He made his Test debut, opening with Froggy Thomson, in the sixth Test, at Adelaide, taking 5-84 and showing a determination that sugested he would be around for a while.

In the English summer of 1971, Lillee turned up at the Haslingden club in the Lancashire League, developing his fast bowling and working on his swing and seam bowling. It was there that he hit a young batsman plumb in front for an lbw only to see his rival remain rooted to the spot. Lillee yelled at him to go and pointed toward the dressing room. But the batsman did not move. He could not. His foot was broken. The fieldsmen carried him off.

Back in Australia, Lillee showed he was no longer just a raw tearaway: he had class. Suffering from a viral infection during the match against the Rest Of The World in Perth, Lillee had to be cajoled by Ian Chappell into continuing after he had dismissed Gavaskar and Engineer in the first innings.

Chappell's pleadings bore fruit, and Lillee's last 15 balls yielded six wickets for nought against some of the finest batsmen in the game. The World side was all out for 59, Lillee took another four wickets in the second innings and Australia won by an innings.

Later in the World XI series, Lillee suffered during

he could knock someone's head off. The swaggering, beer-swilling yobs cultivated by Lillee loved it, and in turn he seemed to need mindless adulation to give of his best. As Lillee ran in, bulging-eyed, with thigh muscles pumping, the more moronic sections of the crowd would chant 'Kill, kill, kill'. Without the helmet, that might have been the case."

Bob Willis said that, though he himself would gladly settle on being the back end of the horse in the theatre that is international cricket, Lillee loved being centre stage, playing the melodramatic villain. More often than not he stole the show.

Long-haired, muscular, with a bandit's moustache,

Sobers' 254 at Melbourne. But he learned from the experience, just as he did when Barry Richards, the South African playing for South Australia, hit 325 in a day against WA, prompting the former England spinner, Tony Lock, to nickname Lillee "Fot" (a flippin' old tart).

Lillee rarely suffered against batsmen as his career progressed. Most of his pain came from within.

In the 1972 Ashes series in England Lillee looked a lot like the old Ashes killer, Fred Spofforth, and had, in the words of John Snow, turned into a "cricketing werewolf". Despite the miracles of Bob Massie, Lillee was still England's chief persecutor, with 31 wickets at a little under 18 in a drawn series, his 10 wickets in the fifth Test at The Oval leaving the series at 2-2.

Back in Australia, he bowled fast against Pakistan in a series that saw the erratic debut of Jeff Thomson.

For the third Test Saeed Ahmed, a former Pakistan captain and veteran of 41 Tests, announced he was unavailable for the match because of a bad back. He and Lillee had traded insults at Melbourne, where

Saeed had made 50 and Lillee made it known he was going to settle the score. Saeed was sent home, his Test career finished.

It was Lillee who really had the bad back. In the Caribbean, he broke down on the island of Antigua playing the Leeward Islands with four stress fractures.

The injury would have ruined a lesser cricketer, and many were prepared to write him off. But, under the guidance of Dr Frank Pyke and after spending six weeks in a plaster cast, Lillee began the long and painful journey back to the bowling mark.

In the 1973-4 Australian season, he spent his cricketing weekends as a medium-pacer and batsman in grade cricket, gradually becoming stronger, fitter and faster. He pronounced himself ready to take on the English tourists in 1974-5, and the selectors gambled

---

BELOW: Dennis Lillee, record breaker and crowd hero.

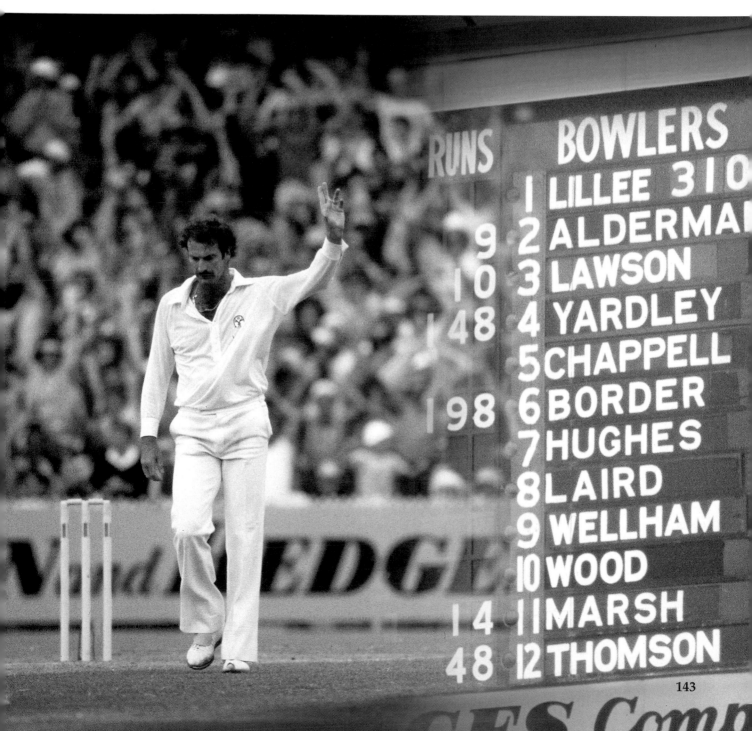

on partnering him and his suspect back with the powerful Thomson, who had done nothing much but send down a lot of fast wides against Pakistan two years before.

After just two Tests, "Lillian Thomson" was the world's most feared fast bowling combination. In the Centenary Test in Melbourne in 1977, Lillee's masterful bowling and 11 wickets allowed Australia to win by 45 runs, the same margin by which it had beaten England 100 years before.

At Perth against England in 1979-80, he came out with an aluminium bat he was trying to market and when the umpires, under siege from English skipper Mike Brearley, prohibited its use, Lillee set a record for throwing such a piece of equipment.

At Perth two years later against Pakistan, Lillee and Aldermen blew the visitors away, Lillee taking 5-18. But Lillee's performance with his boots rather than the ball captured the headlines.

The great bowler seemed to obstruct Javed Miandad as he tried to complete his 30th run. Javed pushed Lillee off balance with his bat and then, when the two argued, Lillee kicked him lightly in the pads. Javed raised his bat, as though to club the fast bowler, and only the intervention of an umpire, Tony Crafter, prevented the incident becoming even uglier.

In England in 1981, Botham's heroics stole the limelight from Lillee and Alderman, who between them shared 81 wickets in the series. Lillee, who had set an Ashes record of 31 in England nine years before, finished with 39 and his best Test figures to that time of 7-89 in the sixth and final Test, at The Oval.

Lillee was Man Of The Match in both the first and last Tests of his final series in England — not bad, considering he had started out with a case of viral pneumonia and a knee injury.

Yet even his monumental efforts were clouded by controversy. In the third Test, in which Botham saved England from an innings defeat and then paved the way for an astonishing victory, Lillee and Marsh both had a small wager on the opposition at 500-1. They won a small fortune despite doing their best for Australia.

Lillee equalled Richie Benaud's Australian bowling record of 248 Test wickets when he dismissed Gavaskar lbw at Melbourne in 1980-1, and again the milestone was clouded in controversy as Gavaskar, disputing the decision, walked off with his fellow opener, Chetan Chauhan.

During his days as Kerry Packer's leading man in World Series Cricket, Lillee picked up 79 wickets of recognised Test players that would have given him 434 Test scalps had the matches been official.

Instead, he retired with 355 Test victims, the same as his inseparable mate, Rod Marsh. Lillee took the wicket of Sarfraz Nawaz with his last delivery in Test cricket to set up a 10-wicket win for Australia over Pakistan at the Sydney Cricket Ground and then he, Marsh and Greg Chappell, who had all started out in the same series, all quit with another win behind them.

Lillee made a comeback bowling for Tasmania, taking the wicket of Andrew Hilditch with his first ball and then went off to play for Northamptonshire.

Len Pascoe
(1950-)

Violence in Motion

It was probably fitting that Len Pascoe's debut as the coach of NSW in 1987 would come as dark storm clouds enveloped the Sydney Cricket Ground. Pascoe was surrounded by tumult throughout his career as one of the most outwardly hostile pace bowlers Australia has produced.

He was the perfect example for any teenage quick with a chip on his broad shoulder. Those who lacked the rhythm and grace of Dennis Lillee or the contortionist's ability to mimic the Jeff Thomson slingshot, imitated Lennie Pascoe.

He was big and mean, and his style was all violence and anger in fast motion. His arms and legs pumped as he pounded towards the crease, his delivery stride began with what could easily have been a rugby league shoulder charge and the slamming down of his front foot and bending of a broad, brawny back finished with a brooding stare that made even the harshest visage of Dennis Lillee seem tepid by comparison.

Leonard Stephen Pascoe was born on February 13, 1950, to Yugoslav parents in Bridgetown, Western Australia, and grew up in the western suburbs of Sydney, changing his surname from Durtanovich. He remembers a teacher trying to show her class of 10-year-olds how to play cricket and ending up sprawled on the ground with the bat knocked from her hands after asking young Leonard to send down his best.

As a high-school tearaway opening with Jeff Thomson, he was inspired to reach for greatness by the deeds of Lillee, the best fast bowler he ever saw. On the field, Pascoe was about as subtle as a stormtrooper, his great pace coming from broad shoulders, a thick, deep chest and a love for seeing stumps fly.

He made his NSW debut against Queensland at Brisbane in 1974-5 and played his first Test in the absence of Dennis Lillee at Lords in 1977, taking five wickets in the match and 13 in the series at 28.

Pascoe spent two years partnering Lillee in World Series Cricket, and when they rejoined the establishment the pair created chaos for a while against India, Pascoe putting their top-scorer in hospital with a bouncer at Sydney.

Pascoe took 16 wickets in three matches at 18.68 in a series Kapil Dev managed to draw for the Indians.

The big man missed the 1981 England tour because of a knee operation, but he returned in 1981-2 to record his best first-class figures, 8-41 against Tasmania at Hobart.

At 31 his days as a top-flight speedster were numbered, but he was still fiery enough to earn a one-match suspension from his NSW team mates for bowling a beamer at Kim Hughes in a match against Western Australia. In 14 Tests Pascoe took 64 wickets at 26.06.

Big Len Pascoe on the rampage.

Sometimes he looked like a big cricketing bully, and occasionally it took a more masterful craftsman to knock him down a peg.

Viv Richards taunted and provoked Lennie at Adelaide in 1979-80 and proceded to paste him for a while when the big man lost his cool. Richards was the master boxer slapping the face of a wild brawler.

But sometimes an enraged Pascoe, goaded by the opposition and the chanting crowds, could land some telling blows of his own.

After a first-innings feud with Ian Chappell, Lennie tore through South Australia in the second innings of their SCG match in February 1980, taking 7-18 and dismissing the visitors for 69. The next season, he took 5-27, including a hat-trick, when NSW visited Adelaide.

Andy Roberts, taciturn and deadly.

Andy Roberts (1951-)

The Rasputin Stare

When Andy Roberts burst upon the English cricket scene bowling fast for Hampshire, he looked unlikely to succeed.

He seemed as tranquil as a lazy day by the Caribbean, and there was no outward fire or devil any fast bowler worth his bouncer requires.

But beneath the shy exterior, the languid eyes, and the bashful smile was a cunning quick man, desperately fast and with enough aggression to make even the most established county heroes shake in their batting boots. At a little under 180 centimetres and, as Dennis Lillee described him, "186 pounds of concrete set in steel", Andy Roberts was a sinewy bowling machine with strength and grit.

But for quite some time many doubted that Roberts could make it. John Snow admits he was skeptical about the quiet man's durability.

"He projects a sense of strain," Snow wrote in the early 1970s. "There is a harshness in his run-up and his actual gather, just before the moment of release, is rough."

But there was a harshness also for every batsmen who ever faced the man responsible for introducing all-out pace into the West Indian attack in the past 15 years.

John Arlott was one man among many surprised that such a gentle character could become such a frightening Mr Hyde when the smell of wickets was in his nostrils.

"He has no such towering physique as Wesley Hall or Charlie Griffith," Arlott wrote, "no such overt aggression as Roy Gilchrist, nor even the muscularity of Learie Constantine or a Manny Martindale. His manner is almost drowsily relaxed, his eyes languid, his voice soft.

"Yet as a bowler he is all cold, penetrating hostility."

There was the catch. The eyes that seemed so serene were capable of a stone-cold-dead Rasputin stare that could, after a savage bouncer or two, make a hard man humble. Beneath the uncomplicated exterior was a fast bowler whose brain ticked over with all the treachery of a master spinner.

Within a few years of his spectacular Test series in India in 1974-5, Roberts was being hailed by Lillee as the finest fast man of his generation.

"He was the most complete fast bowler I have seen," Lillee wrote. "He was fast, damn fast, his line and length were immaculate, and his variation was brilliant. He had inswing, outswing, a magnificent off-cutter and a superb yorker."

Roberts also had a bouncer — two bouncers, the first delivered at full throttle and the second a little slower, to deceive the batsman into playing a false shot and miss-hitting. Sometimes he reversed the order, giving the first bouncer as easy runs and making the batsmen hurry for his life the second time.

The combination was often disastrous for batsmen, among them David Hookes, the cavalier South Australian, whose free scoring was suddenly abated by a broken jaw.

"I believe Andy Roberts was a vital part of the West Indian renaissance in world cricket," Lillee wrote. "He gave them determination. They became mean and tough. I'm convinced Andy had a lot to do with that change in attitude."

Roberts was surprisingly quick. Even when he seemed to be dawdling rather than scurrying to the wicket, his immense strength and suppleness produced deliveries of rare pace.

In Perth during his team's disastrous 1975-6 series, Roberts was feeling poorly but still helped the Windies score their only Test victory that summer with a spell of 7-54 in the second innings.

He took the top seven in the batting order including Alan Turner and Ian Redpath without scoring.

Despite a weakened condition, Roberts' fastest delivery of the match was clocked by electronic means at 93.62 mph (150.67 km/h), and early in his career he rivalled Jeff Thomson as the world's fastest bowler.

Born on January 29, 1951, one of 14 children to a fisherman in Urlings Village on the small island of Antigua, he did not play cricket until he was 16 and, although his parents encouraged him to study as an architect, he played with Viv Richards for the Rising Sun Club and for Antigua. He then journeyed on a scholarship with Richards to Alf Gover's school in London in 1972 to make it as a professional.

He was so quick that after a few weeks with Gover he emerged from obscurity to join Hampshire.

He took 40 wickets in a qualifying season with the Second XI, and in 1974 he played in the county championship on unresponsive wickets but still took 119 wickets to head the English averages.

His arrival and immediate success was welcomed by Hampshire stalwarts, among them Roberts' county team mate, the South African batsman, Barry Richards.

"The arrival of Andy Roberts for his first full season with Hampshire in 1974 made the job of batting outside our home county more tedious than ever," Richards wrote.

"Roberts began that season sensationally. In an early match he tore through Kent's batting line-up — one of the best in cricket — and felled Colin Cowdrey along the way as he destroyed them inside two days.

"The news was out on Roberts before he led us from the field at the end of that match. From then on, Hampshire played away matches on many pitches that were noticeably slower than they were the year before. The host teams were prepared to sacrifice some of their own capability to score runs in order to neutralise or much diminish Roberts's pace and threat."

Roberts made his Test debut against England at Bridgetown in March, 1974, with three expensive wickets. He was the first Antiguan fast bowler to achieve international acclaim, inspiring others from the island, such as Eldine Baptiste and George Ferris, who broke Roland Butcher's jaw.

On the normally unresponsive pitches of India, backed by Vanburn Holder, Keith Boyce and Bernard Julien, Roberts made his first real impression in international cricket, taking 32 wickets at 18 from just five matches, 7-64 and 5-57 at Madras, and then nine wickets in Lahore against Pakistan.

His batting with Derek Murray in the 1975 World Cup against Pakistan saved the West Indies from elimination and allowed them to go on and beat Australia in the final.

Back in England in 1976, he and Michael Holding began their real reign of terror, taking 28 wickets each in the Test series, Roberts skittling 10 batsmen at Lords and twice being denied the hat-trick at Old Trafford.

From the time of his Test debut he raced to 100 wickets in just two years, 144 days; but from the late 1970s he usually had to share his wickets with three other fast men and his personal tally began to suffer.

But at home against India in 1982-3, when there were plenty writing him off at the age of 32, he was the best of the pacemen, taking 24 wickets at 22, his 5-39 at Kingston setting the Windies for a 2-0 series victory.

At tea on the final day, India was 164 ahead with four wickets in hand and the match seemed certain to finish with a draw. But Roberts took three wickets in the first over after tea and finished with four in 20 balls. The home team then made 172 off 26 overs, Viv Richards cracking 61 off 35 balls for a remarkable victory. By 1983-4 Roberts was surrounded by fast bowlers, younger and quicker than he. But he still played in two Tests against India, taking five wickets and at Calcutta hitting 68, his highest Test score.

By then his Test career was finishing and at Leicstershire, where he began playing in 1981 after leaving Hampshire, he was going out as a faithful and deadly servant.

Roberts was a man who will always be remembered for his cricketing deeds rather than for histrionics or scandals. In a craft dominated by explosive extroverts, he was a surprise packet with a fearful bang.

Sarfraz Nawaz (1948-)

Mr Trouble

Sarfraz Nawaz pulled off one of the most amazing escape acts Australian cricket had seen with a spell of superb seam bowling on March 15, 1979, at the Melbourne Cricket Ground.

The Pakistanis had set Australia 382 to win, a tough total on an unpredictable pitch. But, after a century by Allan Border, Australia was cruising at 3-305.

Then Sarfraz, the sometime genial, sometimes stormy, giant with the bandito moustache and stiff wooden-legged run up, gave the performance of his life.

In 33 deliveries he took the last seven wickets for one run, improving his figures from 2-85 to 9-86.

It was an erratic summer for Sarfraz in a two-match series.

He followed his heroic performance at Melbourne with an act in Perth which made many remember him for something other than his great control over line and length.

Run out by the fast bowler, Alan Hurst, when backing up too far, Sarfraz gained revenge of sorts when it came Australia's turn to bat, dismissing Andrew Hilditch for handling the ball after the opening batsman picked it up and

LEFT: The erratic Pakistani Sarfraz Nawaz was capable of some astounding performances with the ball, but is remembered most for an unsporting act in a Test against Austrtalia.

gave it back to the bowler. Sarfraz was always unpredictable.

While playing for Northamptonshire against the touring Australians, he bowled a succession of bouncers at Jeff Thomson, who treated it all as a joke. But Joel Garner could not see the funny side and let Sarfraz have them all back after being fed a spate of short balls in the 1979 Gillette Cup Final.

In the middle of the 1977-8 Test series between Pakistan and England in Pakistan, Sarfraz left the country and headed for England as a protest against his match payments.

Sarfraz made his first-class debut for Lahore in 1967, first played for Pakistan in 1968-9 and joined Northamptonshire later that year.

For 15 years he was a mainstay of the Pakistan team, forming with Imran Khan and Asif Masood a strong fast-bowling attack in the 1970s.

In Australia in 1972-3 the pace bowling attack of Asif Masood and Salim Altaf suffered against the Australian batsmen; but from two Tests Sarfraz took 12 wickets at 25.67.

In 1976-7 he and Imran formed a strong combination against New Zealand, Sarfraz taking 13 wickets at 22 each as his team won 2-0 at home.

After three drawn matches at home against England in 1977-8 the Pakistanis travelled to England for three matches.

Sarfraz was injured in the first two, and Liaquat Ali and Sikhander Bakht could not prevent two innings defeats.

But Sarfraz added the starch to the attack in a match ruined by rain at Headingley. England lost seven wickets for 119 in its only innings, Sarfraz taking 5-39.

At home he and Imran helped Pakistan to a 2-0 win over India with Sarfraz topping the bowling averages, taking 5-70 in a big Pakistan win at Karachi.

Although the 1982-3 series against India belonged to Imran (40 wickets) and to three Pakistan batsmen, Zaheer, Mudassar and Javed, who all scored double-centuries, Sarfraz did his share of the work.

He took 19 wickets at 33, his four-wicket hauls at Lahore, Faisalabad and Hyderabad contributing to Pakistan's dominance in the series.

With Imran injured for the 1983-4 series at home against England, Sarfraz filled in with a pretty good all-round performance of his own.

In three matches he took 14 wickets, his 4-42 at Karachi giving a big help to Pakistan's three wicket win.

In the third Test, at Lahore, Pakistan was still one match up but was in trouble until Sarfraz, with 90, and Zaheer, with 82, came to the rescue.

Controversy was never far away from him, though. In the 1983-4 series against India, Sarfraz was left out of the Pakistan team and claimed it was because he would not go along with plans to draw all three Tests.

After retiring from cricket, he pursued the safer, friendlier world of Pakistani politics. In 1986, he was beaten unconscious by a gang armed with sticks near his home in Lahore after announcing plans to disclose government fraud.

Jeff Thomson
(1950-)

Blood On The Pitch

"Ashes to Ashes. Dust to Dust. If Lillee don't get ya, Thommo must". That slogan became a cricketing catchphrase in that vicious summer of 1974-5.

Don Bradman described the pairing of Lillee and Thomson ("Lillian Thomson", as they became known) as probably "the fastest and most lethal opening pair in Australia's history.

"They possessed remarkable physique, strength and stamina and ability (and may I add within the confines of diplomacy) a willingness to exploit the short-pitched delivery to an extent which would have unnerved any side."

Thomson once described his bowling action to the journalist, Philip Derriman, by saying: "I just shuffle in and go whang."

What a whang the whang was, the fastest whang of all time. Though great fast men of decades past did not have the advantage of sophisticated timing equipment, few of them would ever have approached the 99.7mph (almost 160km/h) Thomson reached in Perth in 1975, a figure recorded in the Guiness Book Of Records as the greatest pace a cricket ball has achieved.

Thomson bowled with a slinging action that owed much to his days as a school javelin champion. Photos of his exaggerated side-on wind-up with his bowling arm disappearing behind his back, hark back to the slingshot action of Tibby Cotter.

Thomson had a slow run-up, almost a gentle jog to the wicket and then one leg would cross the other, the powerful torso would swivel, his right arm would wind out to the small of his back, his left karate chop the sky and then he would uncoil with tremendous thrust and a whoosh of acceleration.

Early in his career he became notorious as a batsman-hater. Before the MCC tour of Australia which catapulted Thomson to fame, indeed infamy, he sat with a Sydney cricket writer, Phil Wilkins, in a portable press box — a Holden car — and gave a controversial interview which he would later play down whenever possible.

Thomson told Wilkins that he enjoyed hitting batsmen more than getting them out, watching them drop rather than seeing the stumps fly.

"It doesn't worry me in the least to see a batsman hurt," Thomson told Wilkins. "In fact, it makes me happy, rolling around screaming and blood on the pitch. The ball hitting his skull was music to my ears."

Yet in his biography, speaking of the time he had flattened the son of a former Test umpire, Reg Lewidge, in a club match with a ball that cannoned into his eye, Thomson said: "It was frightening to see this bloke just screaming and shaking and the pitch splattered

Jeff Thomson burst upon the Test scene like a fireball.

with blood as it poured through his fingers. He was in the intensive-care unit of a hospital for a week. I don't mean to hit (the batsman). I'd rather bowl them out than knock them out."

Though he was deadly quick, Thomson did not go for the overt aggression of a Lillee or a Trueman. He rarely spoke to batsmen.

Lillee described Thomson's stock ball as an over-pitched bouncer. He was fast enough to bruise breast-bones simply by slinging the ball in just short of a length.

"Anyone who said they enjoyed facing him was tampering quite outrageously with the truth," Lillee wrote.

"Jeff was the only Australian fast bowler to whom I ever happily played second fiddle. At his peak he was the most explosive, lethal, and unplayable bowler I have seen. His ball pitched just short of a length would rear so sharply that the lofty Adam's apple of beanpole Tony Greig was in constant danger."

Thommo was so unpredictable that he often had no idea where the ball was going to pitch. He just bowled it as fast as he could and hoped for the best. If he did not know where it was going to land what chance the palpitating man with the bat at the other end who, at Thomson's speed, had less than half a second to sight the ball, decide upon a stroke and play his shot?

Against the Englishmen on their terrifying journey south in 1974-5, he sent many complexions a whiter shade of pale.

Greig was one of Thomson's favorite targets. Thomson loved bowling yorkers at the big English all-

rounder. He called the delivery his sandshoe crusher, and it seemed tailormade for Greig because of his unusually high backlift and the fact he preferred wearing sandshoes to boots while batting.

Born in Sydney on August 16, 1950, Thommo grew up in the city's western suburbs. His father, Ron, had been a pretty good cricketer for the inner-city New-town club but had to give the game away because of a growing family and no money.

His son became a tearaway in the backyard, for his club side, the Padstow Pirates, and at the Condell Park Primary School. There he sometimes played against another local kid, Lenny Durtanovich (later Lenny Pascoe), with whom he would open the bowling for the Punchbowl Boys High School — and years later for Australia.

Thomson was chosen to play for the Australian schoolboys on a tour of the West Indies, but his parents could not afford the air fare so he stayed home.

He began his career proper as a teenage tornado bowling with Pascoe for the Bankstown club.

He was chosen on speed alone for the NSW team in 1972-3 and at the time stood 182 centimetres and weighed 86 kilograms.

He made his Australian debut that year, opening the Test attack with Dennis Lillee against Pakistan at Melbourne in the second Test, coming into the team with another debutant, Max Walker, after the swing king Bob Massie had been dropped

Thomson played with a broken bone in his foot but was so determined to fight his way out of the humble circumstances in which he was born that he told no-one, hoping he could still get wickets. He got none for 110.

He was dropped from the NSW team, and there was talk of his moving to South Australia to try to revive his career.

Instead, after seven matches for NSW he moved to Queensland, where for many years he tried to help the Bananabenders win their first Sheffield Shield without success.

In the summer of 1974-5, he was still regarded as a dangerously quick but erratic paceman; and his selection again to open the Australian bowling with Lillee, this time against England, was considered a big gamble.

Thommo finished the series with 33 wickets (at 17.93) even though he tore fibres playing tennis and could not bowl in the second innings of the fifth Test or in any of the sixth.

David Frith remembers the havoc Australia's terrible twosome caused that season: "Dennis Amiss and John Edrich suffered broken hands in the First Test, Thomson damaged Luckhurst's knuckle and hit David Lloyd a cruel blow in the pit of the stomach, Lloyd's finger was split and Titmus was almost maimed by a ball from Thomson which cannoned into his knee, Underwood was hit resoundingly in the ribs by Lillee, who also bowled a beamer at Willis and was cautioned by the umpire after two withering bumpers at Amiss, Fletcher headed an unplayable ball from Thomson to cover point and John Edrich, dropping earthward from his first ball from Lillee, suffered broken ribs in the fourth Test, which gave Australia the Ashes."

Thomson's pace was reduced slightly in England in 1975 but he still took 16 at 28.

On the harder, faster wickets in Australia for the 1975-6 series against the West Indians, he was again the most successful bowler in the series with 29 wickets.

After colliding with Alan Turner while trying for a catch against Pakistan, he dislocated his shoulder, missed the Centenary Test and became embroiled in court battles to join his mates in World Series Cricket.

He toured England in 1977, played at home against India and toured the West Indies in 1977-8 where he produced some of the fastest bowling of his career in taking a vain 6-77 at Bridgetown.

He drifted in and out of the Australian team as the old fire drained away and, after being left out of the 1981 Australian team to England, he had a season with Middlesex instead, putting the Australian opener, Graeme Wood, in hospital.

After becoming merely an occasional member of the Australian attack, he retired from Test cricket after taking his 200th scalp on the 1985 tour of England when many of Australia's pacemen had elected to tour South Africa.

Thomson's best career figures of 7-27, including a hat-trick, came in the 1984-5 season for Queensland against Western Australia, when he and Carl Rackemann came within a wicket of giving the Sunshine State its first Sheffield Shield

In retirement Thomson opted for a simple life with his wife and family. He became a landscape gardener.

The hard-working, ever-genial Max Walker.

Max Walker
(1948-)

Tangles

Max Walker's amiable grin and quick wit made him hundreds of friends, the hero of the Melbourne Cricket Ground and in sporting retirement, a millionaire media megastar.

There were better Test bowlers than Max Walker but, though some could take more wickets, few had the ability to bowl people over the way Big Max could. He turned a broad smile and a hearty laugh into a small fortune as a public speaker, author and sporting commentator.

He was an ungainly fast-medium bowler who, in the words of the Australian cricket writer Dick Tucker delivered the ball off a 13-pace run as you would expect the three-legged Rolf Harris character Jake "The Peg", would do.

He was known as Tangles on the field because his body was a veritable mess of limbs which, when it uncoiled produced deliveries of pace, accuracy, swing and results. In 34 Tests he took 138 wickets at 27.48, even though he often did not get the new ball, because of the presence of Lillee and Thomson.

Trained as an architect, Walker also had some future as an Australian rules footballer but found that cricket was to supersede both as a livelihood and a life.

He became the anchorman of a national sports programme, a popular author and the good-natured star of witty television commercials.

Walker was the ever-smiling hero of a cricket team known for the hostility of Lillee, Thomson, Marsh and Chappell; and, though he was always a fighter, there was the touch, as one writer put it, of the frisky draught horse about him "aided by a face with a distinctly equine cut".

Maxwell Henry Norman Walker was born on September 12, 1948, in West Hobart, Tasmania. He moved to Melbourne to play football and study architecture, eventually playing as a ruckman for the Melbourne club.

At 190 centimetres and heavily built, he developed into a medium-pacer of nagging accuracy but almost laughable action, crossing his feet in delivery and, in his own words, bowling with a chest-on action that was basically "right arm over left earhole".

Yet he was good enough to make his debut for Victoria in 1968-9, and he achieved such fine results that in 1972-3 he made his Test debut against Pakistan along with a raw speed bowler from NSW named Jeff Thomson.

Walker had much more success than his quicker team mate, taking five wickets in his first match for Australia.

In the next, the third Test, at Sydney, with Lillee struggling from a back injury and Massie struggling with a loss of form, Walker took 6-15 off 16 overs, including a spell of 5-3 off 30 balls.

His clumsy action got results with big inswingers and brisk leg-cutters and he earned a trip to the West Indies. When Lillee's back injury caused a complete breakdown and Massie forgot how to swing the ball, Walker became the backbone of Australian fast bowl-

ing and, with the support of the South Australian, Jeff Hammond, he took 26 wickets at 21 each.

Australia won the series 2-0. After recovering from a groin strain that troubled him in two series against New Zealand, Walker demonstrated his great heart and stamina with figures of 8-143 against Denness, Fletcher, Greig and Edrich in the sixth Test of the 1974-5 series against England.

Thomson was injured, and Lillee started hobbling after just six overs. Australia lost by an innings — its only defeat of a 4-1 series — but Walker emerged as a great supporting player to Australia's big quicks, with 23 wickets at just under 30.

Surrounded by Lillee and Thomson and in the later matches by Gary Gilmour, Walker had a good tour of England when Australia retained the Ashes in 1975 with 14 wickets at 34, and his 5-48 at Edgbaston helped decide the Ashes.

Tangles took five wickets opening with Lillee in the Centenary Test, and later that year he played his final series for Australia on the 1977 tour of England, taking 14 wickets at 39 as Thomson, Pascoe and the young Mick Malone stole much of the attention.

Two years with World Series Cricket taught him the value of marketing and personality and, when the hero of the MCG's Bay 13 finally retired from the Victorian team in 1981-2, he began to make a great deal more out of the game than he did when he was playing.

Bob Willis
(1949-)

Unlikely Looking Hero

Bob Willis was always amazed at his ability to bowl, not only fast, but with durability.

His bowling was full of flaws and defects. On his own admission, he was the original, tall gawky man with all the grace of a camel. He was a pessimist with an inferiority complex about an action that was too chest-on, a clumsy run-up and unimpressive physique supported by a pair of wobbly knees.

Yet Robert George Dylan Willis survived the rigours of 90 Test matches, became England's captain and one of its greatest fast bowlers, taking even more wickets than the man with everything going for him, Fiery Freddie Trueman.

"I suppose the first reason is vital — luck," Willis once wrote. "Lucky with the quality of advice I have received, lucky with the skilled surgery that has saved my career and, above all, very fortunate that I could bowl fast naturally."

He was also prepared to work hard, especially in the later stages of his career.

"I discovered the home truths about training and fitness," he said, "when Tony Greig gave me a lecture at a barbecue in Sydney following the Centenary Test

LEFT: Bob Willis, tall, mean and express-paced, was a tower of strength for England.

which England lost by a narrow margin. He said if I'd been properly trained England would have triumphed. I was 28 and revolutionised my attitude toward training."

Willis has always been an advocate of coaches leaving fast bowlers alone. He has always found it remarkable that he became a genuine speedster in a country where speed is all too often coached out of youngsters, sacrificed for line and length; where medium pace is encouraged; and where medium pace is all most bowlers need on deteriorating wickets.

Willis claimed once that he did not become mentally strong for cricket until he had been playing the first-class game for 10 years. He was an insomniac and even needed hypnotherapy to perform.

Standing 195 centimetres with a shock of reddish hair, he made his debut for Surrey in 1969 and two years later joined Warwickshire because the presence of the established bowlers, Robin Jackman and Geoff Arnold, at Surrey made for limited opportunities. In 1972, he helped Warwickshire to its first county championship in 21 years, taking 8-44, including the hat-trick, against Derbyshire.

Early in his first-class career, the Surrey coach, Arthur McIntyre tried to improve Willis's technique, and believed he could turn the windmilling youngster into a fast man with a textbook action. But Willis's first ball with his new style crashed into the side of the net and his confidence was shattered for weeks.

John Edrich convinced Willis to stay with the style that suited him best, no matter how many spectators chuckled or how many critics cringed. It was the wickets in the book that mattered most.

Two years later, Edrich also had a long talk to Ray Illingworth, convincing the English captain to fly the youngster to Australia as a replacement for the injured Alan Ward in the Test series John Snow was winning.

Willis played four Tests, took 12 wickets and began a long and rewarding association with the England Test team.

Willis was England's most aggressive bowler against the West Indians at home and on tour in 1973 and 1974, and in the losing Ashes series he was England's fastest bowler.

But after that series, in which he took 17 wickets at 31, he returned to England for knee operations and many thought he would go the same way as the injury-prone Alan Ward.

Willis missed the home series against Australia that year, but he returned as quick as ever, slamming the ball down from a height of about 2.5 metres and bowling fast in two Tests against the West Indies at home before taking 20 wickets at a little under 17 on the normally dead wickets of India.

At Bangalore, where Bedi and Chandrasekhar spun India to victory, Wills took 6-53; and at Calcutta his 5-27 helped England to a 10-wicket victory.

By 1977, Willis was in peak form. He took his best first-class figures of 8-32 for Warwickshire against Gloucestershire at Bristol, and against the touring Australians he took 27 wickets at under-20 each, including 7-78 at Lords. He followed up his great work

with good showings against Pakistan, New Zealand, Australia and India.

After a disappointing series in Australia in the summer of 1979-80, he valiantly tried to fight fire with fire against the 1980 West Indian tourists; but backed by Botham, Old, Hendrick, Lever and Dilley throughout the series, his pace was not enough to turn the tide.

Despite more knee surgery and an early return from the West Indies in 1980-81, Willis kept his greatest performance reserved for Kim Hughes' Australians in a match in which Ian Botham set the Australians up and Willis made them come tumbling down.

Botham's majestic 149 as England struggled against an innings defeat at Headingley in 1981 allowed the home team a slender lead of 129, which the Australians seemed more than likely to catch without great distress.

They were cruising at 1-56, and Willis was looking like a spent force.

"It was the biggest crisis of my career," Willis would later recall. "Because of the flu, I had not bowled terribly well in the previous Test at Lords and was not originally selected for Leeds."

But Willis had managed to convince the chief selector, Alec Bedser, that he was fit enough after a bad cold to play at Headingley and was virtually given one last chance. He took 0-72 in the first innings on a pitch where Botham bagged six.

"I knew I would have to pull out something special from the bag in the second innings," Willis said, "Thanks to the brilliance of Botham, we at least set Australia a target of 130."

Even though Willis was the oldest man in the England team, he was still its fastest bowler. But Mike Brearley chose to open the attack without him.

"My pride was hurt and, with Australia at 1-56, it looked like we would all be downcast in a couple of hours."

Willis, who came on as second change and had dropped in a number of no balls, told Brearley he could not bowl as he wanted to charging uphill and into the wind and pleaded for a shot at the Kirkstall Lane end.

On a pitch that was becoming more and more unreliable, Willis got his way and his wickets. Aiming at cracks in the pitch just short of a length, he sent them down in one of the truly inspired spells of Test bowling.

Throughout his career his success had been based more on hard work than technique, and against the Australians his ability to fight adversity was never more evident.

Willis finished with 8-43 off 15.1 overs; Australia lost its last nine wickets for 55 and lost one of the most thrilling Test matches by 18 runs.

For all his match-winning performances, though Willis never once took 10 wickets in a Test match, his best figures being 9-92, which brought up his 300 Test wickets in England's first loss on home soil to New Zealand in 1983. Despite defeat at Headingley, England still won the series 3-1 thanks to 20 Willis wickets at fewer than 14 each.

England lost the return series to the Kiwis, and Willis bowed out of Test cricket after a disappointing series against the West Indies at home in 1984.

Tony Greig
Rates The Bowlers

Of all the fast bowlers I have faced, three stand out on their own.

They are, in jungle parlance, Dennis Lillee the lion; Andy Roberts the leopard; and Michael Holding the cheetah. Here are my assessments of them.

Outright, sustained aggression was Dennis Lillee's greatest attribute and, if that aggressive streak embraced both his physical and verbal efforts, it only served to underline his outstanding prowess.

The state of the wicket rarely hampered Lillee as he had the unique ability to adjust to it as necessary. Normally he was very fast and could maintain his pace for much longer than most, especially if he felt he was on top of the batsmen.

However, I saw him once when he had given his all with pace. He then proceeded to bowl leg-cutters on the flattest of flat Adelaide wickets and bowled them superbly.

Lillee had an agressive run-up and the priceless ability to make the ball leave the bat in the air. These, combined with sheer pace; outright aggression; superb control; a never-say-die attitude; and ongoing, shrewd thinking made him the all-powerful lion of fast bowlers in my book.

Like Lillee, Andy Roberts was extremely fast, but, in addition, he was quite cunning and could be dangerously vicious at times. Roberts showed little or no emotion and, as he rarely uttered a word, gave one the impression of being surly.

He was also able to bowl long spells at blistering speed and was a superb exponent of the subtle change of pace which he used to good effect to stalk and kill his prey.

He would, for example, bowl a slow bouncer to an exponent of the hook shot and immediately follow this with another bouncer at maximum pace and perfectly disguised. David Hookes' broken jaw was one witness to this ploy.

Roberts had a lovely economical approach and also had the ability to swing the ball away in the air. One also felt he always had something extra up his sleeve and I would rate him as the scheming, cunning leopard of the fast men.

Holding was the fastest bowler I played against. While he was unable to sustain his full pace for long spells, he did, however, use it with tremendous effect. He had a quite magnificent approach and his success lay more in hitting the seam than swinging the ball.

A cool, calm customer normally, Holding also had that mean streak common to all great fast bowlers. However, he was always in full control of himself and a good thinker. Sheer, blistering pace was his hallmark and he could be described as the lightning fast cheetah of the quicks.

The most-promising new pace bowler, Pakistan's Wasim Akram.

THE 1980s

A New Breed Charges In

"This young man is G-R-E-A-T. He's the best bowler I've seen for years. I love him." So said Rodney Marsh of Pakistan's then 24-year-old, Wasim Akram, that most vicious of rarities, the left-arm fast bowler. Akram had just taken 11 wickets against Australia at Melbourne, frequently hitting arms, helmets, gloves and stumps, coming around or over the wicket and generating remarkable pace from a whippy action that showed little back but plenty of shoulder.

Australia may have had one of the strongest batting line-ups in the world, but even the century-maker, Mark Taylor, was never really comfortable against Akram, saying after the Test that he was a better bowler than any West Indian he had faced and awfully hard to sight, the ball swinging so late.

As Imran Khan topped Dennis Lillee's 355 Test wickets, Wasim Akram had become the most feared bowler from a side that once found it tough fielding decent pacemen.

With Patrick Patterson, Akram formed a Lancashire opening line-up that could have made Viv Richards, who once said he'd rather face fast bowling than the doctor's needle, wish he were a pin cushion.

Richards, of course, was well used to Balfour Patrick Patterson, an immense Jamaican.

Patterson became a regular at Lancashire in 1985 on the recommendation of Clive Lloyd and, though Malcolm Marshall was deemed the world's fastest bowler in the 1980s, Lloyd claimed after the Jamaican Test against Gower's 1985-6 English tourists, that Patterson was perhaps "a yard and a half" quicker than the little Barbadian.

Like Jeff Thomson, Patterson sprayed the ball around in his quest for speed and, with an array of West Indian quicks, notably Marshall, Garner and Holding, all fast and accurate, the Englishmen had no chance. Mike Gatting had to return home with a fractured nose.

Don Mosey wrote that whether the West Indian barrage of speed was "cricket" in the old-fashioned sense or not, it was difficult to imagine any country not using such a potent weapon if it had the chance.

"Equally, it is difficult to criticise batsmen with the technique, grace and charm of England's top six of being unable to cope with 120 feet per second deliveries on some pitches where a ball was just as liable to rear at the throat as shoot around the ankles."

The Welshman, Greg Thomas, bowled fast in the West Indies but was outgunned by a side that boasted many men quicker. Throughout the 1980s fast bowling was the West Indian domain. They uncovered quick bowlers to fill generations of Test teams.

Another Barbadian, Milton Small, took a wicket with his first delivery in first-class cricket in January, 1984, and before the decade was out Tony Gray, Winston Benjamin, Winston Davis, Eldine Baptiste, Ian Bishop, Curtly Ambrose, Patterson and Courtney Walsh had all emerged to distinguish themselves as international fast men.

Some batsmen defied them. In 1982-3, Mohinder Armanath proved to be one of the world's best players against pace, scoring 598 runs in five Tests against Roberts, Marshall, Holding and Garner. Against that line-up India won the World Cup in 1983 using Kapil Dev, Sandhu, Roger Binny, Madan Lal and Armanath for varying degrees of fast and medium-pace bowling. But the next season in India, Armanath's reputation was smashed to pieces at home when he made one run in six innings against the Windies for the series average of 0.16.

The second Test of the 1980-1 tour, at Georgetown, was cancelled because England had chosen a seamer, Robin Jackman, who was married to a South African and had played there for 11 years. Jackman had been flown to the Caribbean after the breakdown of Bob Willis, and the cancellation of the Test was at least some respite for the beleaguered British batsmen.

Malcolm Marshall always seemed the most threatening of the Windies, putting Andy Lloyd out of the game in 1984, but at Old Trafford on that same England tour Paul Terry's arm was broken by Winston Davis, whom Wisden described as being built like an elongated stick of rhubarb.

LEFT: Patrick Patterson. ABOVE: Swervin' Merv Hughes.

Davis's finest performance in international cricket came in the one-day arena.

His 7-51 against Australia at Headingley in 1983 is still a world one-day record.

The Englishmen tried all kinds of pace variations against the West Indies, using Bob Willis, Ian Botham, Paul Allott, Derek Pringle, Norman Cowans and Jonathon Agnew. But nothing worked.

Eldine Baptiste was a valuable member of that touring team, and, though not as sharp as others in the side, his value as a fourth seamer was never underestimated. Nor was that of the lanky Jamaican, Courtney Walsh, who first toured Australia in 1984-5 supporting Marshall, Garner and Holding. Walsh was back in Australia in 1988-9 to take a broken hat-trick in

Brisbane, a feat later repeated by the favourite of Melbourne's Bay 13, Swervin' Mervyn Hughes.

The big Victorian, whom advertising agencies and headline writers loved to portray as a genuine, captain-kissing walrus-whiskered ocker hero, became the most talked-about character in a team of Ashes champions.

Though his 19 wickets in England in 1989 did not swing the series Australia's way in the manner of Terry Alderman's haul, Big Merv's contribution to Allan Border's triumph was remarkable for a bowler with his share of critics. Like Botham, Hughes has never been afraid to experiment, and against the West Indians he was never worried about pitching short and showing them what it felt like to be scalded by pace in a Test match. Just as easily he could send down a slow leg-break to trap the unwary. To many Australian fans, Hughes should have been joined on the history-breaking Ashes tour by the left-armer, Mike Whitney, who devastated the West Indies on a batsman's wicket in Adelaide.

David Hookes described his omission as being like dropping a batsman after he had scored a double century.

Whitney, one of the most popular of Australian cricketers, first played a Test in England in 1981, when he was with Gloucestershire and the tourists had an epidemic of injuries. The Australians wanted Carl Rackemann, in England on an Esso scholarship, but he was injured too.

A blond behemoth, Rackemann is a farmer's son from central Queensland with a crude, twisting action that put great strain on his powerful body. But he was still strong enough to bowl 30 overs in the Sheffield Shield final of 1984-5, when he and Jeff Thomson almost brought the trophy back to Brisbane.

Two of Rackemann's partners on the South Africa rebel tour in the mid 1980s were the Victorian strongman Rod McCurdy and the Queensland medium-pacer John Maguire a man of great stamina who toured the West Indies with Rackemann in 1983-4.

Richard Hadlee dominated the New Zealand attack in the 1980s even more than he had done in the 1970s. He was the best bowler in England on the 1983 Kiwi tour, but it was Lance Cairns, with 7-74, who bowled New Zealand to their first Test victory on English soil.

The very-much-alive Ewen Chatfield then managed 10 wickets at Port of Spain two years later. As the two medium-pacers began to dwell upon retirement and their 100 Test wickets, New Zealand uncovered more pace bowling talent in the likes of Danny Morrison, Derek Stirling and Martin Snedden.

When England visited New Zealand in 1983-4, Cairns and Hadlee helped the Kiwis win their first series against an English team that called in Tony Pigott, of Sussex, after injuries to Graham Dilley and Neil Foster.

England searched for a pace spearhead like Tyson or Snow when Bob Willis began to show signs of wear, tear and 300-plus Test wickets early in the 1980s. Dilley, its fastest bowler, spent much of the decade helping Neil Foster keep back surgeons in BMWs.

Norman Cowans could be quick on his day, and he played 19 Tests between 1982 and 1985 generating his pace from a gloriously athletic approach.

David "Syd" Lawrence, another hulking black Briton who looks like the heavyweight boxer

Injuries curbed Craig McDermott's effectiveness.

Frank Bruno, and might have made a top rugby league player, looked promising with 84 first-class wickets from a shortened, more purposeful run in 1988. But he had his share of problems, too.

Because of injuries, Gladstone Small played in only the final Test of the 1989 Ashes series, after distinguishing himself in Australia in 1986-7 as a fast-medium specialist.

Despite being born with virtually no neck, he can generate good pace off an economical run and model action.

The English batsmen never came to terms with an Australian pace attack led by Alderman, Lawson, Hughes and the Tasmanian debutant, Greg Campbell. Throughout the series England tried to turn things around using its own quicks, such as Foster, the fading Botham, Angus Fraser, Derek Pringle, Phil DeFreitas and Devon Malcolm.

Despite their reputations, none of them could swing the series England's way as Richard Ellison had done four years earlier with his often unplayable movement, taking 6-77 at Edgbaston and 5-45 at The Oval.

Australia had plenty of fast bowlers to choose

from in the 1980s. One of its best discoveries was the slim, tall West Australian, Bruce Reid, who could make the ball swing and lift from a good length. After 62 wickets from 18 Tests, his back gave out and several operations still could not put him into a team that had developed a great fast-bowling base in his absence.

Craig McDermott made his debut for Australia against the West Indies as a 19-year-old and the muscular red-head bowled with real fire in England in 85. But, after 80 Test wickets in 24 appearances, he too suffered injuries and patchy form.

Chris Matthews, who forms a deadly combination with another left-arm fast bowler, Peter Capes, skittled Pakistan bowling for Western Australia but was sadly wayward when called upon earlier to bowl for his country. Dave Gilbert, tall and slender, could generate surprising pace off an easy run-up with a whippy action and had a Sheffield Shield hat-trick.

Simon O'Donnell survived a bout with cancer to re-emerge as Victorian leader and pace-bowling, big-hitting hero of floodlit cricket. O'Donnell graduated to the Test arena.

India, Pakistan and Sri Lanka all developed as fast-bowling nations during the 1980s, if not necessarily shifting the balance from the great bulk of the Caribbean then at least displaying some potential for revenge in years to come.

At 18, Chetan Sharma, of India, took a wicket with his fifth ball in Tests against Pakistan with his reliable medium-pacers and then 18 wickets against an England side in 1986. Later Manoj Prabhakar would partner Kapil Dev.

Azeem Hafeez performed well on Pakistan tours of Australia, India and New Zealand, bowling fast-medium with a claw-like hand and forming a dangerous combination with Wasim Akram, who also partnered Saleem Jaffer to good effect.

In Australia in 1990, youngsters Aaqib Javed and Waqar Younus were emerging as the future supports to Akram.

The Sri Lankans may not yet have found a man of Patterson or Akram's pace, but even the West Indians had to start somewhere. In Australia they were well served by a trio who could swing and cut the ball as well as anyone — Ravi Ratnayeke, Rumesh Ratnayake and Graeme Labrooy.

One of the great tragedies of modern cricket is that one of the finest fast bowlers of the preceding two decades never made it to the Test arena. Clive Rice, a magnificent all-rounder from Johannesburg, bowled medium-fast in the manner of Richard Hadlee, with whom he opened for Nottinghamshire.

Rice spent 13 seasons at Notts after joining in 1975, taking it to two county championships.

Gangling Bruce Reid battled a back injury.

Terry Alderman, cornerstone of the '89 Ashes victory.

Terry Alderman
(1956-)

The Swinger

In two Ashes series, Terry Alderman took a phenomenal 83 English wickets to prove himself one of the finest exponents of fast-medium bowling to ply the trade in the home of cricket.

Between his first history-making series and his second, he survived a broken collarbone that threatened to end his career and endured a three-year ban for playing in South Africa. He emerged eight years later as the cornerstone of Allan Border's 4-0 series win to take home The Ashes in 1989.

Alderman, originally a schoolteacher from Perth, set a record of 42 English wickets in 1981 and and was thwarted only by bad light from passing that figure eight years later.

On his first tour of England he had been something

of a surprise choice, originally chosen only to do all the hard work in the county games. By the time of his second tour, he was a veteran around whom were a myriad of doubts.

His 1981 record was overshadowed only because Ian Botham chose to redeem himself so lustily after surrendering the English captaincy. In 1989 it was a different story. Botham was a tired and hurting medium-pacer who, like all the other English tenpins, seemed awestruck by Alderman's ability to conjure seam, swing and sustained accuracy.

From the time Alderman picked up his first Test wicket, that of Geoffrey Boycott, outmanouvred by an away-swinger, he has been a joy to behold on English wickets. Even with the performances of such talent as Mark Taylor, Steve Waugh and Dean Jones in England, it was Terry Alderman who more than anyone else won The Ashes back for Australia.

Alderman's 42-wicket performance in his debut series had seemed untoppable, considering it came just two years after Rodney Hogg had taken 41 wickets in his debut in Australia. But had the remaining 26 overs been bowled in the sixth and final Test of the 1989

magnificent slip fieldsman and mediocre bat, was born in Perth on June 12, 1956.

From a cricketing family where even his sister, Denise, played for Australia, Alderman was a star schoolboy with a dreaded outswinger, and at 18 made his debut for Western Australia against NSW in Sydney at the start of the 1974-5 season.

At one stage Alderman had 3-0, and he finished the innings with 5-65. But he broke down in the second innings with a hamstring injury that signalled years of breakdowns and career stalls to come.

He had some remarkable performances for WA, but Alderman was often dropped and then recalled to the State team and sometimes even found his first-grade spot with Subiaco-Floreat under threat.

He idolised Dennis Lillee and early in his career had visions of being a hostile Test speedster like him. Yet it was Lillee who convinced him to concentrate on becoming Australia's most astute and penetrative seam-and-swing exponent.

Alderman had a stint in 1980 as a professional in Scotland and returned to Perth more wily, wise and determined. After fine performances for WA against NSW and Queensland in Perth, Alderman earned his place with the 1981 Ashes tourists under Kim Hughes.

Just as in 1989, Alderman did almost all his bowling in the Test matches where opening with Lillee, and, heeding the great man's advice to hit the seam rather than rely on swing, Alderman set a bowling record for Australians against the old enemy, his 42 wickets costing 21 each.

Botham was the man of the series, but Alderman was named as one of Wisden's Five Cricketers Of The Year and was described by cricket's bible as "a seam bowler of the highest quality".

When the Englishmen toured Australia in the summer of 1982-3, Alderman faced the first serious crisis of his Test career.

A group of about 40 English fans waving Union Jacks and encouraged by amber refreshments and the aggressive marketing cricket underwent in the 1980s, invaded the WACA ground, Perth. Bob Willis had just pushed the English total past 400, and part of one supporter's congratulatory message for the giant speedster was to hit Alderman on the back of the head. The swing king chased his attacker and brought him down in a thrashing heap with a rugby league tackle that went terribly wrong, dislocating Alderman's shoulder.

Alderman was carried from the field on a stretcher, and 30 arrests were made. The match ended in a draw because of England's slow scoring, and Australia won back The Ashes 2-1.

There was little joy for a man eager to prove his form on Australian wickets. Alderman took no further part in the series and, though he was chosen to tour the West Indies, he was bowling with a lower arm than before his assault. His four wickets in three Tests in the Caribbean cost an alarming 92 runs each.

Alderman struggled from then for a place in the Australian team. Against the West Indies in Australia in 1984-5, he took 6-128 on his beloved WACA ground in the first Test, but he was replaced by Craig McDer-

series, at The Oval, Alderman would almost certainly have passed the mark.

Throughout that English summer, Alderman had exposed flaws in the technique of the leaden English batsmen, capitalising on their suicidal tactic of playing against the line of the ball that started moving away and them seamed back in. Nineteen of his 41 dismissals were lbw. Alderman simply pinned the batsmen down, delivered the ball from close to the stumps and never wavered in his accuracy.

Eventually, even Graham Gooch, who would be given the English captaincy after a disastrous series, was so numbed by Alderman's bowling that he asked to be dropped from the team.

Terry Alderman was an overnight sensation when he took 9-130 in his debut Test, at Trent Bridge, where Australia won by four wickets in a series that was to swing sensationally to the side of England and its beefy anchor, Botham.

He may have been an instant hero to the masses, but Alderman had become an "overnight hit" after years and years of hard work and frustration.

Alderman, a little under 188 centimetres, wiry, a

mott after three matches. With much of the lustre seemingly gone from his bowling, he joined a Kim Hughes tour again, this time on the rebel circuit of South Africa for the 1985-6 and 1986-7 seasons, filling in between tours with some fine bowling for Kent in the English county championships, taking 8-46 against Derbyshire in 1986.

In two seasons with the county and then another with Gloucestershire, Alderman primed himself for another shot at Ashes glory, not knowing whether he would ever get the chance to bowl for Australia again.

He held very real fears that his tours in South Africa would be the end of his Test career, but he bowled well for WA in the 1987-8 series and laid his claims to a spot in the Australian team again.

In the 1988-9 series against the Windies, Alderman was left out of the first Test at Brisbane and, more importantly, for the second on the WACA strip, where fast bowlers like McKenzie and Lillee basked long before him.

The fast bowling cupboard in Australia was bare, but it looked as though Alderman's fears of being held in perpetual limbo might prove true. Bruce Reid was injured, Chris Matthews was bowling disastrously, Geoff Lawson's jaw was fractured, and Tony Dodemaide's deliveries no longer had teeth.

Alderman was given a chance in the one-day internationals and then the third Test, in which he took seven wickets.

In England in 1989, there was no Ian Botham of old to ruin his work.

Alderman took 10 wickets in the first Test, at Headingley; nine in the second, at Lord's; three in the rain-wrecked third, at Edgbaston; five in the fourth, at Old Trafford; seven in the fifth, at Trent Bridge; and seven again at The Oval.

His best Test figures are 6-128, taken against the Windies at Perth in 1984-5 and against England at Lords in 1989.

Curtly Ambrose (1963-)

The Natural

He is the natural, a loose-limbed, athletic giant who once dreamed of being a professional basketballer in America and who was discovered bowling a tennis ball on a beach at Antigua.

In less than one year, he went from being an unknown to the most promising fast bowler in the world, a key figure in the demolition of England and Australia.

LEFT: Curtly Ambrose rocketed to the top.
RIGHT: The irrepressive Ian Botham.

When he made his debut against Pakistan in 1989, all he really had going for him was his name — Elconn Lynwall Curtly Ambrose — as lyrical and long as his Antiguan Test predecessors, Anderson Montgomery Everton Roberts, Isaac Vivian Alexander Richards, and Eldine Ashworth Elderfield Baptiste.

By the year's end, Curtly Ambrose showed the potential of an all-time great.

He was born at Swetes a few kilometres from Andy Roberts's home at Urlings Village, and his youth was preoccupied with fantasies of slam-dunking against the Celtics. One of seven children, he quit school cricket at 16. At 17, he left school to work in his

family's carpentry business. In his late teens, he exploded from average height to stand 195 centimetres and weigh a lean and muscular 89 kilograms.

A terror with a tennis ball on the beaches of Antigua, he was encouraged by friends to try to do the same with a cricket ball. Serious cricket and fast bowling seemed like too much hard work, however.

But he had natural talent. In 1985, at the age of 22, he played for Antigua and had a first-class game for the Leeward Islands in 1986. But he could not get a game the following season.

In January, 1988, he had no great reason to expect anything dramatic might happen. But in the Red Stripe Cup competition he took 35 wickets at 15, and in one match against Guyana he took 12 wickets, nine of them clean-bowled, beaten for pace.

Suddenly, with Garner, Roberts and Holding in retirement, the West Indies had a new sensation who might handle the other end from Malcolm Marshall.

"It was pressure from my friends that brought me to cricket," he told the Sydney journalist Mike Coward.

Ambrose joined the West Indian team for a one-day game against Pakistan, took four wickets and then took six more in the next two matches. In two months, he was a Test bowler; and, even though his seven wickets against the tourists cost 55 each, the signs were there that Ambrose and his 16-pace run-up could cause havoc with a little more time and experience.

Though he is compared to Joel Garner because of his height, Ambrose is built more like Michael Holding and his run-up has a similar gracefulness, remarkable in such a big man. The delivery is a little open-chested, causing his stock deliveries to roar in at the batsman's body rather than move toward the slips but he also has an effective outswinger.

He was a marvellous support to Marshall in England, with 22 wickets at 22, and in Australia he gave the batsmen little respite with 26 at 21.

Curtly Ambrose arrived in West Indian cricket at the age of 25 with a body that was still flexible and injury-free because it had hardly been used for bowling before. With Roberts, Holding and Garner all in retirement, he turned up, striding in and letting fly just when the world's batsmen thought it was safe to face the West Indians again.

Ian Botham
(1955-)

Guy The Gorilla

When he was just 20 years of age and not yet a Test cricketer, Ian Botham became fed up with some "Pommie bastard" jibes from Ian Chappell at the Melbourne Cricket Ground pub, threatened him with a beer glass and then chased the Australian hero down one of the city's main streets.

No-one fires up a crowd — or the opposition — like Ian Botham.

Botham, sometimes known as Beefy, sometimes Guy The Gorilla and sometimes the saviour of English pride, was no ordinary cricketer. At 12, he had the strength of a man and won a ball-throwing competition in London, hurling it more than 63 metres.

By the time he succeeded Dennis Lillee as Test cricket's greatest wicket-taker, Botham had been front-page news for more than a decade, often for all the wrong reasons.

He walked the length of Great Britain to raise $500,000 for leukaemia victims, but thumped a police-

man in the closing stages. He swung Test matches with his freakish hitting or his marvellous swing bowling, yet Denis Compton said he presented an awful image to England's youth. He suffered a conviction for drug possession and court appearances for assault. He raced and crashed cars. He drove at high speeds on public roads. Once, he had to make a formal apology for saying Pakistan was a good place to send mothers-in-law.

His arrival as one of England's greatest sporting heroes coincided with a greater emphasis on scandal in

the British press, and he was embroiled in the sex, drugs and rock and roll headlines of the 1984 tour to New Zealand and the 1985-6 tour to the West Indies, where he allegedly broke the bed he was occupying with a beauty queen.

He played soccer with Scunthorpe United Reserves and Yeovil Town, grew his hair long and had it streaked to give himself a more dashing image, began travelling with burly bodyguards and was lampooned for allowing himself to become fat.

He also came under the spell of a manager who dressed him in garish blazers and called him the greatest British hero since Churchill — "Biggles, Raffles and Errol Flynn all rolled into one".

Amid all the hype, many seemed to forget that Ian Terence Botham, born on November 24, 1955, in Heswall, Cheshire, was a cricketer first and foremost, a man who, in the words of Frank Tyson, "was driven by an egocentric fixity of purpose to occupy and dominate centre stage" and did not give a damn about conventional standards.

It is a mark of Botham's greatness as a Test all-rounder that, despite his jousting with Richard Hadlee late in his career for the world record for Test wickets, many will remember him as one of the mightiest hitters cricket has seen. He passed 100 wickets and 1000 runs in only 21 tests, 200 wickets and 2000 runs in 42 Tests (four years 126 days) and in 1984 became the first player to pass 300 wickets and 3000 runs. He hit a record 80 sixes in 1985.

Dennis Lillee once said Botham was much more Australian than English in his attitude to bowling, trying to bowl a team out every time he went on to the field, trying to get a wicket every time he ran in.

His aggression and his willingness to take the challenge to the opposition by presenting them with balls to hit often exposed Botham to a good deal of punishment. But his will to win and his fearlessness in experimenting often resulted in wickets even off bad balls and even at times when it seemed he was chosen for England on reputation rather than form.

Botham first came to the notice of the English cricket fans as an 18-yerar-old playing for Somerset in a Benson and Hedges one-day game against Hampshire. He took the wicket of Barry Richards and, batting at No. 9, hit Andy Roberts for a six over square leg, took the next ball in the mouth, spat out blood and four broken teeth, scored a blazing 45 not out and won the match against impossible odds.

Botham's best delivery was the late outswinger, and at times, such as in the 1985 series against Australia, in which he took 31 wickets, he could bowl very fast, tossing in plenty of bouncers and being warned for intimidatory bowling.

He was already a legendary figure in English cricket when he made his Test debut in 1977 with 5-74 in England's seven-wicket victory over Australia at Trent Bridge.

Two weeks later, Beefy took 5-21 at Headingley as England won by an an innings and 85 runs, thanks also to Boycott's century of centuries before his Yorkshire fans.

The following year, Botham scored a century against Pakistan at Edgbaston and followed it with 108 off 104 balls at Lords against an attack missing Imran and Sarfraz, then claiming his best Test figures, 8-34, to give England an innings triumph.

After England had lost 3-0 in Australia through no fault of his, Botham became the first man to hit a century and take 10 wickets in a Test — in the Golden Jubilee match at Bombay in 1979-80, taking 6-58 and 7-48 and scoring 114 to rescue England again.

His mastery with bat, ball and close fielding made him an obvious choice as England captain. But the captaincy was doomed, with two series against a West Indian side that stormed through English cricket.

Botham did not win any of the 12 Tests in which he led England and, after he made a pair of ducks against the 1981 Australians, many felt he was lucky to keep his place when Mike Brearley was lured back to lead the home side. The loss of leadership inspired Botham to some of his best cricket.

In the very next Test, at Headingley, Beefy took 6-95, then going in at No. 7 with England at 5-87 in reply

to 9-401, and the situation calling for a long, grafting innings, he hit 50 off 54 balls. Kim Hughes enforced the follow-on, and England was a 500-1 against chance of winning, according to Ladbroke's.

At 7-135, Graham Dilley joined Botham, who was using the bat of Graham Gooch — a bat which had scored only two and nought for its owner. Botham proceeded to cart the Australian bowling, farming the strike to protect the tailenders and reaching 103 off just 87 balls. Despite two beamers from Lawson, he eventually made 149 not out from 148 balls — and Australia needed 130 to win.

Graeme Wood hit Botham's first two deliveries for four but was out caught behind to the big man soon after, and Bob Willis did the rest. England became the first team in 87 years to win a Test after having to follow on.

In the next Test, at Edgbaston, Botham was asked to keep things tight and instead took five wickets for one run in an inspired spell of 28 deliveries to beat Australia for the second successive time.

At Old Trafford, Botham was on 28 when Lillee took the new ball, allowing himself two long legs for Botham's big hits. Twice in one over, Beefy hooked Lillee bouncers for six and then again in his next over before dishing it out to Alderman and Ray Bright. He finished his innings with 118 off 102 balls, with six sixes and 13 fours.

Wisden said the "ferocious yet effortless power and dazzling cleanness of stroke can surely never have been bettered in a Test match."

After a disastrous start, England had won The Ashes, Botham had won his third straight award as Man Of The Match, and he finished the series with two centuries and 34 wickets at fewer than 21 runs each.

The big hits contiuued. At Indore a week before the last Test of his masterful 1981-2 series in India, he scored a hundred off 48 deliveries in 50 minutes. The following season, against India at home, he took 5-46 and scored 67 at Lords, belted 128 at Old Trafford and scored a blazing 208 at The Oval, breaking Gavaskar's ankle with a drive and leaving the Surrey Pavilion with a hole in the roof.

By the end of the 1984 series, which England, under David Gower, had lost to the West Indies 5-0, Botham was physically exhausted, having played 71 tests in eight years, 65 of them consecutively. He still performed well, scoring 30 and 81 at Lords as well as snaring 8-103. At The Oval, he, Paul Allott and Richard Ellison had the Windies reeling at 6-70; but the visitors recovered, bowling England out twice and winning by 172 runs.

Botham was the best of the English bowlers against Australia in 1985 with 31 wickets at 27, though it was Ellison's swing which literally swung the series to England in the last two matches.

He had to wait until after a suspension for drug-taking to surpass Lillee's 355 Test wickets, and he was hampered throughout the later stages of his career by a back injury.

He did not play with consistency against Australia in 1986-7, but in the first Test, at Brisbane, he ham-

Sylvester Clarke never received the chance he deserved.

mered 138, hitting Merv Hughes for 22 in one over and, in partnership with Gladstone Small, made sure England kept The Ashes with some fine bowling at Melbourne.

By the time of the return Ashes series in 1989, Botham had big scars by his spine, had left Somerset acrimoniously to join Worcestershire and had been sacked from the Queensland Sheffield Shield team after another misadventure landed him in court.

He bowled little above medium pace and to little effect in three Tests; but, given his ability to turn tragedy into triumph, it is dangerous to write him off.

As the Test spinner, Vic Marks, once wrote: "His life moves so swiftly that within six months everything is out of date. However, whatever happens in the next few years, cricket historians will speak of him in the same breath as Grace, Bradman and Sobers.

"Those off-field escapades will fade from the memory, and people will recall only the power and audacity of his hitting and his indomitable will to win."

Sylvester Clarke (1954-)

The Unlucky One

The best-known delivery sent down by Sylvester Theophilus Clarke, a fast bowler built like a heavyweight boxing champion, did not come in the shape of a cricket ball. It was in the shape of a brick.

On the 1980-81 tour of Pakistan Clarke, Colin Croft, Joel Garner and Malcolm Marshall all helped the West Indies to a 1-0 triumph on tour — their first series victory in Pakistan.

Clarke took 14 wickets at 17 each, but his most publicised performance on tour came in the fourth and last Test, at Multan, where he had the Pakistanis reeling at 2-4 but became infuriated by the crowd's throwing orange peel at his team mates.

Clarke picked up a house brick that had been thrown onto the field and hurled it back into the crowd, landing smack in the middle of a group of demonstrators and sending a student leader to hospital.

Clarke was at his ferocious best with the ball, too.

At Faisalabad, he had Pakistan at 2-2 and then, batting at No.11, he scored 35 not out, including three consecutive sixes off Mohammad Nazir.

But the powerful speedster with the short, sprinting run and the thumping chest-on delivery was in Pakistan only because of Michael Holding's absence and his poor record of 11 Tests in five years as one of the world's most respected fast bowlers made an offer to play in South Africa too good to refuse.

Clarke was born in Christchurch, Barbados, home of Charlie Griffith, on December 11, 1954.

He played his first game for Barbados in the 1977-8 season and made his Test debut a few months later against Australia at Georgetown after the West Indian players involved in World Series Cricket quit the team. Even then, Clarke played in the shadow of Norbert Phillip and Vanburn Holder.

Clarke took six wickets in the match and was chosen to tour India.

He opened the bowling with Philip and was backed by Holder and the disappointing youngster Malcolm Marshall.

He was the best of a beaten Windies outfit, with 21 wickets at 34, but it was a season in which Gavaskar, Vishwanath and Kapil Dev could do no wrong.

At 185 centimetres and 95 kilograms, Clarke was a menacing sight for any batsmen with his pace and lift; but, after joining Surrey in 1979, he seemed to gain extra menace.

Paul Terry (who had his arm broken by Winston Davis) owed his selection in the English Test team largely to the way he could play Clarke in county cricket.

Not many have bowled faster than Clarke when he took 4-6 off six overs as Mike Brearley's Middlesex was smashed out for 80 at The Oval in 1982.

For five years between 1977 and 1982, Clarke was given a Test spot only when one of the bigger names was injured or unable to tour.

But he may have been in line for a regular place in the West Indian side when he decided to tour South Africa on the invitation of Don Mackay-Coghill, a former Transvaal left-arm pace bowler who would have played for the Springboks had it not been for sporting boycotts.

The big man was joined on the tour by Colin Croft, Hartley Alleyne, Ezra Moseley, the whirlwind Franklyn Stephenson, a big-hitting batsman and fast bowler whose results were often as spectacular as his windmill action.

All were profound losses to the West Indian team.

Sylvester Clarke was at his pace-bowling peak.

But sadly for his career, there were hundreds of youngsters in the Caribbean just waiting for their chance.

Kapil Dev (1959-)

India's Stalwart

Kapil Dev was the one player for whom India had been crying out since the 1930s.

India at last had a man whose pace recalled Mahomed Nissar, and an all-rounder whose deeds not only surpassed those of Vinoo Mankad but rivalled those of Ian Botham for explosiveness.

Kapil Dev became the most successful all-rounder produced by India and one of the greatest wicket-takers in Test history.

More than 183 centimetres tall and with a springing run-up of 18 metres, Kapil Dev generates brisk fast-medium pace with a whippy action, that is perfectly side-on and involves a generous back arch and a wrist cocked far back.

He was born at Chandigarh, in the Punjab region of northern India, on January 6, 1959, the son of a prosperous timber merchant.

He made his first-class debut before his 17th birthday, taking 6-39 for Haryana against Punjab, taking 7-20 against Bengal the next year, and 8-38 in an 11-wicket haul against Services the year after that.

In Chandigarh, Dev was coached by Desh Prem Azad, a disciple of the English fast bowler and teacher, Alf Gover, and the young quick learned how to drop in the bouncer, change his pace, the effect of changing the position of delivery and the methods of swinging the ball, old and new.

On the recommendation of Sunil Gavaskar, Kapil toured East Africa with an Indian team and he was part of the Test side to play Pakistan in 1978-9.

Test cricket was not meant to be easy and, despite his potential for Haryana Kapil's Test debut, was a disappointment, seven wickets in three Tests at 61 runs apiece.

Against the West Indian tourists that season, he took 17 wickets; at Delhi he hit 126 not out off just 124 balls against Sylvester Clarke, Norbert Phillip and Vanburn Holder.

The 1979 season in England saw his skills developing, and in the 1979-80 series against Australia and Pakistan he took 60 wickets in 12 Tests, with 7-56 in an 11-wicket haul against Pakistan at Madras.

He fell 16 runs short of becoming Test cricket's first man to take 10 wickets and hit a century in a Test, something he would do at Bombay a month later.

In 1979, he took 74 wickets from 17 Tests, breaking the record 72 of Graham McKenzie. In the sixth Test against Pakistan, his 25th match, he took his 100th Test

RIGHT: With his brisk medium pace and flashing bat, Kapil Dev is India's most successful all-rounder.

wicket in the record time of one year 105 days, beating Ian Botham. At 21 years and 25 days, he was the youngest player to reach the milestone; and when in the same match he passed 1000 runs, he became the youngest player to reach that figure, too.

He failed dismally with the bat in Australia and New Zealand, but at Melbourne, encouraged by the bowling of Kharsan Ghavri, he took 5-28, bundling Australia out for 83, 60 runs short of a victory Lillee and Pascoe seemed to have set up.

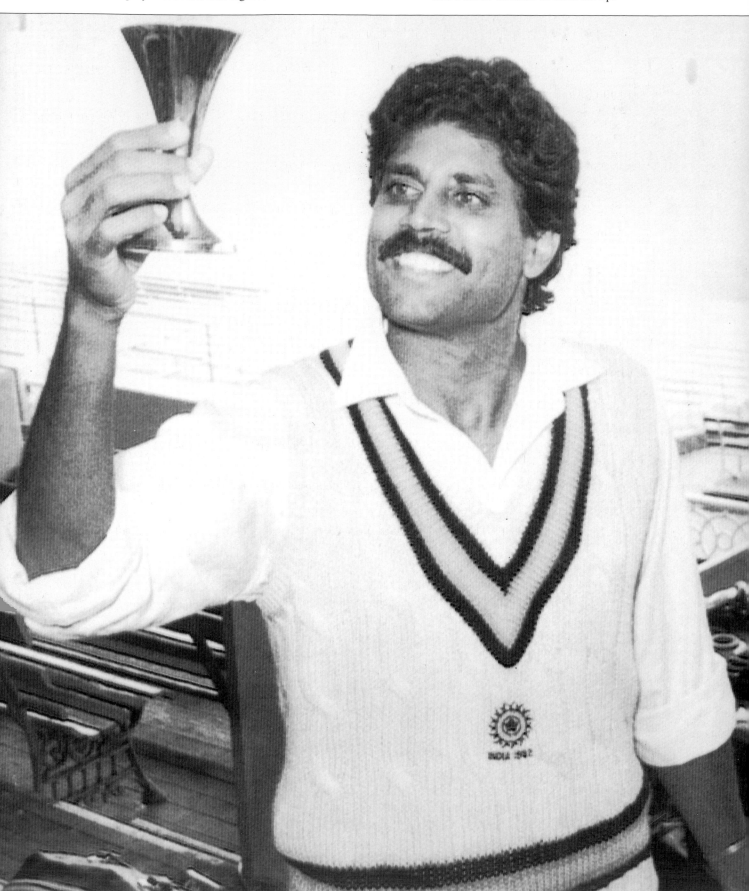

Dev rescued India repeatedly in the '80s

The win squared the series, and in 1981 the Indian all-rounder was hired by Northamptonshire, though he played in only three championship matches that season.

Against England the following season, Kapil took 22 expensive wickets in a series India won after the first low-scoring match at Bombay, where he and Madan Lal bowled England out but could not stop Botham chalking up his 2000 runs and 200 Test wickets.

At Calcutta, Dev took 6-91 in a match watched by a world-record crowd of 400,000, and at Kanpur in the final Test Dev showed he was back to his big-hitting best, blasting 116 off just 84 balls.

At Lords in 1982, he was just 11 runs and 12 balls short of Jack Gregory's 70-minute century when caught at mid-wicket.

At Old Trafford, he hit 50 in 30 balls. At The Oval, he scored 97 in 93 balls. But he could not do everything, and England won the series 1-0.

In 1982-3, Dev succeeded his old mentor, Gavaskar, as Indian captain but would go 21 Tests, including a loss to Sri Lanka, before he led his talented band to a victory, at Lords in 1986.

In the West Indies in 1982-3, he had great personal success but his team was beaten 2-0.

In the first Test, at Kingston, he passed 2000 Test runs. In the second, at Port of Spain, he passed 200 Test wickets in his 50th match — at the age of 24 years 67 days.

In the second innings, he hit 100 not out off 95 balls against an attack of Holding, Roberts, Marshall and Garner. At St John's, he hit 98 and then finished the series with 19 wickets at 23.

No matter what the opposition or the circumstances, the man could never be underestimated. In the World Cup preliminaries of 1983 at Tunbridge Wells, Kapil had gone in to bat against Zimbabwe with the score at 4-9 and before long it was 5-17.

India was in danger of dipping out against a side that did not even play Test cricket. But in three hours Kapil hit six sixes and 17 fours to post a World Cup record of 175 not out and India had made 8-266. India then went on to beat Australia and England, then tossed the Windies in the final.

Dev was not just a hero of the big occasion, either. In the 1983-4 series in Pakistan, in which Zaheer, Mudassar and Javed all averaged more than 100 with the bat, Kapil never surrendered taking 24 wickets in the losing series in long, arduous spells. He followed 5-102 at Karachi with 7-220 at Faisalabad and 8-85 at Lahore.

Against the West Indians, looking for revenge in the same season, he took 29 wickets; but even his Test best of 9-83 at Ahmedabad could not stop the West Indian speed machine from sweeping the Indians away for a 3-0 victory.

Not everyone was thrilled with Kapil's cavalier attitude. Against England at Calcutta the next year, Gavaskar had him left out of the team for having holed out after hitting a six off the fifth ball he faced at Delhi. But, upon a defiant return at Madras he hit the first ball for four and made 53.

Graham Dilley
(1959 -)
The Lone Hand

Graham Dilley was only 21 when Clive Lloyd called him the fastest white bowler in the world.

If the big fast man of English cricket had been blessed with a stronger skeletal system and the support of another genuinely quick bowler throughout the 1980s, England would probably have enjoyed a great deal more Test success.

Lloyd's praise for the youngster came after an inspired spell of express bowling in Jamaica.

But, instead of bowling with similar speed against the rest of the Test-playing countries, Dilley seemed to spend most of his promising career at home with a sore back.

Graham Roy Dilley, born at Dartford, Kent on May 18, 1959, missed the next two series after his first burst in the Caribbean and many more important matches when England was crying out for a truly quick bowler to complement the likes of Willis, Botham and Neil Foster.

He had one of the most awesome actions in cricket. Little wonder that his back completely surrendered. After a thrusting run-up, his action finished in a high-stepping delivery as he raised his left foot almost above head height and brought it crashing down to the turf with all of his powerful 190 centimetre frame behind it.

Dilley first played for Kent in 1977, and he played there for 10 years before joining Worcestershire, which he helped to the county championship and the Sunday League crown in 1988.

He made his Test debut in Australia in 1979-80, and at Perth added his name to the scorecard with Lillee, caught Willey, bowled Dilley.

In the West Indies, he took 10 expensive wickets but bowled fast enough to impress such judges as Lloyd; and in 1981, in Botham's Ashes triumph, he took 14 wickets at 19 each. His best, 4-24 at Trent Bridge, came in the only match Australia won.

In 1984, Dilley and his doctors feared his career was finished because of back trouble, and from February, 1984, to June, 1986, he played no Test cricket.

But he worked hard on his strength and fitness, and out of the turmoil came a renewed paceman. In 1985, he played with Kent and had a season with Natal in South Africa, refining his delivery and his changes of pace.

In 1986, Dilley took 10 wickets at 30 against India but Vengsarkar was unstoppable with the bat and India won the series 2-0.

Against Australia in the 1986-7 series, his 5-68 at Brisbane helped England retain The Ashes, and Dilley's determination was reflected when Pakistan made 708 at The Oval in 1987, Dilley's 6-154 an indication of his refusal to give in.

Graham Dilley had genuine pace in an era when England cultivated seamers.

At Lords in 1988, he had his great outswinger working to full effect, having the mighty Windies at 4-24, with Haynes, Greenidge, Richardson and Richards back in the Pavilion.

Malcolm Marshall had the final word, but Dilley took nine wickets and gave the tourists a rare taste of

the medicine they doled out throughout the 1980s.

When Dilley was fit and well, few men bowled faster.

But, sadly for English cricket, he was all too often unable to play. He took just five expensive wickets in two matches against the 1989 Australians.

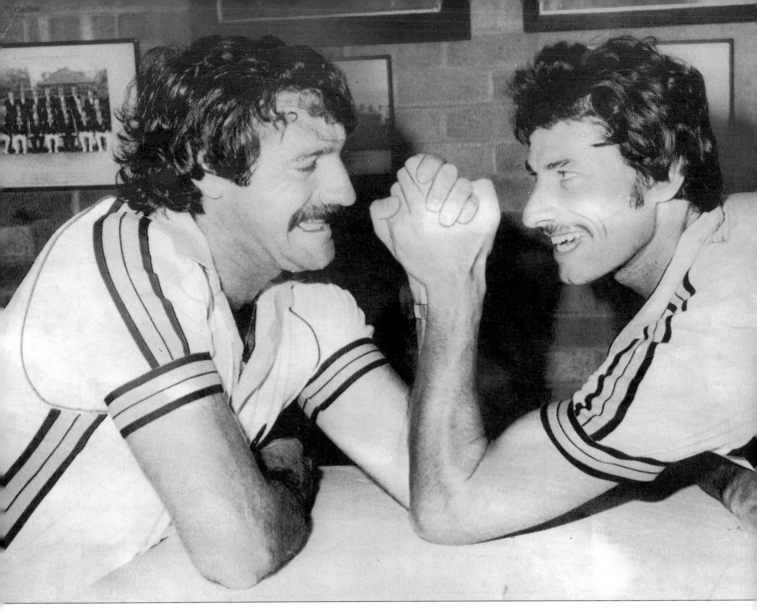

Rivals in bowling and arm-wrestling — Richard Hadlee and Dennis Lillee.

Sir Richard Hadlee
(1951-)

The King of Swing

Richard Hadlee is the son of an accountant and cricket captain of New Zealand. But, even with an hereditary head for figures, few cricketers have so defied logic and arithmetic as this slender, sinewy man.

As he approached the age of 40 with more than 400 Test wickets Hadlee confounded all theories on fast bowling and physiology.

The finest cricketer New Zealand has produced, and Test cricket's greatest wicket-taker, Hadlee was the main factor in turning the Kiwi cricket team from being the international easy-beats to a side that could win Test series against England, Australia and the West Indies.

Though something of hot-head in his young days when some saw him as a trans-Tasman cousin of Dennis Lillee, Richard Hadlee became as cool, calculating and seemingly as ageless as Sydney Barnes,

attacking the task of fast bowling with all the sublety and deep thought of a master spinner.

As he grew older and wiser, Hadlee became a meticulous man with a sharp, analytical mind for detail, especially when it related to chinks in a batsman's armour.

When he decided in the 1980-1 series against Australia to cut his approach from 23 paces to 15 and later 10 in an effort to preserve his body for its 11 months of cricket each year, he was criticised at home for not trying.

Yet Hadlee's decision led to him becoming a more durable speedster capable of great variation and becoming the first New Zealander to match the immortals of the game. It took him 25 Tests to take his first 100 wickets, but in 45 more he had matched exactly Lillee's 355 in 70 matches.

While Lillee retired to nurse his creaks and strains, Richard Hadlee kept rolling in, whipping the ball over with his classical action and snaring wickets all over the world as he chased number 400.

Hadlee was born in Christchurch on July 3, 1951, one of five boys, the son of a former New Zealand Test skipper, Walter Hadlee. His brother, Barry, was part of New Zealand's 1975 World Cup squad and, despite back trouble, losing a toe to a lawn mower and having one leg shorter than the other after a soccer accident, another brother, Dayle, was often the senior partner when he and Richard opened the Kiwi attack.

Walter Hadlee laid a concrete-and-malthoid pitch for his boys at their first home and laid a turf wicket at their next.

Richard debuted for Canterbury at 20, and took a hat-trick in his third match, against Nelson. He made his debut for New Zealand against Pakistan in 1972 and toured England in 1973. In both series his brother, Dayle, was a superior performer.

For the next few years, Hadlee, with his curious sideways shuffle at the start of his long run, was an indifferent performer at the international level. But he had a good series at home to Australia in 1973-4, and two years later he confirmed his place as a New Zealand mainstay against India at Wellington.

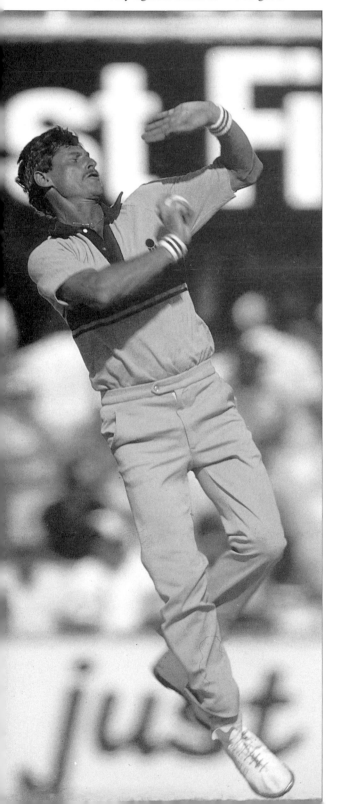

With one match gone to India and the second drawn, Hadlee saved the series for New Zealand, taking 4-35 and 7-23 as New Zealand won by an innings. It was his first great effort, but ironically his selection for the match as the fourth pace bowler at the expense of the spinner, Hedley Howarth, caused some controversy, since Hadlee had been a disappointment in the series.

In the second innings, New Zealand picked up six wickets for six runs, five of them to Hadlee in 30 minutes of cricket the likes of which had seldom been seen in New Zealand.

At Wellington in 1977-8, the Kiwis were in trouble in their first innings against Boycott's England, which needed just 137 in its second innings to win the Test. But, backed superbly by Richard Collinge, Hadlee, bowling in a gale, took 6-26 (for match figures of an even 10 for 100), and England was out for 64. Hadlee had turned a potential hiding into New Zealand's first triumph over England in 48 matches and 48 years of effort.

The next season, Hadlee again toured England with much greater success than the disappointment of five years earlier and was so impressive that he signed with Nottinghamshire. There, under Clive Rice, he developed his gifts further and further until in 1984 he became the first man to pass 100 wickets and 1000 runs (including a double century) since the county championship had been modified in 1969.

In what became the sour summer of 1979-80, Hadlee calling it "the most bitter and controversial series I've played in", he was the architect of New Zealand's first series win over the West Indies, taking 11 wickets and hitting 51 at Dunedin and then hitting a century off only 86 balls against Roberts, Holding, Garner and Croft in the second Test, at Christchurch.

The series also marked the first home rubber New Zealand had won after 50 years of Test cricket.

For Nottinghamshire, Hadlee was just as much a match-winner. In 1981, he helped it to its first county title since the days of Larwood and Voce 52 years before, and he topped the English bowling averages, taking 105 wickets at 14.89, the only bowler that year to pass the century mark.

Two years later at Headingley, he went wicketless; but he scored 75 in the first innings against England and was at the crease in the second when New Zealand won their first Test on English soil.

Even though the series was lost, Hadlee's hero status was confirmed. He passed 200 Test wickets on the tour and was master with bat and ball, finishing the four matches with 21 wickets and averaging more than 50 with the bat.

He found himself besieged by demands on his life and time. For a private man it became almost too much to bear. To be or not to be the centre of attention? He suffered a nervous breakdown. Frank Tyson compared Hadlee to another hero, Hamlet.

"Hadlee contained his tensions until he was wound up as tightly as a watch spring," Tyson wrote. "He

Richard Hadlee in action.

could make mountains out of molehills — the classical sign of stress. Small wonder, then, that he could seriously admit that the problems emanating from a 'mere game' once assumed such significance for him that at one stage (he) questioned living."

But Hadlee was able to make the pressures pay off. Against England at Lancaster Park in 1983-4, he hit 99 off 81 balls before being caught by Bob Taylor off Bob Willis.

In his first turn with the ball he sent down 17 overs to take 3-16, and in the second innings he whipped down 18 overs, taking 5-28. England was bowled out for 82 and 93, the first time this century that England had been bowled out for less than 100 in each innings, and it made Hadlee's 99 look pretty good.

A lifetime's ambition for all of New Zealand's cricket followers had been reached when the third Test, at Auckland, was drawn and New Zealand had beaten England in a Test series.

Hadlee then went for a picnic in Sri Lanka, taking 23 wickets in three Tests at 10 each. He helped New Zealand gain revenge over Pakistan at home for an earlier series loss and even, though his fine bowling in the West Indies in 1984-5 could not thwart the local batsmen, he did succeed in shaking some up with the bouncer, causing Garner and Marshall to unleash their own fire and break the arm of Jeremy Coney.

By 1985-6, when the Kiwis arrived in Australia, Hadlee was unstoppable, taking 33 wickets in three Tests at 11 each.

In the humidity of Brisbane his swing was mocking in its subjugation of the batsmen, and he finished with 9-52, the fourth-best Test analysis ever. The only wicket he missed was that of Geoff Lawson, who was caught by Hadlee on the boundary. In the next innings, Hadlee took 6-71. He also hit 54 just to be sure he won the Man Of The Match trophy and the Test.

He took, for him, a mere seven wickets at Sydney, including 5-65, but he was back in form at Perth with 5-65 and 6-90. New Zealand won the series 2-1.

Greg Matthews, the ebullient Australian all-rounder, would recall that, though Hadlee said little or nothing to batsmen on the field, he was able to beam "bad vibes" by a menacing presence, his confident walk and eye contact that spoke a thousand volumes of intimidation.

In England in 1986, in he took 19 wickets in three matches and, although England won the series, Hadlee knocked out wicket-keeper, Bruce French, and forced England to use three substitutes before he was fit to resume duties.

Hadlee's worth to New Zealand cricket was immeasureable.

BELOW: New Zealand's finest, Richard Hadlee.
RIGHT: A ferocious appeal from the New Zealand champion.

Imran Khan
1952-

The Lion Of Pakistan

Imran Khan is tall, dark, handsome, rich, an unassuming yet aristocratic sex symbol, champion athlete with a degree in political science and economics from Oxford University.

As one commentator remarked, "There had to be *something* wrong with him". But, whatever flaws Imran might have had, they rarely showed up on the field, certainly not from the early 1980s on when he consistently proved himself to be one of the greatest all-rounders in the game's history.

Imran Khan had been a Test cricketer for seven years before a couple of astute coaches moulded him into a fast bowler who could compete with Thomson and Holding for pace and who would go on to become one of the most successful fast bowlers.

They took a fast-medium bowler with a windmill action and a stock inswinger, and taught him to run and jump and deliver the ball with a whip of his lean, muscular body to produce not only the fastest bowler Pakistan ever fielded but one of the fastest to play the game.

In 1978, Tony Greig took Imran and his aged Sussex partner John Snow to Australia for World Series Cricket and Imran came under the influence of both Snow and Mike Procter.

The burly South African taught Imran the importance of the run-up, and Snow worked with him developing his delivery action and helping him master swing bowling.

The result was a bowler of extraordinary speed and accuracy who generated his terror from a long, prowling, stooping run and a spectacular final leap that culminated in a heave of his muscular shoulders.

The great Khan was born to an aristocratic background in Lahore, son of a wealthy landowner, on November 25, 1952. Although he found cricket boring as a child and was hampered throughout his career by an arm injury suffered when he fell from a tree as a boy, Imran was bred for the game. His was a regal cricketing family, with eight cousins playing first-class cricket. Two of them, Majid Khan and Javed Burki, captained Pakistan.

Like his wealthy Indian contemporary, Kapil Dev, Imran made his debut in first-class cricket as a 16-year-old fast-medium all-rounder, playing for Lahore. His captain was his cousin, the chairman of selectors his uncle.

Imran Khan could generate extraordinary speed, helped by an idiosyncratic pre-delivery leap.

His early performances were not great, but at 18 he toured England with the Pakistan team. His debut and only Test was a disappointment. He was run out for five in a score of 7-608 and took no wickets for 55 at Edgbaston. But he did bowl with great control, backing the medium-pacer Saleem Altaf and at one stage conceding just 36 runs from 23 overs against the likes of Edrich, Cowdrey and Amiss.

Imran had sufficient potential to be signed by Worcestershire in 1971 and was schooled at Worcester Royal Grammar and then at Oxford, where his reputation as a dashing hero with matinee looks was confirmed. He won Blues between 1973 and 1975 and captained the university in 1974 when he hit 117 not out and 106 against Nottinghamshire and then 170 against Northamptonshire.

He was still something of a disappointment when he joined the Pakistan tourists that year in England but he did at least take his first Test wicket among five in three Tests at an expensive 52 runs each.

In 1976, he was involved in a bitter feud to leave Worcestershire for Sussex and in the players' dispute in Pakistan; but neither drama really affected his form once he was chosen as a Test regular.

At home to New Zealand, he and Sarfraz dominated the bowling as Hadlee struggled to contain prolific scoring from the local batsmen, led by Javed Miandad. Pakistan won the first two Tests and the third at Karachi, where Imran was taken off for bowling too many bouncers, was drawn.

In Australia that season, Imran's pace and direction were improving and he presented grave problems for batsmen, slanting the ball in from wide of the crease and making it leave the bat at the last moment.

He took 18 wickets at 28 from just three matches, including 12 in the third and final Test, at Sydney, where Pakistan won to square the series. At the time Australia was riding high after nine wins and just two defeats in the series against England and the West Indies, but no-one counted on Imran bowling so well.

The West Indians were given a taste of their own fire at Kingston when he took 6-90 as part of his 25 wickets on tour at 31 each, claiming the wicket of Viv Richards four times in nine innings.

During the World Series, Imran developed his ability to bowl close to the stumps, propelling his outswinger at great pace from his big final leap and strong upper body. In a competition to decide the world's fastest bowler, he finished third behind Thomson and Holding. Dennis Lillee believed there was not much between all three at their peak.

Despite chronic back pain, Imran took 33 wickets in two series against India in 1978-9 and 1979-80, and two years later, after solid results at home to Australia, he took his best Test figures, 8-58 in a 14-wicket haul against Sri Lanka at Faisalabad.

By 1982, Imran had succeeded Fazal Mahmood as Pakistan's greatest wicket-taker and amid great strife in the politics of Pakistan cricket, he was chosen to lead his country against England. The captaincy brought out the best in him, and he produced the kind of all-round performance that became typical of him in the

LEFT and ABOVE: Imran Khan, long one of the world's most accomplished — and popular — cricketers.

1980s, taking 21 wickets at 18 and averaging 53 with the bat.

At Edgbaston, he took 7-52 and scored 65; but ultimately it was the batting of Mohsin Khan and a spell of 6-32 from the gentle medium pace of Mudassar Nazar that gave Pakistan its victory at Lords in a series they lost 2-1.

Imran then led Pakistan to a 3-0 victory against the Australians under Kim Hughes during a season in which Zaheer and Mohsin Khan made the Australian bowlers tremble before Imran and his little mate Abdul Qadir bowled their team out.

Against India in that same 1982-3 season, Imran showed just how much he was enjoying the responsibility of leadership, averaging 62 with the bat and taking 40 wickets at 14 in six Tests.

Bowling faster than Ian Botham ever did, he took 8-60 at Karachi and then matched Beefy's big double with 6-99, 5-82 and 117 at Faisalabad.

Imran made his first retirement after the 1987 series in England, going out with a bang as he and Wasim Akram, together with the fine batting of Javed, gave Pakistan a 1-0 victory in five Tests. Imran took 21 wickets at 22 and, despite a great spell of bowling by Neil Foster at Headingley, Imran's 7-40 saved the day.

Earlier in his career, a shin injury had stopped Imran playing against India and England; but such was his standing that he was retained as a middle-order batsman and captain in the 1983 World Cup and for the tour of Australia.

When his injury healed, he was quickly back into the fray, taking a superb 6-14 against India at Sharjah in a one-day game. Although he talked about retirement for the last half of the decade, he was still a popular and at times devastating leader when the Pakistan team arrived in Australia in January, 1990.

He became the third player, after Botham and Kapil Dev, to pass 300 wickets and 3000 runs in Test cricket.

Geoff Lawson
1957-

Henry

Like the heavyweight boxing champion, Larry Holmes, Geoff Lawson never truly received the respect he deserved because he had such a hard act to follow.

Just as Holmes had to box in an era immediately after that of Ali, Foreman and Frazier, Lawson not only had the brilliance of Terry Alderman to contend with but he became a Test bowler on the boot heels of Lillee, Thomson and Rodney Hogg.

At 190 centimetres, Lawson possesses a long-striding run-up and a spectacular goose-stepping delivery stride that turns his body into a human catapult. Sometimes his follow-through is so exaggerated that you feel he will land flat on his face.

He never dominated the Australian attack, as his early promise suggested, but Lawson still became the fastest bowler in Australia in the early 1980s and one of the most successful of Australia's Test cricketers.

He was a vital cog in the Australian Ashes machine of 1989, partnering Alderman in repeated assaults on the English batting, finishing the series with 29 wickets at 27 each and winning the Man Of The Match award at Old Trafford with 6-72 and 3-81.

Nicknamed Henry after the 19th-century Australian poet, Lawson was born in the NSW regional centre of Wagga Wagga on December 7, 1957, the son of a service-station owner.

He was playing senior cricket by the age of 14 and made his debut in 1976-7 for Sydney University, where he studied to be an optometrist.

He first played for NSW in the 1977-8 season, against Western Australia, after being acclaimed the fastest bowler in the State and after just three first-class games.

Bob Simpson called him the best fast-bowling prospect NSW had unearthed in 15 years. That season, he dismissed Geoff Boycott at the SCG and was warned in the second innings for bowling too many bouncers.

In 1979, he had a season with Heywood in the Central Lancashire League and played one match for Lancashire against Cambridge.

He was sent to Pakistan as an emergency replacement but had to wait until November, 1980, to make his Test debut at Brisbane, with three wickets against New Zealand.

Because of his extreme back arch, Lawson suffered a great many stresses and strains even early in his career.

But, despite a nagging back complaint, he had some remarkable success on the 1981 Ashes tour, taking 12 cheap wickets supporting Lillee and Alderman, and finishing with 7-81 at Lords, better figures than Lillee ever took in a Test.

In the return series in 1982-3, he was voted Man Of The Series, filling the void left by the injured Alderman in taking 34 wickets in five matches at 20 runs each, and was the man most responsible for Australia's 2-1 triumph to regain The Ashes Botham's side had won in England.

That same season, he took 65 first-class wickets and helped NSW win the Sheffield Shield for the first time in 17 years.

Like most fast bowlers who followed Lillee, he had his petulant moments. Sometimes they backfired. He was twice fined for bad behaviour in 1984-5, once at Melbourne after his dismissal of Gordon Greenidge.

In 1982-3, when Australia lost 3-0 in Pakistan, the touring fieldsmen were pelted with stones at Karachi after Lawson exploded with anger after a disallowed appeal.

But more often than not his aggression paid off.

Lawson was again the best of the bowlers in the 1983-4 summer against Pakistan, supported by Lillee, playing his last series, and the often injured Carl Rackemann.

Lawson took 24 wickets and Australia won the five-Test series 2-0.

Only a few months later, Australia was ducking for cover against the Windies' bouncers in the Caribbean, watching with dismay as their own deliveries were scattered to all parts of the West Indies.

Lawson was the most successful of the Australian bowlers, but his 12 wickets cost more than 50 each.

His figures were much more impressive when the Windies toured Australia the following season but, despite 23 wickets at a little under 26 runs each, the West Indies still won the series 3-1, with the spinners, Bob Holland and Murray Bennett, finally doing what the fast men could not.

Lawson showed his fighting qualities throughout the series, going wicketless at Perth, then taking six in Brisbane and then 8-112 and 3-69 at Adelaide.

In England in 1985, his 22 wickets cost 38 runs each, and he and Craig McDermott were unable to keep The Ashes with Australia.

For the next couple of seasons, Lawson had to contend with repeated injuries.

But in England in 1989, bowling with a little less pace but more variety than in his prime, Lawson helped make the dreams of every Australian cricket fan come true.

After an early career as a firebrand, Geoff Lawson mellowed into a dependable, if injury-plagued, Test stalwart for Australia.

Malcolm Marshall (1958-)

West Indian Rubber Man

There was nothing particalarly menacing about young Malcolm Marshall to suggest he would become the most feared fast bowler of the mid-1980s.

Like Ray Lindwall he is not a big man — just 175 centimetres and about 76 kilograms, much of it in his shoulders. But as the West Indian Rubber Man, his flexible little body could twist in all directions and from a charging, bounding run-up and an acrobatic chest on wind-up, he became the fastest bowler in the world and the greatest wicket-taker in West Indian cricket.

Like Lindwall, Lillee and Holding, he was able to cut down his run-up after the age of 30 and still achieve phenomenal results by his mastery of swing and cut, taking 35 cut-price wickets in England in 1988 though never reaching the express speed of previous duels with the English batsmen.

Malcolm Denzil Marshall was born in the village of St Michael, near Bridgetown, Barbados, on April 18, 1958.

He had played only one first-class match, the final of the 1977-8 Shell Shield, in which he took six Jamaican wickets, when he was chosen to tour India the next year during the absence of the World Series Cricket stars.

Fuelled by a desire to succeed Thomson and Holding as the world's fastest bowler and to emulate Andy Roberts, whom he succeeded at Hampshire, Marshall developed into a paceman with a lethal, skidding delivery and the fire to bounce even the most inept tailender.

He made his West Indian debut in the second Test, at Bangalore, in December, 1978, bowling with Sylvester Clarke, Norbert Phillip and Vanburn Holder.

The match was drawn when riots broke out in the city over the arrest of the former Prime Minister, Indira Ghandi.

Marshall did not have a good series on slow wickets, and the West Indians were beaten 1-0, his three wickets in three matches costing nearly 90 runs each.

In England in 1980, the West Indians had their big five — Roberts, Holding, Garner, Croft and young Malcolm, who took 15 wickets in the series at 29 and was starting to show signs that he would one day be the best of the bunch.

In Pakistan later that year, Marshall's 4-25 at Fais-

Malcolm Marshall is a ruthless and implacable foe who bowls to take wickets and to terrorise.

alabad helped the Windies to their first series win in Pakistan; and against India in 1982-3 after Croft had defected to South Africa, Marshall finished close behind Roberts in the tour figures with 21 wickets at 22 each, a best of 5-37 coming around the wicket at Port of Spain.

The hapless Indians suffered against him on their own wickets the following year when he took 33 wickets at 19, this time with Holding and Roberts supporting him.

At Kanpur, where the Windies won by an innings, he scored 92 and took 4-19 and 4-47. At Calcutta, he hit 54 and then tore the heart from the batting with 6-37, causing another innings victory. The Indians had already been battered when members of the 80,000 crowd attacked them for their meek submission.

Such was the speed of Marshall that in 1984, when the Englishmen lost 5-0, even helmets were of little use. At Edgbaston, he hit the opening bat, Andy Lloyd, with a bouncer and, despite the helmet, Lloyd suffered a hairline fracture near his eye, was plagued with double vision and was put out of cricket for some time.

Marshall forced Graeme Fowler to retire with a bruised arm at The Oval but, despite repeated bouncers, he was not warned by the umpires, Constant and Meyer, even though in the previous season the spinner Phil Edmonds had been warned for too many short deliveries.

At Headingley, Marshall showed he not only could dish out the pain but could take it too.

He had taken 6-85 at Lords but, after fracturing his left thumb while fielding, Marshall ignored doctors advice and came to the crease for the last wicket at Leeds to help Larry Gomes hit his century, even cracking a boundary himself while he was there. Then, with his hand in plaster and bowling off a short run, he decimated the English batting, taking 7-53 and even collecting a difficult caught-and-bowled off Fowler, the top-scorer.

After taking 5-35 at The Oval, Marshall finished the finest series for the West Indies to that time, with 24 wickets at 18, forming with the giant Joel Garner an irresistible partnership of opposites.

The pair were at it again in Australia in 1984-5, having cut the locals to pieces in the home series a year earlier.

At Adelaide, Marshall took 10 wickets and, with 28 in the series at 20 each, was voted the best player of the summer.

Then it was the New Zealanders who had to suffer as Marshall punished them for a series won amid controversy and ill-will five years before.

At Bridgetown, he took 7-80 and scored 63 and in partnership with Garner and Winston Davis won the series 2-0. The spate of bouncers Marshall and Garner unleashed in the fourth and final Test at Kingston resulted in a broken arm for Jeremy Coney and another West Indian win by 10 wickets.

In four matches, Marshall had taken 27 wickets, and he added another 27 against England at home in 1985-86 during the second successive blackwash.

His 5-33 at Lahore a year later helped draw the

series against Pakistan, where another new fast-bowl-ing star, in Tony Gray, emerged. In 1982, he took 134 wickets for Hampshire, the most by anyone since the reduction of the country program in 1969.

In an era when fast bowlers came out of the West Indies quicker than the Joel Garner yorker, Malcolm Marshall was always there when the wickets were falling, surpassing his idols as the most succcessful Calypso Killer when he passed Lance Gibbs's 309 Test wickets.

Malcolm Marshall, always there when the wickets are falling.

Greg Chappell
Rates The Bowlers

Wasim Akram and Curtly Ambrose are the world's best young fast bowlers. In all conditions Wasim is the better all-round paceman.

If the wiry Pakistani can show anything like the durability of Richard Hadlee he could very well go down in history as the greatest left-arm fast bowler of them all.

Although his run-up and action don't look threatening, his pace is derived from supple strength and perfect balance. Somewhere between the actions of Akram, John Snow and Jeff Thomson lies the perfect fast bowling action – an economical run-up and an action which has the arms close to the body, ensuring perfect balance and explosive speed.

I would say Akram and Malcolm Marshall are the two fastest bowlers in the world today. Malcolm's greatest asset is his shock value. He runs quickly into the wicket but is one of the few fast bowlers who, like Mike Procter, can run right through his action, not stopping to gather himself to release the ball.

Marshall is quicker than Curtly Ambrose who, in turn, is quicker than Joel Garner but not as accurate. (Joel was the most accurate quick bowler I played against.) Curtly will never be a great swinger of the ball but he does have the height and bounce to trouble any batsman.

In the 1980s Richard Hadlee became a role model of reliability, accuracy and resilience. He was not a robust man and he realised pretty early in his career that he would not have a long future as a tearaway quick. Playing in England helped him become a master of seam bowling.

Richard also had the greatest weapon a pace bowler can have — the ability to bowl the quicker one which was an asset that also belonged to a great fast man I faced early in my career, Graham McKenzie.

Imran Khan was the best swinger of the ball among the genuine fast bowlers I encountered but like Dennis Lillee he had an action that placed great stress on his back. Imran tended to throw his front arm out towards the offside and it placed a lot of strain on his spine. (Dennis, by the way, was the greatest fast bowler of my time, followed by Andy Roberts.)

Patrick Patterson can be very fast on his day and when everything clicks, he can be a dangerous proposition for the batsman. But if you sweat on him for a while he presents a lot of scoring opportunities. His pace relies on sheer brute strength.

Merv Hughes derives his speed from a high energy commitment but his balance is not good. The same can be said about Craig McDermott, who has such potential but has always been an enigma.

Bruce Reid is a great left-arm bowler when he's bowling, but his injuries prove that a fast man can't be too thin. Many of Graham Dilley's injury problems can be traced to an arm action that is all over the place. Like West Australian Chris Matthews his bowling arm is a long way from his body and tends to tip him off balance. I always believed that like Patrick Patterson, Dilley could not maintain a lengthy spell of sustained accurate fast bowling.

The same can't be said of Terry Alderman. Although he is not as quick as some of the guys around these days, Terry is a fine new ball bowler with tremendous control. He's another man who is not a big swinger of the ball but who proves an important point about the art of quick bowling. When you have control, the ball only needs to swing three inches to hit the edge of the bat.

Bibliography

Arlott, John; *John Arlott's Book of Cricketers,* Angus and Robertson, Sydney, 1979

Arnold, Peter; *The Illustrated Encyclopedia of World Cricket,* Golden Press, Sydney, 1986

Arnold, Peter and Wynne-Thomas, Peter; *The Illustrated History of the Test Match,* Sidgwick and Jackson, London, 1988

Australia's Yesterdays; Readers Digest; Sydney; 1974

Brittenden, Dick; *The Finest Years — Twenty Years of New Zealand Cricket;* A.H. and A.W. Reed; Wellington; 1977

Bromby, Robin; *A Century of Ashes;* Resolution Press, Sydney, 1982

Crowley, Brian; *A History of Australian Bowling and Wicketkeeping 1850-1986,* Macmillan Australia, Melbourne, 1987

Crowley, Brian; *Cricket's Exiles — The Saga of South African Cricket;* Angus and Robertson, Sydney, 1984

Derriman, Philip; *Bodyline;* William Collins, Sydney, 1984

Derriman, Philip; *The Top 100 and The 1st XI,* The Fairfax Library, Sydney, 1987.

Duckworth, Leslie; *S.F.Barnes — Master Bowler;* The Cricketer/Hutchinson; London, 1967

Dunn, John; *How to Play Cricket — Australian Style;* Rigby; Adelaide; 1974

Foster, David and Arnold, Peter; *100 Years of Test Cricket - England v Australia;* Hamlyn, London, 1977

Frith, David; *Pageant of Cricket;* Macmillan, Sydney, 1987

Frith, David; *The Fast Men;* Van Nostrand Reinhold, Berkshire, England, 1975

Goodwin, Clayton; *West Indians at the Wicket;* Macmillan; London; 1986

Heads, Ian; *Backpage — Australia's Greatest Sporting Moments;* Lester-Townsend Publishing, Sydney, 1989

Heads, Ian and Lester, Gary; *200 Years of Australian Sport — A Glorious Obsession;* Lester-Townsend Publishing; 1988

Huxley, John; *Border's Heroes;* Lester-Townsend Publishing, Sydney, 1989

Lee, Alan; *The Wisden Book of Cricket Heroes — Bowlers;* Stanley Paul; London, 1989

Lemmon, David; *Cricket Mercenaries;* Pavilion Books, London, 1987

Lillee, Dennis; *Over and Out;* Methuen; Sydney; 1984

Lillee, Dennis; *The Art of Fast Bowling;* Collins; Sydney; 1977

McFarline, Peter and Sparke, Garry; *Cricket in Australia;* Garry Sparke and Associates; Melbourne; 1981

McGilvray, Alan; *Backpage of Cricket;* Lester Townsend Publishing, Sydney, 1989

Manley, Michael; *A History of West Indies Cricket;* Andre Deutsch; London, 1988

Marks, Vic; *The Wisden Illustrated History of Cricket;* Angus and Robertson; Sydney, 1988

Martin-Jenkins, Christopher; *The Complete Who's Who of Test Cricketers;* Rigby Publishers; Adelaide, 1980

Mosey, Don; *Botham;* Methuen; London; 1986

Page, Michael; *Bradman,* Sun Books, Melbourne, 1988

Piesse, Ken and Main, Jim; *Calypso Summers;* Wedneil Publications; Melbourne; 1981

Phillipson, Neill; *Cricket Cavalcade;* The Craftsman Press Pty Ltd; Melbourne; 1977

Pollard, Jack; *The Pictorial History of Australian Cricket,* J.M.Dent Pty Ltd in Association with Australian Broadcasting Corporation; Melbourne; 1986

Pollard, Jack; *Australian Cricket: The Game and The Players;* Angus and Robertson; Sydney; 1988

Ross, Gordon; *A History of West Indies Cricket;* Arthur Barker Ltd; London; 1976

Sheppard, John, *Cricket: More Than a Game;* Angus and Robertson; London; 1975

Tatz, Colin; *Aborigines in Sport;* The Australian Society for Sports History; Adelaide, 1987

Trueman, Fred; *The Thoughts of Trueman Now;* Macdonald and Jane's Ltd; London; 1978

Tyson, Frank; *The Test Within;* Century Hutchinson; Melbourne; 1987

Whitington, R.S.; *The Courage Book of Australian Cricket,* Wren Publishing, Melbourne, 1974

Willis, Bob; *Fast Bowling;* Willow Books; London; 1984

Willis, Bob and Murphy, Patrick; *Starting with Grace;* Stanley Paul in Association with the BBC Hulton Picture Library; London; 1986

The superb high action of John Snow

PHOTO CREDITS